James Graham

Maryam Philpott

James Graham

State of the Nation Playwright

Maryam Philpott
London, UK

ISBN 978-3-031-59662-9   ISBN 978-3-031-59663-6 (eBook)
https://doi.org/10.1007/978-3-031-59663-6

© The Editor(s) (if applicable) and The Author(s), under exclusive license to Springer Nature Switzerland AG 2024

This work is subject to copyright. All rights are solely and exclusively licensed by the Publisher, whether the whole or part of the material is concerned, specifically the rights of translation, reprinting, reuse of illustrations, recitation, broadcasting, reproduction on microfilms or in any other physical way, and transmission or information storage and retrieval, electronic adaptation, computer software, or by similar or dissimilar methodology now known or hereafter developed.
The use of general descriptive names, registered names, trademarks, service marks, etc. in this publication does not imply, even in the absence of a specific statement, that such names are exempt from the relevant protective laws and regulations and therefore free for general use.
The publisher, the authors and the editors are safe to assume that the advice and information in this book are believed to be true and accurate at the date of publication. Neither the publisher nor the authors or the editors give a warranty, expressed or implied, with respect to the material contained herein or for any errors or omissions that may have been made. The publisher remains neutral with regard to jurisdictional claims in published maps and institutional affiliations.

Cover credit: Wil Wardle Photography/Getty Images

This Palgrave Macmillan imprint is published by the registered company Springer Nature Switzerland AG
The registered company address is: Gewerbestrasse 11, 6330 Cham, Switzerland

If disposing of this product, please recycle the paper.

Contents

1 **Introduction and Early Works**   1
    1.1 *Delegated Authority*   6
    1.2 *Assumed Power*   15
    1.3 *Early Works*   23
       1.3.1 *Experimenting with Form*   23
       1.3.2 *Youth and Tradition*   27
       1.3.3 *Power and Leadership*   29
       1.3.4 *Social Decline*   37

Part I   Legitimately Delegated Power

2 **Democracy**   51
    2.1 *Political Parties*   54
    2.2 *Elections*   70
    2.3 *Parliament*   80

3 **Anarchy**   99
    3.1 *Inside the System*   101
    3.2 *Outside of the System*   116
    3.3 *Anarchy in Dramatic Form*   135

Part II   Assumed Power

4 **Famous Faces**   147
    4.1 *Incidental-Celebrity*   150

		4.1.1	*This House*	150
		4.1.2	*Ink*	156
		4.1.3	*Quiz*	162
		4.1.4	*Best of Enemies*	166
	4.2	Celebrity-Protagonists		170
		4.2.1	*Create and Be the Change*	171
		4.2.2	*Last Chances*	179
		4.2.3	*Troubled Times*	186
5	Television			197
	5.1	Television Justice		204
	5.2	TV News		219

Part III The State of the Nation

6	Writing for Television	243
7	**Conclusion: The State of the Nation**	259
	7.1 Working-Class Masculinity as the State of the Nation	268
	7.2 Britain Today	273

Bibliography	285
Index	291

CHAPTER 1

Introduction and Early Works

James Graham is one of the UK's most important contemporary dramatists whose work across two decades has profoundly understood and sought to explain the nature of Britain today, how power is distributed in modern society and patterns of politically driven social and economic decline that have shaped national identity and Britain's capacity to respond to the demands of twenty-first century living. No other playwright has either been so consistently acclaimed nor been able to so precisely define and present the changing face of Britain onstage, analysing and dramatising the pulses shaping the country since the Second World War as the rise of new technologies facilitates different kinds of public communication while, beset by human error and the dangers of ambition, political systems and institutions have struggled to provide effective governance in response to the challenges and issues that the writer defines. Graham's collective work has become a byword for political analysis, charting a course through the history of the last 70 years of State development, exploring the compromises and failures of functions such as Parliament, political parties and the justice system with legitimately-delegate power to plan, manage and shape society. Across the writer's work, the breakdown of political and legal efficacy at all levels is stark and through plays including *This House*, *Tory Boyz* and *Labour of Love*, Graham has explored the inherent fragility of Britain's brittle democratic structures and ways in which their purpose and effectiveness

© The Author(s), under exclusive license to Springer Nature
Switzerland AG 2024
M. Philpott, *James Graham*,
https://doi.org/10.1007/978-3-031-59663-6_1

can be derailed or misdirected, further weakening the role and stability of governments. Graham's work identifies the far reaching and deeply rooted implications of this by dramatising the growing distance between the government and the governed.

But Graham's importance is assured through his exploration of growing soft-power authorities in contemporary society, the media organisations and television channels that have created and propelled populist forces in order to wield considerable influence over public information. By utilising a manufactured hunger for content to drive ratings, his plays show that this has important implications for the effectiveness of democratic institutions who lack that reach and impact, and in their place these companies assume control. *Ink*, *Quiz* and *Best of Enemies* provide detailed anatomies of such organisations, explaining how perspective, fact and notions of truth have become malleable, with shifts in the last 60 years that have fundamentally shaped public narratives with major implications for concepts of public interest, how this is reported and the influence of media in determining how governments respond to crises. Graham's work explains how, driven by a commercial, ratings-based agenda, these organisations came to establish such a dominant role in modern public life and why these unelected and unaccountable forces that shape public opinion, voter behaviour and even government policy pose as great a threat to the enfeebled political system as they do the lives of individuals pitted against them. These plays enact examples in which the writer demonstrates how the might of print and television media is levelled against an individual in a disproportionate battle in which the Goliath conglomerate defeats the powerless David unable to contend with the multifaceted tricks and perils of engaging with so complex and wily a foe. As Graham untangles the influences that keep power with the already powerful, there are deeply personal consequence for his protagonists, and the plays act as a public, political and personal warning about the problems of unchecked influences in modern society.

Born in a Nottinghamshire mining village in 1982, Graham's drama has been infused by the causes and consequences of strikes, closure and community division emerging from those circumstances with its political and economic aftermath having fundamentally shaped the writer's output with his debut play *Coal Not Dole* (2002) performed at the Edinburgh Fringe during his drama degree at the University of Hull while several of his subsequent works including *Labour of Love* (2017) and *Sherwood*

(2022) were also set in the Midlands, noting the aftermath of government decision-making in former industry-led communities. 'I remember growing up in a time when it was tough because mines were closing. We had four pits in our village and they all closed in the early 90s,' Graham noted in an interview for *The Observer* in 2015,[1] telling the *The Standard* 'I remember what it felt like to grow up in a post-industrial town in the 1990s and feel voiceless… but I was very lucky because my family encouraged me to be creative.'[2] Graham became the Finborough Theatre's writer in residence where he staged his first professional play, *Albert's Boy* in 2005. Graham continued to work at the Finborough, producing *Eden's Empire* in 2006, *Little Madam* (2006), *Sons of York* (2008) and *The Man* (2010) as well as joining the Royal Court Young Writer's programme alongside now established contemporaries Jack Thorne, Lucy Prebble and Laura Wade, and mentored by Simon Stephens. During this period 2005–2010, Graham also staged Early Works at the Soho Theatre (*Tory Boyz*, 2008), Theatr Clwyd (*A History of Falling Things*, 2009) and the Bush Theatre (*The Whisky Taster*, 2010), with further works *Relish* for the National Youth Theatre, *The Tour Guide* (Edinburgh Fringe) and *Bassett* (National Theatre Connections) following in 2010–2011. Graham made his West End debut with *This House* at the National Theatre in 2012, entering a major works phase which is the subject of this volume. Graham is a multi-award-winning writer earning Olivier Awards for *Labour of Love* and *Dear England*, and has received multiple Olivier, Tony, BAFTA and Emmy Award nominations for his stage and television work in the UK and America. He remains the only contemporary playwright to have two productions running side-by-side in the West End – *Labour of Love* and *Ink*. In 2020, he was awarded an OBE for services to drama and young people.

Badged as a 'political playwright' following the success of *This House* in 2012, Graham's dramas take place at important moments of change, when a crisis or nexus occurs that sets society on a different path. Frequently, these are times of upheaval in which one way of living is about to be replaced by another. In Graham's first published play *Eden's Empire* from 2006, the writer sets his story in the mid-1950s when the transition from Winston Churchill's leadership to Anthony Eden's brief time in office precipitates the final decline of Britain's imperialist policy and sets in motion styles of premiership that no longer keep pace with their age. The plays further suggest that all Prime Ministers since have lived in a lost past while the country moves on without them. Later, the arrival of

Margaret Thatcher is used as another watershed moment in the shaping of modern society, setting several works around that crucial change of political leadership and direction. Plays exploring this crucial transitional phase include the crumbling minority administration of *This House* during the 1974–1979 Parliament, *Monster Raving Loony* that sweeps through much of post-war Britain but focuses particularly on the Thatcher era when David Sutch had the greatest public profile, and *Little Madam*, an unpublished play about Britain's first female Prime Minister. But Graham also defines less obvious moments in which significant societal shifts take place, two of these occurring in the late 1960s as changes in print and television news media take place, simultaneously shaping public appetites for populist content that continue to evolve and drive public discourses. An arguably disproportionate media response to televised content in *Quiz* in the mid-2000s has, the writer shows, also created equivalent interest in big media court cases and the phenomenon of trial by television. Defining these turning points, the events that led to them and the relevance of these stories to audiences now is fundamental to understanding Graham's importance as a contemporary commentator, how his drama operates and why it is so illuminating.

At what point to assess the work of such a prolific writer and how best to summarise their evolving contribution is a key question for this book. Graham's career has now extended to almost 20 years and it is more than a decade since the writer moved into his major works phase beginning in 2012 with *This House*, his first West End production at the National Theatre. This book therefore examines Graham's published plays between 2005 and 2023, exploring the key themes, concepts and theatrical techniques emerging from his writing during this time and how this work has evolved to position itself at the heart of stage approaches to defining and explaining the state of the nation. It argues that the writer's collective output during this period has provided a systematic analysis of Britain's power structures and the ways in which power has been held, transferred and influenced since the Second World War, creating cycles of decline that Graham has examined and explained through the construction and management of his drama. This analysis explores the ways in which Graham has applied different dramatic devices and audience engagement techniques within the themes and narratives of his work, ever conscious of his own authorial voice in the presentation of historical events, and the use of entertaining shortcuts and constructs to deftly convey complex historical contexts and debates. Although Graham may continue to produce work for several decades to come, this volume provides a model that can also be applied to future output, to understand its likely themes, approaches and focal characters. Ultimately, this book will show that Graham has uniquely and consistently articulated an important state-of-the-nation commentary that defines Britain today and offers solutions for the future.

The importance of Graham's work, then, is in distilling and repackaging the central tensions in British society between formal constitutional authority enacted by those with delegated power to govern within its renewable and accountable democratic mandate, and those who assume power through public reach and global communication platforms that link beyond the needs of individual governments and societies, setting-up alternative authorities that challenge, undermine and sometimes misdirect British democracy. The specificity with which Graham is able to take amorphous and overwhelming concepts and filter them through the more relatable notions of human drama is particularly skilful, examining the human weaknesses and stories that undermine the processes and systems that constitute democratic representation and effective governance. This much larger context of historical and social forces frames plays like *Best of Enemies* and *Monster Raving Loony*, as well as explaining less tangible ideas of what power is and who has it that play out through the carefully constructed and tightly bounded scenarios and character relationships that Graham creates. And it is this focus on the personal that makes these works so successful as theatre, helping audiences to make the causal connections between tiny misdemeanours or change attempts and the much wider consequences this has for the issues and challenges facing contemporary British society. When Kirsty misappropriates ballots in *The Vote* or when Charles Ingram changes his delivery style in *Quiz*, Graham clearly articulates the ways in which these slight shifts relate to, affect and start to define broader definitions of power and the effective functioning (or misfunctioning) of State systems. Even more importantly, Graham draws a direct line between Kirsty's actions and those of Charles Ingram, who become far more than two isolated individuals from separate stories acting in ways that create entertaining stage drama, but two people whose personal motivations and intentions, well-meaning or not, have the power to affect the robustness of those State functions and their perceived propriety. The writer's importance lies in this ability to recognise and dramatise the complicated, messy, varied and often silly experiences of people operating within the same stacked power structures.

Each play, therefore, balances the personal consequences for individuals engaging with systems bigger than themselves as well as the fragility of the democratic institutions designed to protect them from the soft-power organisations whose influences increase as a result of their actions.

1.1 Delegated Authority

The effectiveness of State institutions has been an important theme in Graham's work throughout his career, reflecting on the compromised existence of often very long-standing and old-fashioned institutions whose ability to reflect contemporary society is hampered by institutional structures and approaches to governance that prevent their effective and consistent operation. While Graham's work remains generally optimistic about the existence and purpose of those entities when operated effectively, the capacity for human error as well as the effect of ambition proves so deeply rooted as to subvert the functioning of democracy and justice, rendering it ultimately quite fragile. Graham's work examines the interrelations between different parts of the Establishment and the extent to which small-scale compromises eventually result in a broader misfunctioning of democratic and governance systems in which limitations or problems filter both upwards through the hierarchies of power but also affect local and national interests when these interact with personal needs. These create crisis points or stagnation within a system that in Graham's writing seems chronically incapable of change or renewal. Looking across his democracy and anarchy-focused plays—*Monster Raving Loony*, *The Angry Brigade*, *Labour of Love*, *The Vote* and *This House*—several clear concerns emerge with significant ramifications for Britain's capacity to function and develop as a nation.

The central tension Graham identifies is between short-termist electoral cycles and longer histories and traditions that shape the behaviour, beliefs and deep divisions within political parties. A constant refrain in Graham's plays is that the Conservative Party's self-belief secures its continued return to power while the tendency of the Labour Party to engage in ideological battles actively deters voters. When Jim in *The Angry Brigade* argues that the history of British politics in the twentieth century is of Conservative power as a steady state, occasionally interrupted by other parties, Graham suggests a national picture that is inherently right leaning, at least at the level of national politics. Much of this emerges from an innate confidence within the party driven by class and education that produces a type of politician that appeals to UK voters but, as Graham's work explains, will never effect the kind of change a teetering country requires. The writer frequently offers examples of Prime Ministers since the Second World War following the Public School to Oxbridge model of education establishing a particular path to power, a power that is predicated on an assumption of right or fitness to rule. The desire to stay in power as the primary driver of Parliamentary business emerges directly from this supposition and is an important connection across Graham's plays that links theoretical discussions in *The Angry Brigade* of how roads to power are created with how they operate in practice that the writer explores in *This House*. As a result, it has a significant impact on the effectiveness of the legislative agenda, a programme driven by short-term, often reactive thinking. While *This House* examines a majority / minority / coalition Labour government, the activities undertaken by both Whips' offices explored in the Democracy chapter are essentially a vote-by-vote scrap to retain governmental control rather than a coherent and vision-driven programme of social improvements that underpin their time in office. Obvious parallels exist in the present day, but Graham uses *Labour of Love* to consider the long-term failure of Parliamentary democracy to deliver sustained change or regeneration in areas of decline. Across the years of this play (1990–2017), the focal region of the Midlands loses its key local industry, opens and closes a data centre intended to bring new skills and opportunities to the constituents, and struggles to understand how its future fits into the purpose of twenty-first-century Britain. Linking the two plays together, Graham's comment on these short-term investments is the result of short-term-focused Parliaments seeking re-election, a notion that speaks to decades of decline and lack of opportunity created by the misgovernment of modern Britain described in *Monster Raving Loony*.

But although electoral patterns change and Graham references developments in the demography of political parties in the last 50-years—both the elected representatives themselves and the people who vote for them—Graham's work is far less optimistic about the capacity of political parties to overcome their internal differences and to fully represent either their constituents, party membership or ultimately to deliver national programmes of improvement. The result is to reinforce the status quo rather than offering new ways of governing. The current state of British politics as analysed in the writer's work, then, is a complicated mix of personally ambitious politicians placed in safe seats to facilitate their place in the central party leadership and contentious power struggles between party membership, central leadership, fee-paying stakeholders and lobby groups as well as voters. Expanded in *Labour of Love*, the writer is unambiguous about the challenges of overcoming these multiple interests and, for the Labour Party in particular, the cycles of influence that shape policies as the leadership of the party struggles to make itself electable. Meanwhile, *Tory Boyz* highlights the assumptions and traditions that affect the Conservative Party. Together, these works paint a picture of limitation and stagnation within the electoral system with party development hampered by long-term grievances, policy disputes and factionalism that inhibits change.

Underpinning all of this is the question of personal ambition and careerist objectives that often undermine democratic representation and, by extension, detract from State interests. The process of bargaining and threats practised by the Whips office in *This House* is part of a system that uses reward and promotion as the tools of compliance with only the Member for Coventry South West refusing to compromise her principles or her constituents needs to side with the government when required to do so. But looking across the group of plays devoted to democracy and anarchy, Graham returns many times to the career prospects of individual characters as well as the inter-relationships between different levels of governance within the UK system. There are multiple examples of local councillors who want to be Members of Parliament, of Civil Service and party officers seeking selection, of Council Workers hoping for promotion to senior electoral offices and constituency agents nominated as local candidates for national office. Once someone becomes an MP, their ambitions only continue to grow as *This House* notes when the Member for Thurrock demands a place on the Science Committee in return for loyally voting with his Parliamentary party, and again in *Labour of Love* when David Lyons holds a ministerial role for a time. The romantic notions of MPs and councillors joining parties on purely ideological grounds and representing the views of their communities are not the picture of modern Britain that Graham suggests. Instead, personnel and policy changes in party leadership undermine the effectiveness of political parties and the philosophies they claim to represent. The question of evolving demography is salient here as Graham questions whether existing approaches and structures are fit for purpose when a single party in *Labour of Love* struggles to appeal consistently to working-class communities in the traditional heartlands of the Midlands and North of Britain as well as the urbane metropolitan intellectuals of the south.

Graham's work also repeatedly notes the lack of distinction between the UK's main political parties in which Labour representatives are increasingly drawn from Public Schools while Conservative MPs have working-class backgrounds. Neither party fully acknowledges these shifts, preferring to present their traditional face to the electorate, but both *This House* and *Tory Boyz* unpick the fuzzier distinction between the parties while *The Vote* and *Tory Boyz* include voters and schoolchildren who dismiss them as 'all the same.' In *Monster Raving Loony*, when Sutch complains that the Labour Party has deliberately adopted a strategy of acting and dressing like Conservative Party representatives, the realistic chance of gaining power is the given excuse, because they are the steady state of UK politics. Even within Sutch's own allegedly anarchic party, one of his team switches allegiances because he wants real power. Party distinctiveness in contemporary Britain is based largely on history and habit rather than ideology, policy or even personnel in Graham's work, which removes or undermines even the simple binary choice presented to the electorate because the Conservative Party will eventually win sufficient seats to govern even when other parties have shifted to resemble them. But this appearance of similarity is also the cause of voter apathy and disillusionment with the effectiveness of democratic systems speaking to narratives of British decline that Graham uses to frame debates about political legitimacy.

Other parts of the Establishment are no better prepared for the influences and assaults of contemporary Britain and Graham looks at how shifts in societal power and those wielding it has affected State functions also invested with delegated authority to protect the rights and freedoms of citizens. The primary focus has been on the workings of the UK's criminal justice system which, in the very recent past, buckles under the pressure of television and public expectation to deliver guilty verdicts based on scant evidence and a flimsy prosecution case dramatised in *Quiz*. When Kirsty in *The Vote* argues that the appearance of propriety is more important in the electoral system that the strict application of electoral process, she speaks to the same conclusion that Woodley QC comes to at the end of *Quiz*, that justice must be seen to be done, an ideal that is more important than justice actually being done. Beneath the entertaining and perhaps frivolous surface of the *Who Wants to Be a Millionaire*-framed play sits a deeply important state-of-the-nation drama about the compromised operation of the justice system and its responsiveness to unaccountable influences from beyond the confines of the police investigation and trial—namely television and a media-influenced pressure exerted by public opinion. A catalogue of mistakes in the collecting and management of evidence as well as the context in which the trial of Charles and Diana Ingram, and co-conspirator Tecwen Whittock, was carried out, Graham's play demonstrates that justice was fundamentally unbalanced by the considerable external interest creating pressure for a conviction before the Jury had decided, an outcome shown to be vastly disproportionate to the sentence then handed down by the Judge. While Graham's play concludes with the scales of justice being partially rebalanced, it highlights the inherent weakness in the UK system that allows a case to come to trial without sufficient evidential grounds, largely to mitigate a version of events maintained by an undemocratic entity with a vested interest in the outcomes of the case and with considerable unaccountable social influence—television.

This link between innocence and fairness is an important one for the effective operation of justice, and the possibility that it can be derailed or shaped by external influences is symptomatic of the wider concerns that Graham raises across his work about broken social functions and their consequences for individuals caught up in their failure to perform. *Quiz* demonstrates that the fundamental basis of UK justice, that individuals are innocent until proven guilty, feels like a hollow claim in practice, particularly when subject to the pressures exerted by television, a complex and relatively faceless collection of production companies, television channels and well-known personalities all with individual and collective interests to protect. Crucially, they are able to redeploy the full resources of the media to sway public opinion in ways that influence proceedings in the courtroom. The smallness of the Ingrams and their reasoning is significant in this context, unable to change a national narrative about themselves and their time on a quiz show. Graham uses this story as a proxy for wider concerns about the misapplication of justice and the ease with which more favourable narratives can be created and used to redirect social power. The disproportionate nature of this response relative to the crime committed is also notable for UK justice. Does cheating on a gameshow—if that is indeed what happened—warrant a campaign of hatred directed at the couple before, during and after the trial? Is UK justice a fair weighing up of the evidence tested against established laws or a witch-hunt driven by uninformed public opinion based on an episode that was never actually seen? Graham clearly demonstrates that a trial and trial by television do not have quite the same basis in modern Britain.

And that becomes even clearer during the police interviews dramatised in *Quiz* as part of the Case for the Defence. The police are the third strand of the Establishment that Graham has examined across multiple works, a body also holding officially delegated authority to protect citizens and uphold the principles of justice. In *Quiz*, the police are not quick enough to question the evidence presented to them and, as shown in Chapter 5, accepted the television company's version of events without question and without applying the institutional rigour of their function. In *The Angry Brigade*, The Branch fare better, a crack team tasked with the discovery and investigation of a series of anarchic attacks in 1970s London. But although they achieve their aim through careful police work, evidence gathering and dedication to the task, Graham nonetheless presents a picture of deep conventionality and traditionalism, more in keeping with earlier eras of British society than the one they exist within, unable to understand the needs of people completely different to themselves. Like the politicians of *This House*, the police are the infinitely replicated product of the same type of background and social conditioning, openly acknowledging how little they have in common with the people that they are investigating beyond a similarity in age. Brief though it is, this commentary is an insightful one, creating an impression of modern Britain that is governed by inherited systems and ways of living that are unable to respond to the changing face of society but seek instead to reimpose a pre-existing order on each generation. This collective desire to replicate rather than evolve looks to the past for models of governance and behaviour that continue to shape a very different and, as Graham demonstrates, changed present against which existing systems and rules strain.

In one of Graham's earliest works, *Eden's Empire*, it is clear how completely the intersection of politics, justice and British identity has troubled the writer since the beginning of his career. Early in the play, it is Eden himself that gives voice to this essential tension between past and present, and the difficulty of encouraging choice in a country governed by traditional values with one foot in the past:

> Eden: Sometimes I just despair of the whole wretched thing. As much as Rab, Harold and I try to push forward, it's no good until we get rid of all these old dinosaurs on our front bench.[3]

In this play, Graham aligns Eden's declining health with Britain's failure to address its role on a global stage in the years following the Second World War and Eden is beset from all sides, pressed to take a difficult military position urged on by continual reference to the country's tactical strength during the previous conflict. This is frequently alluded to by Eden himself who recognises the moderation and nuance required by the country's position in a system now bounded by international relations and inter-country authorities such as the United Nations who are given nominal power to intervene and negotiate crises. But Eden is ultimately driven to act by pressure from others based on inherited political and military tactics and, as part of the Establishment that created him, is required to comply:

Caricaturist: One of them. Born into it and all that. Eton.

Reporter: Oh yeah. Money.

Caricaturist: Buy yourself into it, can't you?

Reporter: Hmm.

Caricaturist: Pay for it. I could have been a gentleman if my old man had paid for me to be one.[4]

And it is the persistence of this hegemony that Graham so acutely analyses along with a refusal to understand that Britain has changed as a result of the war, a subsequent decline that Eden and his Cabinet cannot stop:

Eden: Well, all in all we haven't been producing enough. We're consuming too much of domestic production ourselves, leaving not enough to export.

Macmillan: I've ordered the banks to reduce advances to customers. Local authorities are to cut back on spending.

Eden: But despite world trade expanding at a healthy rate, Harold, Britain is scarcely managing to balance its payments. (*Facing the Queen's portrait.*) We're the fathers of industry, Harold. Architects of modern manufacturing and commerce. Now everyone has caught up and is leaving us behind. How is a small island to cope?[5]

And soon, Eden becomes the man blocking progress, perceived as a barrier by the younger generation including Foreign Office Minister Nutting who notes 'we're of a different generation. You and I. We see the future when all they see is the past.'[6] Graham alerts the audience to a continual cycle in British politics since the 1950s that shows what Britain was, what it aspires to be and what it can realistically be, are not in alignment. Making the pieces fit and trying to forge a different kind of role is something that Graham's work has charted, as those given legitimately delegated power by society fail to use it effectively.

The chapters in this book work in pairs, the first examining the political playwright label that has followed Graham for more than a decade by focusing on the plays with a political subject matter. These democracy-focused works look across the hierarchy of governance institutions in a multi-layered political structure in *Labour of Love*, *The Vote* and *This House* to first consider how Graham presents the formation, organisation and purpose of political parties. Graham's plays regularly cite the messy transition between Labour and Conservative governments as a determining factor in British social experience since the Second World War and this section considers the writer's reflections on the role that political parties play and the ideology they represent in contemporary Britain as a result of their construction, membership and voter base as well as influential lobby groups inside the major parties that affect decision-making. But, as Graham shows in *Labour of Love*, the party entity is beset by a number of challenges that derail or actively hinder their effectiveness as democratic units, placing the role of the local MP and the pressure of constituency business in the wider context of the directives and expectations set by central party leadership along with the demands of elected government. The *Democracy* chapter explains the effects of human error and ambition in the functioning of democracy in Graham's work as well as the requirements of changing policy demands that render the political party an often-inconsistent constituency presence. The second part of this chapter examines the writer's views on the efficacy of the electoral process, its customs and regulations as well as its role as the public face of the democratic process. Using stage farce to structure these observations, *The Vote* is set in a polling station in which the writer exploits the misdirection of the ballot, and Graham's management of the escalating humour and what this means for British voters is examined in this section through scenes in which political tradition and modernity collide within the process, and the manifold problems arising from direct engagement with the voting public. Consistent with Graham's analysis of political parties, here too, the writer creates ambitious characters tightly woven into potentially conflicting forms of local and national government that reflects on these unresolved tensions, and links this to his broader commentary on the effectiveness of the individual parts of the democratic system as well as their relationship to one another. Finally, the *Democracy* chapter completes the governmental lifecycle with *This House* and the activities of parliamentary leadership in which Graham's creations prioritise the needs of the Parliamentary party to retain power at all costs and thereby actively subvert the business of government within the drama. Here, the tactics applied by the Whips' Office in *This House* to cajole and coerce MPs to vote with an ailing administration raise important questions about representation, the government's mandate and inability to deliver programmes of either national improvement or even a coherent legislative agenda. Across this work on the components of democracy, Graham charts a process of unresolved compromise and decline, setting these plays across several decades in which the weaknesses at all levels of Britain's system of governance are only compounded by short-term approaches to retaining power while failing to resolve the questions of party identity and representation that continue to affect contemporary politics.

The partner chapter to *Democracy* is *Anarchy* which considers Graham's wider analysis of political processes and responses, focusing on two plays that present direct challenges to existing forms of democracy from those working both inside and outside of the system to effect change in governmental practice. These plays open out the concept of political playwriting to respond to and react against restrictive social conventions beyond the institutions and personnel of traditional politics. This second thematic chapter thus explores the role of dissenting voices and organised groups working to subvert conformity in these plays and the ways in which Graham's version of democracy responds to attempted incursions. Here, Graham expands his interest in political function to consider the ways in which society is constructed, the opportunities it creates for social progression and the effects of control mechanisms applied to ordinary members of the public with differing reactions to compliance. Graham is sympathetic to anarchic voices in his plays, although equally pragmatic about their effectiveness, so the first section of this chapter considers a character working inside the political system using the existing rules and organisations of democracy to push a new or more radical agenda. The semi-biographical story of David Sutch in *Monster Raving Loony* is an opportunity to re-examine the political lifecycle from Chapter 2 from a different perspective as the party leader builds a manifesto and a political entity against a backdrop of economic decline and social stagnation that speaks to Graham's thesis on the failures of post-war national government and political change. The second part of this chapter looks more broadly at inherited social conventions and expectations in Graham's work using anarchic characters working outside of the system to effect change by violent means against focal targets beyond traditional political institutions with legitimately delegated power, and instead attack wider economic and consumerist objectives. Using *The Angry Brigade* as the basis of analysis, this section explores the dynamic that Graham creates between the organised group and the deeply conventional police team tasked with tracking and deterring them to explain how society functions and the expectations it places on young activists to comply. In both examples, Graham's democracy reasserts control, even convincing some of the anarchic individuals to fulfil inherited expectations of what their lives should be. In performance, both *Monster Raving Loony* and *The Angry Brigade* present particular challenges for a company staging them, so the final part of this chapter analyses Graham's approach to introducing anarchic concepts into the structure and presentation of both of these plays, upturning dramatic convention and actively restraining his own authorial voice in ways that mirror the action, experimenting with different theatre-making techniques to challenge the determining role of the playwright. Although democratic components are weakened through the events of these plays, albeit temporarily, this chapter shows that there is insufficient momentum in either the social or theatrical anarchy that Graham introduces to prevent State and theatrical convention from eventually reasserting control.

1.2 Assumed Power

Part of the reason for that is the pressure exerted by social bodies with considerable assumed power to influence and direct democracy and subvert the business of delegated authorities. In *Eden's Empire*, Egypt's president Nasser warns:

Nasser: Astonishing! This new thing of tele… television. Still, it is not all so good for the people to see so much into the government working. In Egypt, I think we will not let them see so much. They might find things they do not like.[7]

Graham's work has explored in detail the populist shifts in media organisations that has given them a reach that extends far beyond that exercised by traditional democratic organisations through a direct access into people's homes that allows the media to influence and actively shape public opinion, beliefs and even the outcome of democratic and societal functions that should operate independent of these external interests. Here, Graham pits the traditions and backwards-looking Establishment against the emergence of new power bases actively working to effect change in the ways that information is both structured and disseminated. Like Parliament, focal media organisations in Graham's plays seek their own longevity by also reinforcing their power and protecting their unaccountable influence at any cost. But the writer also shows that these organisations are better able to reflect the desires of the public and feed the appetites they create. So, while politicians, cocooned within their carefully controlled class and educational backgrounds, struggle to understand and appeal to an increasingly apathetic population, newspapers and television by contrast are able to both manufacture and direct the public mood. The cost of this unchecked social influence is the subject of Graham's work, and the writer identifies key moments at which media organisations of the 1960s unleashed rapacious social forces that quickly move beyond their control, fundamentally altering the ways in which people engage with one another and the nature of public political discussion, including reflections on British identity and social accountability. Yet the media's scale and reach place it in an unassailable position to shape the state-of-the-nation narrative and determine who is responsible for Britain's perceived decline.

The transfer of power to these assumed authorities began in the 1960s and Graham examines the media companies that set out to deliberately disrupt the status quo, win ratings and decide their own future, one in which their own power is enhanced. The parallels between actions undertaken by the characters of Rupert Murdoch and Larry Lamb at *The Sun* in *Ink* (2017) and Elmer Lower and William Sheenan at ABC news in *Best of Enemies* (2021) are clear, both teams setting out to overturn their position as underdogs by abandoning the usual rules of their industry and applying new approaches to business operation that have far reaching consequences for modern Britain in Graham's work. Conventionality in the political sphere, anarchic principles and approaches may be corrected by and eventually subsumed within democracy, but in the unregulated worlds of journalism and television, the anarchists win, changing how their sector operates by directly responding to a perceived public mood that they have manufactured. The ways in which media organisations create, develop and sustain narratives in order to generate sensation and drama drive their own sales figures, regardless of the cost to individuals, and this is a central tenet of Graham's plays, a theme the writer returns to repeatedly. Like the tranche of politically focused plays, these also seek to examine how changes in organisational policies and culture have personal consequences for the individuals involved. The growth of populist approaches fundamentally alters the purpose of news and media organisations in Graham's plays as well as creating appetites in public consumption that become increasingly difficult to satisfy. And it has a twofold effect: first in the growing influence of alternative sources of societal power that actively challenge and seek to sway the legitimately delegated authority awarded to Establishment institutions, but it also influences how society engages with itself, affecting public discourses through the polarisation of individual opinions and perspectives on identity. Both of these notions contend across shows like *Ink* and *Best of Enemies* as characters press ahead with small-scale innovations that have long-lasting effects on British society, balancing character-driven stories with a wider analysis of how we engage with one another as a result.

The rebalancing of authority between the justice system and television in *Quiz* was explored earlier in this chapter in which Graham outlines the consequences of manipulating and managing factual evidence as concepts of truth and fairness collapse under the populist pressure exerted by the media frenzy the Ingram case elicited. That pressure, Graham argues, was partially manufactured by the creation of newspapers like *The Sun* in its current form, detailed in *Ink*, a process in which fact and truth were blunted by a new interpretation of 'public interest.' Although the phrase is not explicitly used in the play, the character of Larry Lamb and his team manufactured a concept of public interest by applying the techniques of episodic drama and entertainment to sell newspapers. By appealing to populist forces and not heeding the warning of rival Editor Hugh Cudlipp that their actions will unleash a hunger that the industry will never satisfy, Graham takes the audience through a series of incremental changes that destabilise the boundaries and rules of traditional journalism, building to the serialisation of Muriel McKay's abduction and murder in which *The Sun* plays an active role by printing missives from the kidnappers that maintain the story's momentum, building public demand with continual revelations across days of attention-grabbing and morally-outraged headlines. What Graham is actually charting here is the transfer of power from a societal organisation tasked with investigating the case and protecting the public—the police—to a media company which sets itself up as both authority on the conduct of the public body and moral guardian of national values. In deciding that an active criminal investigation was in the public interest and by communicating its progress in a public and sensationalist style designed to generate repeat custom from readers, the writer shows a shift from established print approaches and factual reporting practised by the traditional Fleet Street newspapermen to a stage in which national newspapers have positioned themselves as unelected arbiters of societal management, dispensing advice on how national activities should be conducted and sitting in judgement of them all under the banner of the public's 'right to know.' This control and use of information as well as the national and international platforms that media companies operate gives them a reach far beyond the political sphere in Graham's plays allowing them to actively control the operation of society and manipulate how the public respond to news reporting.

Taking this concept further, Graham unpicks the changed purpose of television news in *Best of Enemies* to explain the fractious and increasingly entrenched mode of public engagement in which tolerance and difference have evolved into outraged extremes of opinion with no space for middle ground solutions. The abrasiveness of the central series of debates between Gore Vidal and William F. Buckley is couched by the writer in similar commercially driven concerns about ratings that, like Lamb's work in *Ink*, propel the US television channel ABC from last to first place in the ratings by adopting an equivalent populist approach to generating news content. This transition in 1968—notably set a year before *Ink*—precipitates a subsequent shift in which sound factual reporting of the news is blended with entertaining and purposefully combative styles of public interactions facilitating the rise of celebrity commentators seeking a public platform for their views and ambitions, encouraged by the ratings to take these opinions to extreme and unreconcilable positions. The outcome, Graham shows, is not the representation and diversification of viewpoints but to make good TV, the long-term effects of which have shaped the manner in which public conversations take place in British society today. The transition that occurs in *Ink* and *Best of Enemies* is from dispassionate and balanced reporting of the news to media organisations becoming content creators who shape the conditions around the facts, control information and decide when and how it should be shared.

As well as redefining definitions of public need and the ways in which news content is managed and distributed, media organisations in Graham's work are also filled with equivalent desires for individual self-promotion and advancement. Much as councillors, party workers and politicians use the electoral and governance structures of democracy to enhance their own careers, so too do those engaging with or working for media organisations use television and newspapers as a platform for their own personal aspirations or ambitions. At times, these two worlds intersect with individuals using television to bolster their political importance, reignite or launch political careers. As shown in Chapter 5, both Gore Vidal and William F. Buckley hope to use the ABC news debates to initially reinforce their position as political commentators and intellectuals in the hope of receiving recognition and even endorsement from their respective parties that will facilitate a return to political life, and with it the attainment of legitimately delegated power through the electoral process. This interaction between official and unofficial power is one of many examples in Graham's work in which a media profile is closely aligned with and a steppingstone towards power even if it ultimately hinders political decision-making. This commentary on what is given airtime on news programmes and the motivation for doing so is an increasingly pertinent one for contemporary Britain where the boundaries are blurring between opinionated celebrity commentators and those with official delegated authority to publicly contribute to national debates—or conversations that assume a national importance because they are covered on television. Sitting beneath *Best of Enemies* is not only a question of who is selected to speak about these topics and the credentials they have to act as an expert, but also what is discussed at all. It is principally the characters of Vidal and Buckley who set the agenda for their own discussions, shaping what is and is not said based on their own interests, knowledge and ambitions with very few interjections from moderator Howard K. Smith to manage this agenda. In *Ink*, it is Lamb and his team who determine what is printed and the importance attributed to the stories through placement and tone, eventually basing decisions on their personal and quite compromised association with a major criminal storyline involving their own chairman—something they cannot report with any rigorous independence. What Graham shows is not only the significant influence that unelected and unaccountable bodies exert on national debates through the selection of compromised individuals as commentators and editors, but that it is media organisations rather than elected representatives who determine what those national debates ought to be and use their enormous public influence to decide how they are conducted.

That all of this is driven by ratings and sales rather than measurable improvement in standards of living or national prosperity is extremely pertinent, and both plays conclude with those propagating innovative forms successfully leaping from last to first place, achieving economic and social influence for their industries. But, as Graham concludes, this leaves a troubled legacy for modern society now contending with the overmighty influence of unelected power bases able to reinforce their own position at the expense of established democracy and societal authorities just by controlling the conversation about them, deciding who can speak publicly and determining what it means to live in contemporary Britain.

This close examination of Graham's work demonstrates that the 'political playwright' label is too narrow a definition of the writer's output given the broader focus on social authority and the effects of traditional politics on everyday life. This work on the rise of undemocratic soft-power organisations is especially enlightening, situating Graham at the heart of analyses of contemporary Britain. Part II of this book, Chapters 4 and 5, therefore considers other kinds of social influences in the writer's work and how these are managed within the drama. Famous faces have become an important focus for Graham, and although not writing about celebrity culture directly, they are increasingly a major feature of his plays with famous faces acting as both protagonist and important secondary characters. Most importantly, they are indicative of broader political forces being unleashed in society that these characters often instigate or are swept up in. Chapter 4 first considers the role of fleeting celebrity appearances which have been a feature of Graham's work for more than a decade. Badged here as 'Incidental-Celebrity,' these background characters have a particular contextual purpose in the writer's work, acting as a dramatic shorthand to summarise a period of time or cultural direction that is essential to understanding the impact of the play's events on modern society and the growing influence of non-political forces in shaping Britain. This chapter examines how the use and proliferation of Incidental-Celebrity has evolved over time across these collective works, the juxtaposition of their role in the plot in support of the narrative requirements in each play and their interaction with Graham's second category of famous faces, the 'Celebrity-Protagonist.' The second part of this chapter therefore looks at *Ink*, *Quiz*, *Best of Enemies* and *Dear England*, works in which the lead character (or characters) is a 'celebrity,' usually a distinction they have earned through their actions in the scenarios that Graham dramatises in the play. By exploring turning point moments in their careers, Graham's Celebrity-Protagonist creations follow a similar trajectory of ascendency and decline. The writer uses this as an opportunity to harness audience preconceptions of these individuals based on their subsequent reputation and works against this by recasting their original intentions as early innovators and change makers in their field, as well as examining the personal and professional stakes for each of them. Crucially, each Celebrity-Protagonist has a role to play in unleashing new social forces, often by accident, which have significant consequences for contemporary society and public debates on soft-power organisations and their growing influence.

The fifth chapter expands this part of the writer's focus with an assessment of Graham's television-focused plays that explore the unaccountable influences of programme makers and news broadcasters, applying a case study analysis of *Quiz* and *Best of Enemies*. Graham recreates the television studio in both works, putting the theatre audience in the dual position of television viewer in these plays to explore notions of perspective, composite versions of truth and the shaping of national and public narratives. *Quiz* seeks to understand the soft-power might of television as a complex, unaccountable body that affected the legal process—an important State function that should operate independent of coercive self-interest—as well as the individual whose life is permanently altered by their television appearance. The consequence of this for the justice system is significant in *Quiz* and the first part of the chapter explains how different perspectives are actively managed within the play to recast the events around the *Who Wants to Be a Millionaire* trial against Charles Ingram and how these events gained momentum when different versions of truth are created by television. The writer explains how public perceptions are manipulated by television's techniques through an investigation of trial by television, in which Graham applies a variety of theatrical devices including the recreation of broadcast television while also imagining content behind the camera. This is enhanced by the application of audience participation tools that show how television is created and its consequences for justice and perceptions of justice in Britain. This case unleashed public appetites that, Graham argues, continue to demand and consume manipulated realities. This chapter's second case study focuses on *Best of Enemies* and the rise of celebrity commentators in television news. Graham has identified a moment in which factual news reporting and authority became increasingly acrimonious, feeding a polarisation of public discourses that affects the role of news media and perceptions of truth in the modern day. Once again blending broadcast debates and off-camera moments, Graham's play carefully stages the political ambitions of its Celebrity-Protagonists in a drama-laden gladiatorial format that pushes characters to adopt extreme positions. Chapter 5 examines the approaches used by Graham to understand the concept of 'good television' and the binary simplification of public narratives. The protective might of media companies to affect social change at this turning point moment in 1968 provides a particular opportunity to explore overlapping perspectives and the important of narrative control in staging this work as a theatrical rather than a televised experience.

The conclusion draws together these different strands to assess and explain Graham's state-of-the-nation commentary across the writer's collective works, arguing that there is a consistent and clear articulation of the economic, political and historical challenges inherited by contemporary society and their consequences for a British identity that is couched in tradition. Expanding the 'political playwright' label, this chapter focuses on *Dear England* (2023) and *Boys From the Blackstuff* (2023) to explore the nature of identity in twenty-first-century Britain, the changing expression of working-class masculinity—which Graham has often used as a proxy for state-of-the-nation concerns—and the role of a national sports teams in defining and embodying a consistent but backward-looking concept of Englishness based on tradition and ritual since 1945. This chapter explains the persistent and uninterrupted cycles of decline that have affected Britain since the Second World War, characterised in plays from *Eden's Empire* in 2006 to *Dear England* in 2023, and the problematic nature of short-term political and social thought which occur repeatedly in Graham's writing, providing an anatomy of State power and its long-lasting effects. Finally, this chapter considers Graham's reflections on British identity emerging from his analysis of the last 70 years of British history and what hope exists for the future by looking within the very systems and structures that his work has investigated. This deep understanding and interest in exploring how society operates and its consequences for holders of power—legitimate or assumed—has been a feature of Graham's writing since his earliest works making him far more than a 'political playwright' and instead provides a structure and foundational directiveness that makes his work so vital to understanding the state of the nation today.

1.3 Early Works

An early work can be defined in many ways; it might be a chronological definition applied until a particular level of success or influence is gained by a writer, or something more fluid that aligns with where the work is produced. A writer may not be in a major works phase until multiple plays have opened in the West End or there could be a numerical benchmark based on volume of output or the age of the writer. For simplicity here, early works refer to those prior to Graham's first West End production in 2012, *This House*. Like all playwrights, Graham's early works are experimental, tackling a broad range of subjects and staging ideas as the writer found his tone and style. There is no single trajectory from early to major works and not every play a writer produces charts a linear career progression of settled ideas or even the formulation of a singular 'voice,' but are a response to the period in which the play is produced, the opportunities and funding available to stage it and sometimes passing interests in exploring different kinds of characters or stories. As a result, the more cohesive pattern of Graham's writing since 2012 is reflected to varying degrees within his earlier output as the writer investigated different forms and worked in venues around the UK. Graham's developing analysis of the political, social and economic challenges facing modern Britain is not always the primary focus of plays such as *A History of Falling Things* (2009) and *The Whisky Taster* (2010), which include only fleeting contextual reference to these broader themes and instead try out different staging techniques and approaches, explore the creation of different character relationships and respond to cultural and technological influences at the time of writing.

1.3.1 Experimenting with Form

The History of Falling Things is an Internet-focused play in which the protagonists, Robin and Jacqui, are confined to their homes by debilitating agoraphobic conditions resulting from trauma. They engage instead via chat rooms and webcams in this one-act play about falling in love with someone they cannot meet in person. Written as a side-by-side drama, *A History of Falling Things* is a social-media age two-hander in which characters Robin and Jacqui make an online connection despite living a few streets away, speaking regularly but never meeting in person due to Robin's agoraphobia and keraunothnetophobia—the titular fear of satellites falling from the sky—that prevent him from leaving the home he shares with his mother. Likewise, Jacqui who has returned home following a traumatic experience during the 7/7 bombings in London where she was trapped in a tube carriage shows symptoms of depression remaining in doors with her single father. First performed in 2009 at Theatr Clwyd directed by Kate Wasserberg, the drama anticipates the writer's later perspective-based plays which use this structural device to guide audiences through different points of view, controlling how and when information is released to an audience and its effect on narrative certainty. Elisabeth Mahoney's three-star Guardian review described the play as 'a little sentimental' but recognised the potential in Graham's writing noting the 'many moments to savour.'[8] Later works expand the techniques used here beyond a singular relationship, applying it to complex social and cultural debates in plays including *Quiz* in which the blending of evidence from different points of view is integral to Graham's unfolding drama about television justice and truth, as well as unpublished piece *Bubble* (2021) that imagined two alternative versions of a relationship, one in which the central characters spent lockdown together and one who, like Robin and Jacqui in this early play, communicate via video calling platforms. The back-and-forth interaction created in *A History of Falling Things* is also essential to establishing the independent circumstances of each character outside of their engagement with one another, an approach that Graham would later apply to the structure of *Best of Enemies* in which the protagonists Gore Vidal and William F. Buckley exist in a similar construct, created as two separate individuals with their own lives, motivations and reactions but also fully integrated into each other's trajectories and the play's overall narrative.

Reflective year-in-the-life drama *The Man* utilises a formative audience engagement technique in which Graham experiments with different ways to create and present a narrative using a box of receipts given to the audience as the substance and frame of the single-actor monologue. First performed at the Finborough Theatre in 2010 and built around the completion of an Inland Revenue self-assessment form, each receipt prompts a different part of Ben's story, expanding on grief, family connections and the day-to-day anxieties of establishing himself in a major city but in an order that is entirely random depending on the document selected and the individual choices of the actor during the performance. Described as 'pre-scripted while having the remarkable feel of an improvisation' by *The Telegraph*'s chief critic Dominic Cavendish in his four star review,[9] Graham's approach to handing over control for some aspects of the performance to the company and the audience is a technique the writer would revisit in both *The Angry Brigade* and *Quiz* where the authorial voice is restrained but not fully absent in determining the overall shape of the narrative. *The Whisky Taster* has a similar character-focused purpose set in a marketing office in London during a campaign to promote a new brand of vodka for which the staff consult a mysterious whisky expert from Scotland. 'When I first moved to London during the run-up to my first Finborough outing, I got a job in a theatre press and marketing agency run by Guy Chapman,' Graham recalled in the introduction to this play written in 2012, 'it gave me a taste of the world of advertising.'[10] Drawing on this, there are scattered political references throughout but the play is primarily concerned with the central relationship between two friends drawn to each other in the workplace. The writer plays with different forms of reality in the creation of character intimacy as protagonists Nicola and Barney put on an 'act' as part of a game between them:

> Nicola (*as Barry*) Someone's gonna be jumpin' into his shoes, know what I mean, you get what I'm saying, kiddo?
>
> Barney: (*as Keith*) Jump in his grave as quick, would cha, fuckin' 'ell, love, blimey.[11]

This drama has a playful and illusory quality, depicting a light-heartedness and trust in their friendship in which Graham creates moments of separation from reality as the characters step outside themselves to engage with one another in ways that exclude others. 'This dynamic duo work well together, and their chatter is punctuated with in-jokes and funny voices' theatre critic and writer Aleks Sierz explained in his review for The Arts Desk,[12] and while Graham applies it lightly in *The Whisky Taster*, the approach foreshadows a character construct applied in an extended form in later work *The Angry Brigade* in which the central anarchist characters Anna and Jim assume performative roles as more conventional versions of themselves to mock the social expectations of conformity that they are protesting, discussed further in Chapter 3. Graham's work here is beginning to probe the connection between his fictional characters and different versions of societal power they are enacting, developing some nascent thinking about the influence of soft-power organisations that would become a key mode of analysis within the writer's major works. In *The Whisky Taster*, Graham notes the assumed power of advertising to shape society, ideas that would later emerge more fully formed in *Ink* and *Best of Enemies* but have their origins in this play, looking at how products are packaged and commercialised to shape what people think they need:

> Nicola: Exactly, no, we're trying to build it up little by little, softly, softly, that's why we don't want a massive, bling bling campaign, full of fireworks, we want it to develop, or *seem* to develop, organically. Even though it's not, even though we're 'managing' it. But I know what you're thinking, 'Well, that's cynical marketing', that's still… 'Grr, the evils of advertising, brainwashing,' but it's not, any more, is it, Barn? It's all changed now.[13]

The consumerist pressures that lay behind advertising are an idea that would expand considerably in Graham's work in the years ahead, looking more clearly at media outlets and organisations that operate a new kind of authority and social influence through printed media and television to influence British social values and measures of political success. This experimental approach to different kinds of storytelling and staging techniques lay the foundation for many of the innovative methods applied to audience management and storytelling in Graham's later works. 'Wanting to write a play about being the age I was, in the city I was, feeling, as I did, that sometimes the whole thing was just too loud and too colourful, the prospect of the play began emerging.'[14] Along with the developing socio-political commentary and studies of power, across these early plays Graham is also testing out thoughts, scenarios and dramatic techniques that give the writer a platform for the more directed approaches to narrative control, character development, the management of perspective and audience engagement within the works that follow, establishing clear themes about the exercise of political authority at all levels of society, the long-term effects of government failures as well as the soft-power influences that shape Britain. And while these experimental forms and topics are important, Graham's most significant published plays between 2005 and 2010 indicate a writer thinking about formative ideas of power, leadership, social decline and the inherited expectations of conventionality that will be explored in this book, conversations that begin and are underpinned by these early works.

1.3.2 Youth and Tradition

A significant thematic strand within Graham's early works unpicks divisions between the needs of youth seeking changes to society in the post-war era and expectations set by the Establishment to maintain social control, a feature of the later anarchy plays in particular. Originating in *Eden's Empire*, Graham twice pits the ambitious younger generation against older era politicians seen to be clinging to power beyond their time. Initially, it is Churchill who stands in Eden's way, promising to resign but inventing ever more excuses not to do so. Eden complains of this early in Act One frustrated that 'Cabinet's a mess, no one believes he knows what he's doing any more,' going on to describe the once eminent Churchill as 'That silly old man!'[15] Later it is Eden himself who has become the old-guard and in just a couple of years is viewed as the block to progress. Graham's later work creates narratives in which 'youth' is a distinct category of society, a group of people who, like Sam in *Tory Boyz* and Barney in *The Whisky Taster*, are seen as somehow 'other.' In the latter, manager Malcolm actively designates this group as 'People your age' during a meeting beginning a conversation that actively marks out the focal generation as economically different to those that came before with quite different needs and fewer opportunities, offering early echoes of the impassioned speeches made by activist characters in the 1970s set *The Angry Brigade*. Advising his staff to assume young people drink more, Malcolm explains his rationale:

> Malcolm: I just wonder whether... because it's the one thing, in this age of, in this time of economic... it's the one thing that is sustain - not only sustaining itself, flourishing, amongst you lot, because... well. You're still rich, aren't you? By the standards of... and your disposable income, it ain't going on houses, is it, because you can't. Or savings, because...[16]

Nicola, herself one of the 'young' members of the team, also exploits this connection between youth and disposable income, imagining a style of contemporary living that makes the group a core advertising target:

> Nicola: what about also… young professionals. At home. Gorgeous modern flat. The lights of London in the background, they're high, high up, they're doing well, Habitat furniture. Abercrombie and Fitch clothing. It's the evening, they're kicking back, shoes off, massive corner sofa, vodka.'[17]

Warming to this particular theme, the character of Malcolm returns to the distinctions of this age group at the end of Act One, attempting to define Generations X and Y but instead discovering a similar feeling of disconnection that occurs between grandfather Terry and grandson Mark in *Sons of York*, one with important effects on public narratives:

> Malcolm: Boggles my mind. Honestly. Never have people spoken to each other so often, and yet all it's exposed is an absolute absence of anything worthwhile to say.[18]

Later in the play, Graham gives Malcolm an extended monologue that associates long-term state-of-the-nation changes with the creation of a distinctive youth experience that has notably limited the target generation:

> Malcolm: No, I don't blame them, fuck it, if I were your lot, I'd fucking drink. Can't get a house, aw sorry, we've got them all, and shit, sorry, we've spent all the inherited wealth that's been passing down the generations on second homes and cars and holidays. But that's OK, you've been very patient, waiting your turn, but now – oh no! – there's no money left, we spent it, and there's less jobs, crikey, so tighten your belts. I would go away, travel, escape, but you can't really because we did that too much and now the planet needs saving. But the tragic thing is, the real crime, Barney, whatever you hate me for or blame me for, the biggest fucking crime of all is that none of you are angry enough to do anything about it.[19]

As the character of the Whisky Taster goes on to explain, conformity is inevitable: 'Distillation is, by definition, reducing and removing. To make the same. It is the uniform for school children. It is the state restricting the man.'[20] A thought that recurs in *The Man* when character

Ben considers the transition point at which a conventional adulthood begins:

> Ben: Grow up, I suppose. But I.... I didn't – it didn't feel. Right, Erm. Because I suppose that literally really is becoming a grown-up, isn't it? Saying bye to being young, to being... saying bye to the future being possibly *anything*. And instead saying, no, it's going to be specifically *this*. For ever.[21]

This idea is an important one, evolving through Graham's major work to come and their state-of-the-nation considerations. This analysis is later reflected in the principles behind The Brigade's challenging of social control and conformity in *The Angry Brigade*, as well as the eventual resumption of democratic and conventional behaviours that defeat anarchic intrusions against the State. But this association between youth and the challenge of social convention begins in the early works as Graham expands a broader analysis of social structures and their definitions, beginning to form impressions about inherited conformity and its effects on the opportunities available to each new generation, and the traditional democratic structures that confine them.

1.3.3 Power and Leadership

One of Graham's earliest plays from 2006 is *Eden's Empire*, the story of Anthony Eden's patient wait to become Prime Minister during the 1950s when Winston Churchill refused to retire. Couched in British foreign policy in the aftermath of the Second World War when America's international influence began to superseded its former ally, the Egyptian government's military claim on the Suez Canal and Eden's eventual handling of the crisis and mistimed attempt to invade Egypt came to define his premiership and, in Graham's version of events, is symptomatic of Britain's failure to recognise its newly reduced world status. 'The Suez Crisis has haunted a number of key stage-plays – from John Osborne's *The Entertainer* to David Hare's *Plenty*,' critic Paul Taylor wrote in his review for *The Independent*, finding Graham's interpretation 'a lucid and gripping account of the background and course of the crisis.'[22] Staged at the Finborough where Graham was writer in residence, the play may be close to twenty years old, yet remains a sprightly two-Act historical drama that laid the foundations for topics including the nature of governmental power and styles of personal leadership that the writer would continue to analyse in his later democracy plays *This House*, *Labour of Love* and *The Vote*. The story of Anthony Eden's brief premiership and the loss of the Suez Canal with which he is most associated, *Eden's Empire* is really a play about the transfer of power between leaders that reinforces how little has changed in the democratic weakness and state-of-the-nation concerns that Graham identifies between the period of the play and the time it was written. It considers the development of Prime Ministerial reputation in which three successive Conservative party leaders worry about their place in history while navigating difficult economic and international circumstances. Identifying notions of post-war decline, Britain's uncertain place in the world and how Parliamentary politics should be conducted, this play is the template for Graham's ongoing interest in the effective functioning of democracy and the uneasy balance of power at the top of government.

Transitions of power are quite marked in *Eden's Empire*, looking at why individuals seek to hold on to it long after their regime or the individuals themselves have proved ineffective, a subject Graham would explore again in the weakened administration of *This House* and its consequences for effective governance. But here the writer generates an interplay between personality and a singularity of power invested in the role of Prime Minister in which the freedom to choose when to hand over the reins of government and who to work against the broader needs of the party and even the country. The dominant figure of Winston Churchill marks a shadow over the play as the experience of Anthony Eden is measured against his predecessor throughout the story by himself and by other characters. The author too uses Churchill as a yardstick for assessing Eden's effectiveness by controlling the way in which information is constructed for and related to the audience, a comparison that Eden becomes increasingly agitated about:

> Lloyd: Perhaps a stirring speech in the Commons, Anthony. Bolster their patriotism. Think of Winston, think of all he would have –
>
> Eden: WINSTON CHURCHILL IS NOT THE PRIME MINISTER! I AM![23]

Churchill appears as a dominant figure throughout the two-Act drama, a celebrated war leader setting a standard for what a Prime Minister must look like, a pointed allusion to then Prime Minister Tony Blair and the Iraq war that recur throughout the drama. Yet, Graham's play argues that Churchill has created an infeasible template for premiership built around particular and high-profile military success that has endured since:

> Churchill: Remember. Indecision is a most fatal vice. Better act wrongly but quickly... than lose the chance of acting at all. I have not chosen you, Anthony. History has chosen you. You will find out... soon enough... why...[24]

And despite all that happens in the play and the failure of Churchill's own final months in office, Graham notes the leader's reputation remains undimmed at the end of the action:

> Eden: Winston's funeral, Fred... the whole nation. Mourning. Did you see? All the cranes in London, bowing their head... as his coffin sailed across the Thames. The whole city, the whole country... leaning with them... onto their knees.[25]

Eventually, Eden's successor, Macmillan, is forced to acknowledge the full implications of the Suez Crisis, an international relations disaster for Britain, when the US refuses to underwrite the currency and so precipitates a major shift in Britain's international standing that will shape subsequent political administrations and the lives of individual characters in Graham's later works. The 'real villain of the piece is Eden's ambitious Foreign Secretary and then Chancellor Harold Macmillan,' Taylor writes, gleefully enjoying Graham's 'artful mix of historical reconstruction and mischievously handled hindsight,'[26] in which Eden's replacement is no more fortunate. Having adopted a strident warmongering position over the Canal crisis, as Eden's Principal Private Secretary Bishop notes, Macmillan soon creates issues of his own claiming he has 'run into a few problems with his "Never had it so good" claim.'[27] In the writer's assessment, this systematic failure to address the inheritance of the past and the tendency of Prime Ministers to make the same mistakes in different scenarios is a consequence of the brutal cycle of usurping and replacing leaders in which each new Prime Minister brings a fresh wave of optimism about the new perspective they represent and a chance to reset—only, the problems facing Britain explored in *Eden's Empire* are never solved.

The writer shows how the action of this play, and the sequential leadership exchanges it depicts, only exacerbates national decline and proves a stumbling block for every Prime Minster to come. They are all in the shadow of Churchill who, in Graham's drama, could barely live up to his own reputation during his second attempt to lead the nation. With the notion of Britain's great empire already long gone in the 1950s, by the time of Eden's premiership, first ministers are already seeking to emulate Churchill and secure their own place in history. Graham suggests this is a consistent failure to grasp the vastly changed reality of post-war Britain and the national requirements of leadership at the time they hold power. Those who seek power desperate to be remembered, the writer argues, are doomed to make the same mistakes all over again.

That template for leadership and its relationship to inherited forms of political culture is something Graham examines on a much smaller scale in other early works, notably *Tory Boyz* (2008) and *The Whisky Taster* (2010) in which fractious professional connections between colleagues are used to consider the disastrous effect of weak or prejudicial management and its consequences for the individual. In *Tory Boyz*, Graham creates a micro-hierarchy within a Parliamentary researchers' office, a structure in which power can be exercised in both legitimate and inappropriate ways through a line management relationship that is used to characterise the experience of working for a particular political party in a manufactured and directed office culture. Through the character of Nicholas, the Chief of Staff, protagonist Sam's direct manager, Graham creates an impression of power that Nicholas believes is casual and without consequence but with the result that attempts to be engaging create a toxic working culture in which difference is isolated rather than embraced. The audience's first impression is of a character trying very hard to seem relaxed and fun when discussing a colleague's civil partnership ceremony which Sam cannot attend:

> Nicholas: All right, Tetchy Von Sensitive. (*As 'street'*.) Take a chill-pill in' it (*Beat*).[28]

But later Graham reveals the underlying and deeply rooted defensive and offensive nature of the character in response to Sam's interest in developing a career in politics:

Nicholas: And they will have a black, Islamic wheelchair-bound liberal as Prime Minister before we see a fella kissing his other half on the steps of Number 10. And you know I'm right. (*Pause.*) Christ, I'm just saying if you want to climb that ladder, don't make it an issue.[29]

There are many ideas compacted into these exchanges about the continued traditionalism and conventionality of the Conservative Party as well as the unassailable position of men like Nicholas who, Graham shows also crave elected office, to say and behave in any way they wish without acknowledging the boundaries of appropriateness. But Graham is exploring a much larger issue here about the sustained nature of culture and power within democratic entities, some of which will emerge in the problematic behaviour of the Whips in *This House* (2012) using bribery and coercion to secure votes. This discussion is foregrounded in *Tory Boyz* in a parallel stream of action that dramatises the experience of Ted Heath, a Prime Minister in a far earlier era who may have concealed his sexuality as Sam is encouraged to do. But the Heath character has another, larger purpose in Graham's work by using his personal position of power as Prime Minister to ensure individuals vote as he needs them to:

Ted: Look (*Serious*). We are hanging on by a thread, do you understand? We are literally under attack in there every single day. It's a barrage. And whether or not it's a Bill to regulate the size of grass or a Bill to invade Canada, the Opposition will divide the other way every single time. All it takes is a handful of our chaps to get a cold, sprain their ankle, or miss the bus, and we couldn't pass the parcel, let alone a law.[30]

His tactic is to use his private and Prime Ministerial influence over his colleagues to encourage their conformity:

Ted: Write on it: 'Marital problems' stop. Brackets 'adultery', question mark.

Frank: Well. When we bump into old tearaway Turnbull later I'm sure we won't have to worry which way he'll be voting, now will we?

Ted: The information we record is not for the purposes of blackmail, Frank, it is to foresee the potential for scandal and to nip it in the bud before it blossoms. Make sure we get him in this afternoon, will you? (*Small beat.*)

And incidentally, yes, make sure he does understand that he'll be voting with us.[31]

That these embedded power structures seek to replicate themselves through the selection of similar candidates for political office is an idea that recurs through Graham's work, and while the line management relationship described in *Tory Boyz* is a fairly unusual one in the writer's output, the underlying analysis of the closed way in which political parties work and the failure of demographic changes to fundamentally alter entrenched traditions and leadership styles is an important contention across Graham's democracy-focused plays. Described as 'timely and thoughtful' by Lyn Gardner when the play transferred to the Ambassadors Theatre in October 2013, (a year after the premiere of *This House*), Gardner's three-star review notes the relish with which Nicholas tries to stymie Sam's career and his sexuality.[32]

> Nicholas: You're on a timer with me now, boyo. So I don't want any fuss, any accusations about things you think I may or may not have said during our little chat the other day. I don't want any threats; I basically just don't want you around. We don't like each other, Sam. Do we? If we're honest? Or at least I don't think you like me and I can't stand people who don't like me. You've got your references. Get a position somewhere else. And leave. Make it soon, make it quiet, but make it quick.[33]

Graham creates a similar concept of power and control between a manager and an employee in *The Whisky Taster* in which the writer gives manager Malcolm a false light-heartedness to disguise a much harder personal dislike of worker Barney:

> Malcolm: (*still trying to be friendly, and casual*) Barney, please don't... interrupt. When I'm...
>
> Barney: ...

But when Barney stays silent, Malcolm's impatience becomes apparent:

> Malcolm: You can speak, Barney; it's interrupting when you talk over someone, not when someone has stopped talking and / is waiting for you to –

Barney: Malcolm, I'm sorry, / I wasn't –

Malcolm: That's interrupting, what you did just then. OK? That's interrupting. (*Beat. Softens...*) Now it's turned into this... like a, huh, like a serious... and it's not. (*Laughs.*)[34]

In his review, Aleks Sierz considered this one of the best scenes in the play as 'two generations of ambition clash in a telling account of our current political apathy,'[35] and in both *Tory Boyz* and *The Whisky Taster*, Graham creates scenarios in which the older Establishment figures react against younger employees perceived as 'other,' Sam because he is homosexual and Barney because he has a neurological condition called synaesthesia. The exploration of Sam's sexual preferences creates a discussion in *Tory Boyz* about concealment within politics and the need to 'fit in' or conform with the prevailing culture, expected notions of what political power looks like and what it must represent in order for Sam to win support within the party that will aid and guide his career development and selection. Graham presents Nicholas's behaviour towards Sam in parallel with Ted Heath's trajectory from young boy to Prime Minister in which speculation about his sexuality resurfaces. This reinforces the pressure Sam feels within the office culture, a pressure that spills over into a conversation with a school group that he is working with:

Ray: Can I ask you sumfin? Do you hide that you're gay 'cause you're in politics and that?

Sam: I never said I was gay.

Ray: You never said you weren't.

Sam: Well. Um... in certain quarters of life, erm... tolerance advances slower.[36]

The consequence of leadership styles and the desire to replicate existing norms has considerable impact on the ways in which political parties engage with the electorate in Graham's work and the growth of voter apathy resulting from governance processes that seem confusing and old-fashioned to his non-political characters. A strand of *Tory Boyz* takes place in a school classroom as protagonist Sam engages a group of teenage music students to work on a Schools' Bill being amended by the Opposition Minister he supports. And while the writer often dramatises the work and experience of politicians, rarely has this included direct interaction with members of the public—not even in *Labour of Love* which is set in a constituency office. Although Sam is not a politician, this is a place where Graham brings together governance and the governed to explore the broad disinterest in politics, its exclusionary nature and the inherent suspicion that shapes the view of these individuals before they enter the electoral system.

> Sam: Right, so when you reach voting age, more of you will choose to vote in *The X Factor* than at the next general election.
>
> Muznah: That's because what's the point, nothing changes.[37]

In *Tory Boyz*, then, Graham is starting to explore the culture and behaviours that determine what modern party politics looks like, helping to maintain their traditional demographic appeal reinforced by existing leadership styles. In the public forum that the writer creates with schoolchildren, these characters have inherited concepts of party preference from their parents, largely based on traditional notions of class and privilege that become Sam's primary experience of working for the Conservative Party. *Tory Boyz* begins a strand of work that unpicks the nature of party politics, its membership and ethos. 'My way in was that I had a friend who was gay, northern, and Conservative,' Graham noted in his introduction 'to a world of young, often working-class, and predominantly gay, staff researchers behind the scenes of the Conservative Party, completely contradicting the image of the stuffy old "nasty party".'[38] The anatomy of the party as a democratic entity is a topic the writer revived in *This House* and *Labour of Love*, but many of the ideas about the relationship between class and party association, the link between educational opportunity and public office and the strength of party tradition are formed in *Tory Boyz*. This play establishes a more expansive commentary in Graham's later work that extends the practical application of party politics, the changing demographic make-up of party staff and membership, and Parliamentary operation. There are also nascent ideas here that touch briefly on voter apathy and the careerist ambitions of staff at all levels of the party structure whose desire for personal power and influence determine character action in this play, underscoring and shaping the writer's analysis of the political weaknesses and failings within an increasingly brittle democratic structure.

1.3.4 Social Decline

The most important contribution Graham's writing has made to contemporary drama is in establishing a basis for and understanding the effects of long-term social decline that has blighted Britain's development in the years since the Second World War, outlining the failure of social policy as well as of political and economic decision-making that has failed to improve the lives of citizens. This has been the focus of the writer's major works and is a concept that has its origins in *Eden's Empire* which dramatises the failure of international relations during a 1950s administration and Eden's desperation to preserve some vestige of Britain's global influence via a number of diplomatic discussions with representatives from France and America, a physical and metaphorical dance imagined by Graham to analyse Britain's relative and rapidly diminishing influence. As Foreign Secretary Eden engages in a series of 'tangos' with equivalent politicians throughout the play constructed by the writer to summarise the complicated decisions about the world being made among these men with significant implications for the country's future influence. The writer depicts the growing influence of America in determining what Britain is allowed to do, an outcome that affects the stance Eden takes on the Suez Canal debate when the US withdraws support, leaving the protagonist—and through him the nation itself—isolated and humiliated. Here, military presence and political influence clash with the changing world order as old notions of empire and superior British governance crumble within the period of this play. The writer thus places Eden in the same disassociated positions as later Prime Ministers, worrying principally about 'My place in history'[39] instead of making the most appropriate or even morally-sound decision depending on the contemporary circumstances. The reality of British decline is ultimately voiced by the character of Foreign Office Minister Anthony Nutting who fears Eden's 'premiership will be such an anomaly he will barely be remembered at all.'[40] When Eden's successor Harold Macmillan insists Britain is still a force to be reckoned with—a position Graham implies he will falsely take into his own premiership and thus begin the cycle again—the play shows that Eden's era originates a feeling of distrust between the government and the governed, a feature of post-war Britain that starts to emerge in this period, a broken fealty that the writer suggests is symptomatic of the long consequences of the Suez crisis:

> Eden: I have, I have Cabinet members resigning, a country divided, a parliament nearly in revolt. Our Commonwealth against us! And the press![41]

Graham's earliest published work further analyses the changing nature of political governance, the relationship between individual failures of leadership in the moment and its consequences, comparing that to the changing definition of British identity both inside and outside the country, exploring challenges to tradition that affect the country's economic prosperity, its position in international relations and its consequences for individual family units in the decades following Eden's resignation. *Sons of York* was Graham's most intimate work until BBC drama *Sherwood* appeared more than a decade later, exploring the complex masculine relationships between a grandfather, father and son brought together by a family emergency and financial straits during the Winter of Discontent, a pivotal period in the post-war story of modern Britain that recurs with some frequency in Graham's work and would later become a partial setting for *This House*. In his introduction to the play published in 2012, Graham noted this was 'certainly the most autobiographical I have been.... I imagine the trauma the family in this play goes through is universal.'[42] In *Sons of York*, staged at the Finborough Theatre in 2008, the family dynamic is depicted as a small-scale version of the state of the nation, a major turning point in their lives in which a fractious Labour government makes way for Thatcher's change regime, a transition that the family shown in this drama already know will destroy their way of life and signal the end of a version of Britain that its oldest members cling to. Graham's text includes a strand in which grandmother Val is transformed by dementia from the women she used to be into another kind of existence entirely, one that the family must accept and respond to, mirroring the societal shifts happening outside the household, both of which are beyond their control. Graham makes Val the link to a particular version of working-class life that had existed since the Second World War, representing an era of Britishness coming to an end in this moment and more directly in this living room setting. Although Michael Billington remained unconvinced in his three-star review of the play published in *The Guardian*—'I can't help feeling that Graham's quarrelling Yorkists have to bear too much symbolic weight'[43]—the former Chief Theatre Critic underestimated the complex inter-relationships that Graham builds into this play and the collective commentary of his work on this period of British post-war history. As he would many times in the future, Graham places this personal crisis in a broader context to explore notions of past, present and future colliding at an individual and national level simultaneously with consequences for the economic stability and the opportunities experienced by this family, as well as the changing nature of working-class masculinity across this period. 'How men share pain became a preoccupation and driving impulse behind *Sons of York*,' Graham concluded, the piece combining 'the political with the personal.... [and] setting a family at a crossroads against the backdrop of a nation that is likewise at a turning point in its political and social development.'[44]

The family dynamic is not a scenario that the writer has often reached for or made the primary focus of his drama, with *Sons of York* providing one of the only published examples of this set-up. The play's focus on three generations of men is integral to Graham's exploration of political and social change since 1945 and the expectations placed on them by those who came before, along with the lives they expect their descendants to have as a result. Subjects that infuse Graham's later works have foundation in the conversations created between these characters exploring the shift in circumstance, attitude and opportunity that prevent sons from inheriting the profession of their father and affects their political affiliations. So, while Jim works in the same truck business as father Terry, grandson Mark is on a separate trajectory completely, looking to education as a means of achieving a different kind of future, and Graham charts the period in which manual occupation careers are replaced by service roles and, in this case, creative outlets. Graham's 1978-set drama suggests that this is both the direct choice of grandson Mark and the result of the foreshadowed social changes signalled by the impending inevitability of Margaret Thatcher's government elected in the following year. In his study of popular theatre, Aleks Sierz defined the characteristics of a family play which must 'involve at least two generations, and they usually explore two types of tension: one is the balance of power between the parents, mother and father; the other is the generational struggle between the older family members and the younger ones.'[45] Applying these tropes to his own play, Graham's characters attempt to preserve the veneer of family unity, son Jim and grandson Mark spend much of the play pretending to comply with Terry's wishes, implying that Mark is working at a factory instead of studying:

> Mark: Rubbed me arms and hands down in some 'ot shit he were throwing out, make it seem like I've done a proper day's work for a change. Ha ha. Good eh?
>
> Jim: You silly prick.
>
> Mark: What? Only meant to be funny; thought you'd be pleased. Keeping t' secret.[46]

This belief in tradition, of subsequent generations inheriting and indeed wanting the kind of life that he had, becomes an important refuge and statement of identity for Terry as it will for other Graham characters during moments of flux, at a point when the life Terry recognises and has lived for decades is about to undergo a permanent and drastic personal and national change. Terry's related reluctance to allow Val to be cared for outside the family home is symptomatic of the loss of control the character feels in all aspects of his life which the writer associates with major state-of-the-nation developments and social shifts instigated in this period. Terry's long-held ambition of owning his own truck to pass on to his son, regularly referenced throughout the text, becomes increasingly unlikely as the play unfolds. Terry's primary motivation is directly undermined by Mark's quite separate plans for his career which more broadly symbolises the ending of an old way of life in Britain and the resultant unfulfilled aspirations of working-class experience that characterise the projected political future that the writer anticipates in *Sons of York*. Graham has created a scenario in which old assumptions and expectations no longer apply, and uncertainty replaces stability and surety by the end of the play. All of Graham's major works utilise dramatic irony, telling the story of a moment in history that actively requires the audience's foreknowledge of what happened next to create pathos for the characters who then have little hope of fighting back, and this gives the writer the option to subvert expectations about how those narratives develop, constructing drama that looks backwards and forwards at the same time, creating a driving sense of inevitability within his plays that make character behaviour and their soon-to-be frustrated expectation all the more tragic when the truth emerges:

Jim: Mark's... got work to do, Dad. He's studying / He's got exams.

Dad: Studying? What? / What you on wi'?

Mark: Dad don't, you're right, it in't time.

Dad: What about factory?

Jim: There in't one. And he in't taking driving lesson, not yet. We just... didn't want to tell you yet. / 'Cause of Mam. I'm sorry....

Dad: I don't... I can't... Yer what? Just... look. Can we... why do you have go and, and, and ruin everything?[47]

'Most families have a secret or secrets, which divides the characters into those who know the truth and those who don't,' Sierz explains, meaning the 'revelation of this secret, or lie, is inherently dramatic and provides the fuel for emotional charge.'[48] That charge eventually explodes in this scene with the idealised version of the past that Terry has created crumbling as reality sets in and, with the impending arrival of Thatcher casting a shadow over the action this play, even Terry's hope is soon destroyed. This domestic clash anticipates a longer process of destruction for the family in the months and years beyond the end of the play which will alter or damage the known structures in which they exist. To reinforce this change moment, Graham dramatises aspects of Terry and Val's earlier life in several fantasy/memory scenes that take them back to the Second World War when they were both club singers, a dreamlike remembrance that Terry evokes several times, clinging both to the woman his wife used to be and to the clearer, perhaps more optimistic, man he also was then. It provokes an excitement and happiness in the character that is not present in any other interactions:

> Dad: Eh, crikey, it's a year and a half since jubilee, in't it? God! (*Clapping his hands.*) Remember that? (*Rearranging her clothes, straightening her out.*) Out on the street. You remember that Jim? Christ, never seen owt like it, streams of flags going from house to house, zig-zagging down the street. We've gorra plate, an't we, wi' that on? Scullery, somewhere. Eh, 'ark at me calling it scullery. Kitchen. (*Calling.*) Brenda? (*Back to Mam.*) Victoria sponge, that were yourn, oh my God, people were licking their lips for days, bloody days. (*Laughs.*) Which you renamed Elizabeth Sponge,

remember? And that's… hold on, am I right, or… yeah that's right in't it? Thinking I were gerrin mixed up over VE Day then. Remember that, Val? Eeh, dear, some good parties though, we've had eh?[49]

For this character his best times are behind him rather than in the future and this feeling that an idealised past has been lost but can be reclaimed is vital to the work that Graham would go on to write, as tradition and ceremony—here at a family rather than a national level—infuse ideas of what Britain is and ought to be. It also represents a meaningful version of nationhood in Graham's work, one that has changed little since *Sons of York* was first performed in 2008, or since the 1970s when the play is set. Graham's characters are always looking back to a better world several decades before. This has important consequences for the type of man that Terry is and the ways in which the reality of Britain's social decline directly resulting from the country's failures to address the challenges of the post-war years provoke feelings of rage and powerlessness in working-class lives. It is an idea that would also emerge fleetingly in *The Whisky Taster* as character Nicola expresses similar feelings of powerlessness and political apathy during a discussion about watching the news declaring 'I can guess what has probably happened today, Barney. I can guess that things probably Got Worse. I'd guess that things are probably worse today than they were yesterday, but that they aren't as bad as they're going to be tomorrow.' When Barney optimistically attempts to expand her knowledge of current affairs, Nicola insists 'I Can't Change It, Barney. I just can't. Can you?'.[50]

In *Sons of York* then, Graham uses Terry's character as proxy for an internalised version of this debate, concerned with how his life has developed as a result of the political direction of the country, giving him that symbolic weight that Michael Billington frets about, by finding the human and personal consequence for the man and his family during a time of large-scale social crisis. Terry turns this in on himself and his family in the final section of the play, a man bounded by his age and background in which a reference to D.H. Lawrence in Act One, Scene Two is deliberate. Several of the novelist's constructions evoke hyper-masculine elders with limited access to education but have developed strong practical and manual skills that reinforce a deeply gendered lifestyle. Graham echoes Lawrence in the interactions between these men and the more sensitive and worldly younger male characters offering a very different interpretation of masculine behaviour. In the confrontation that takes place in *Sons of York*, Graham therefore contrasts Terry's often violent outbursts with the gentler bookishness of grandson Mark and places Jim between them to create a continuum of masculine transformation that reflects the eras in which each family member grew up. Mark explains this by quoting lyrics from a song by The Clash:

> Mark: (*turns it off*) It's just about the whole thing, Grandad, how we're bloody, frigging stuck in a rut and can't afford no houses and job opportunities rubbish and just all t' stuff our Mum and Dad's had, with their money and their flowers and hippy peace shit in t' sixties we an't… mean, it's – we're more like your lot, Grandad, not taking no shit.[51]

Graham utilises this idea in his final early work, 2010 play *The Man* in which protagonist Ben assumes the authorial voice to reflect on this same sense of male politicisation associated with the era in which the men of his family were raised:

> Ben: I see both sides, probably because of my family. Dad and Granddad, God couldn't be more different. Maybe it's just that generation thing. Grandad, of the war mindset, Atlee and all that, everything nationalised, 'we're in this together' kind of thinking. Lifelong member of the cooperative group. Dad a child of the sixties, I suppose, wanting to keep more money for himself.[52]

And this changing perspective of post-war masculinity and expectations of manly behaviour is something that the writer returned to with his 2023 football-based play *Dear England*, discussed in Chapter 7, that grapples with imposed and inherited concepts of sportsman-like behaviour and male mental health. Because of the type of man that he is, the eventual explosion of Terry's violence is inevitable in *Sons of York*, an outlet for the frustrations and impotence he experiences, and this tendency to react through physical contact is something which Graham seeds early in the story when 'Jim grabs Mark by the collar' in Act One Scene One. In the next section, a secret day out that Val spent with Jim as a child leaves Terry feeling aggrieved, resulting in a passive aggressive aside that sets him against his son—'No, I don't bloody care,' he declares, and then to himself '(Nowt to me. Do what you want).'[53] Terry's performative masculinity continues with arm wrestling competitions against his male family members along with a dogged refusal to continue with their day until Mark defeats him, an encounter that quickly escalates as indicated in Graham's stage directions for this scene:

> Dad *starts pushing* Mark's *hand the other way. He grabs* Mark *by the back of the neck and starts pushing his whole body down on the table.* Mark *yells out a bit.*[54]

This competitiveness assumes its full political resonance when Mark refers to his grandmother as an 'Iron Lady' in the climax to Act One provoking Terry who '*grabs* Mark *by the neck and yanks him to the floor*,' pushing his head into a tub of water.[55] The bristling aggression that Graham feeds through the text sits under Terry's every interaction, a tendency for explosive violence that escalates until the final decisive altercation in Act Two, Scene One at a belated Christmas dinner in which the simmering tensions finally erupt:

> Dad: You aren't man of this house, Jim, I am! And she, she is... (*Struggling.*) She is My Wife! You've no right. She's My Wife! Now, SIT!
>
> Jim *doesn't move.* Dad *grabs him by the back of the neck and pushes him down.*
>
> Brenda: Jim!
>
> Mark: Grandad, don't! Dad, I'm sorry!
>
> Jim *breaks free and stands back up. He can't look* Dad *in the face.* Dad *hits him.*[56]

After a further scuffle, Terry insists 'You'll do as you're bloody told! This is my house!'[57] Graham actively connects these physical encounters to the external political context of a general strike which causes division within the family who debate its value:

> Dad: I'm not having her cross any picket line, you hear? Nurses. Police. Teachers. Gritters. Postmen. Bloody sandwich-makers. Buggering stamp-lickers. General Strike means General Strike. One out, all out. Don't want no one from my house breaking that pact. It's sacred, Jim -[58]

As the vaunted day arrives with widespread industrial and public service action taking place, Graham allows Jim and wife Brenda a private moment to question its impact on their personal circumstances, bringing the story back once again to the debated intersection of national and individual interests that combine so powerfully in this play:

Jim: What do you want me to do? Eh?! Money's run out, / there's nothing –

Brenda: And why has the bloody money run out? Is it because folk like him intimidate folk like you to stop working?[59]

These conversations anticipate a much more detailed examination of the miners' strikes in the 1980s and their consequences for working-class communities which the writer explored with *Sherwood* in 2022 and *Boys from the Blackstuff* in 2023. In partnership with *Eden's Empire*, *Sons of York*, then, lays the foundation for Graham's work on social decline to come, exploring how larger social forces accumulating over decades affect the lives of his characters, shaping not only their gendered behaviours but also the feelings of impotence and abandonment they feel in moments of significant upheaval. The family in *Sons of York* may be able to overcome their deep divisions, at least on the surface, but Graham argues the wounds this era inflicted are still shaping Britain today. Addressing these patterns of long-term decline across several decades once again in his final early work, *The Man*, reveals the uncertainty created by sustained instability and political flux at a national level. Ideas first proposed in *Eden's Empire* come to fruition in a speech establishing the lack of effectiveness resulting from two party politics and its consequences for national identity, an examination of political balance that Graham would further explore in his major Democracy and Anarchy plays:

Ben: That's why I like history, it gives you 'the long view'.

I don't know. Just seems like after decades of flipping between one idea and another – one election, Labour, collectivism, chucking in more; next one, Conservative, individualism, chucking in less… I guess I naively thought that we'd reach a kind of national consensus. But now it seems like we're split again, fifty-fifty, and suddenly we're not just arguing about tax, it's kind of… it's like what we're actually arguing about is literally, 'What do we believe in?' 'What are our principles?' Our ideology, for the way we're going to live.[60]

In Graham's work, this instability stems from the failure to manage the post-war era, anticipating discussions in the writer's major works about the places where political failure and social decline interact with and shape state-of-the-nation experiences.

Notes

1. Rawnsley Andrew. 2015. Writer James Graham talks to Andrew Rawnsley about his TV drama Coalition: 'I Love Humanising Politics'. *The Observer*, March 22, https://www.theguardian.com/stage/2015/mar/22/james-graham-interview-coalition-x-y-finding-neverland.
2. Manzoor, Sarfraz. 2018. James Graham Interview: My Town Was One of the Top 10 that Voted Leave—I Have to Represent Both Sides. *The Standard*, September 20, https://www.standard.co.uk/lifestyle/james-graham-interview-my-town-was-one-of-the-top-10-that-voted-leave-i-have-to-represent-both-sides-a3938766.html.
3. Graham, James. 2006. *Eden's Empire*. London: Methuen Drama. Act One, p.13.
4. Ibid, Act One, p.35.
5. Ibid, Act One, p.41.
6. Ibid, Act Two, p.72.
7. Ibid, Act One, p.20.
8. Mahoney, Elisabeth. 2009. A History of Falling Things. *The Guardian*, May 16, https://www.theguardian.com/stage/2009/may/16/review-history-falling-things.
9. Cavendish, Dominic. 2010. The Man at Finborough Theatre, Review. *The Telegraph*, June 2, https://www.telegraph.co.uk/culture/theatre/theatre-reviews/7797433/The-Man-at-Finborough-Theatre-review.html.
10. Graham, James. Introduction. In Graham, James. 2012. *James Graham: Plays*. London: Methuen Drama, p.xx.
11. Graham, James. *The Whisky Taster*, Act One, Scene One. In Graham, James. 2012, p.234.

12. Sierz, Aleks. 2010. The Whisky Taster, Bush Theatre. *The Arts Desk*, January 27, https://theartsdesk.com/theatre/whisky-taster-bush-theatre?page=0%2C1
13. Graham, James. 2012. *The Whisky Taster*, Act One, Scene Six, p.272–273.
14. 'Graham, James. *Introduction*. In Graham James. 2012, p.xx.
15. Graham, James. 2006. *Eden's Empire*, Act One, p.26.
16. Graham James. *The Whisky Taster*, Act One, Scene Two. In Graham, James. 2012, p.249.
17. Ibid, Act Two, Scene Three, p.311.
18. Ibid, Act One, Scene Six, p.271.
19. Ibid, Act Two, Scene Three, p.313.
20. Ibid, Act One, Scene Six, p.275.
21. Graham, James. *The Man*. In Graham, James. 2012, p.341.
22. Taylor, Paul. 2006. Eden's Empire, Finborough Theatre, London, 93.2 Fm, Royal Court Theatre, Upstairs. *The Independent*, September 12, https://www.independent.co.uk/arts-entertainment/theatre-dance/reviews/eden-s-empire-finborough-theatre-london-93-2-fm-royal-court-theatre-upstairs-london-415671.html.
23. Graham, James. 2006. *Eden's Empire*, Act Two, p.76.
24. Ibid, Act One, p.29.
25. Ibid, Act Two, p.87.
26. Taylor, Paul. 2006. *The Independent*, September 12.
27. Graham, James. 2006. *Eden's Empire*, Act Two, p.86.
28. Graham, James. *Tory Boyz*. In Graham, James. 2012, p.6.
29. Ibid, p.41.
30. Ibid, p.43.
31. Ibid, p.44.
32. Gardner, Lynne. 2013. Tory Boyz—Review. *The Guardian*, October 3, https://www.theguardian.com/stage/2013/oct/03/tory-boyz-review-gay-tories-westminster.
33. Graham, James. *Tory Boyz*. In Graham, James. 2012, p.55.
34. Graham, James. *The Whisky Taster*. In Graham, J. 2012, Act One, Scene Six, p.270.
35. Sierz, Aleks. 2010. The Whisky Taster, Bush Theatre. *The Arts Desk*, January 27, https://theartsdesk.com/theatre/whisky-taster-bush-theatre.
36. Graham, James. *Tory Boyz*. In Graham, James. 2012, p.61.

37. Ibid, p.26.
38. Graham, James. Introduction. In Graham, James. 2012, p.xviii.
39. Graham, James. 2006. *Eden's Empire*, Act Two, p.68.
40. Ibid, Act Two, p.73.
41. Ibid, Act Two, p.74.
42. Graham, James. Introduction. In Graham, James. 2012, p.xix.
43. Billington, Michael. 2008. Sons of York. *The Guardian*, September 8, https://www.theguardian.com/stage/2008/sep/08/theatre2.
44. Graham, James. Introduction. In Graham, James. 2012, p.xix.
45. Sierz, Aleks. 2021. *Good Nights Out: A History of Popular British Theatre Since the Second World War*, London: Methuen Drama, p.83.
46. Graham, James. *Sons of York*, Act One, Scene Four. In Graham, James. 2012, p.115.
47. Ibid, Two, Scene One, pp.151–152.
48. Sierz, Aleks. 2021. p.83.
49. Graham, James. *Sons of York*, Act, Two, Scene One. In Graham, James. 2012, pp.139–140.
50. Graham, James. *The Whisky Taster*, Act Two, Scene Two. In Graham, James. 2012, p.305.
51. Graham, James. *Sons of York*, Act One, Scene Two. In Graham, James. 2012, p.92.
52. Graham, James. *The Man*. In Graham, James. 2012, p.344.
53. Graham, James. *Sons of York*, Act One, Scene Two. In Graham, James. 2012, p.99.
54. Ibid, Scene Two, p.103.
55. Ibid, Act One, Scene Four, p.126.
56. Ibid, Act Two, Scene One, p.152.
57. Ibid, Act Two, Scene One, p.153.
58. Ibid, Act One, Scene Four, p.118.
59. Ibid, Act Two, Scene One, p.133.
60. Graham, James. *The Man*. In Graham, James. 2012, pp.343–344.

PART I

Legitimately Delegated Power

CHAPTER 2

Democracy

The 'political playwright' badge has followed Graham throughout his career based on a suite of plays set in political institutions but it is a label that the writer has not always embraced, noting in an interview with fellow playwright Anne Washburne in 2019—'I feel like I don't write political theatre.... I just write theatre about politics which is a different thing.'[1] Graham's work instead sits at the intersection of political and the populist play, two forms of theatre-making which have not always been in alignment. Political theatre, of the kind ascribed to Graham, is a playwrighting tradition that stretches back to the early part of the twentieth century, and Jason Price notes Bertold Brecht was one of the first writers to bridge 'past and present' by 'dramatizing historical events in order to comment on the present.' A continually evolving form, more recent writers like David Hare have placed greater responsibility upon audiences, using historical settings to provoke reflections on the present and encourage the viewer to consider possible solutions to contemporary political impasse, writer John F. Deeney notes, much as Graham's work does.[2] Yet, definitions of political theatre are broad and not widely agreed upon. Critic and writer Aleks Sierz in his 2021 book sees a sharp divide between wholesome political theatre with its strict criteria or characteristics and populist forms, while writer Price in his own work on popular theatre sees a much closer alignment between them across the last century, emerging originally from social gatherings and cabaret.[3]

© The Author(s), under exclusive license to Springer Nature Switzerland AG 2024
M. Philpott, *James Graham*,
https://doi.org/10.1007/978-3-031-59663-6_2

Sarah Grochala goes further still, broadening the scope of political playwriting to encompass a more complex relationship between subject matter, the writer's 'political intentions' and the extent to which a play's themes chime with current events. The existence of any one of these things, Grochala argues, can give a play 'political character' regardless of the writer's intentions. Like Hare's appeal to the audience, Grochala too suggests that the experience of the viewer and the circumstances of production also help to define the political character of a performance.[4] If all theatre is political in its construction, performance and reception as Grochala asserts, then art, writer Joshua Abrams suggests, helps to 'draw neat lines around the key political, moral, economic and structural issues of the day.'[5] In a 2013 introduction to *This House*, Graham explained, 'I never wanted it to be a museum piece. Instead, I hope to use the period to create something more timeless than that, something more universal.'[6]

Graham's plays about political subjects therefore exist in this longer continuum, seeking to bring together plays about political topics with popular and accessible forms. The vehicle for this has predominately been recent historical setting which positions his work between past, present and future. Using a post-Second World War history play model allows the writer to emphasis the cyclical nature of British politics, placing contemporary political problems in much longer histories of political behaviours and ingrained power dynamics to consider alternative solutions for how political institutions should operate and what functional relationship they should have to wider society to improve their effectiveness as tools of governance. Sierz has argued that history plays, of the kind that Graham writes, 'makes no demands on the present' and 'don't really give a true insight into real factual history,' mere escapism for audiences keen 'to have fun, to enjoy a good night out.'[7] Yet Graham sees the seeds of the present in the past experiences that his work recreates, places 'where seismic changes in the political landscape can be traced back to the very personal stories of human frailties, desires or mistakes,' explained in an introduction to *This House*.[8] Graham's balanced playwriting does the same across the democracy dramas considered in this chapter—*This House*, *The Vote* and *Labour of Love*—the writer continually navigating a space between representing the past, imagining the future and challenging the audience to think for themselves about the substance of the UK's political structures and a desire to change them.

The changing nature of democracy, its structures and challenges is a key concern across Graham's work and whether his subject is Parliament or local authorities, the problematic nature of contemporary democracy is the subject. Often influenced by unelected social bodies, the political hierarchies, ideologies and realities of functional democracy are shown to be under threat from those actively attempting to hijack due process for their own ends and the sustenance or enlargement of their own sphere of influence, as well as the unleashing of populist forces that overwhelm traditional democratic institutions and push them in alternative directions. Some of these factors, including television and celebrity, are discussed in later chapters, exploring the role of socially cultivated influences on the creation and presentation of facts, and how they generate populist outcomes that have wide-ranging consequences for the independent functioning of State bodies, and how public knowledge is channelled as a result. But Graham is principally interested in the intrinsic compromises built into our established political structures and the challenge these pose to fairness and democratic responsibility, often using historical settings in the recent past as proxy for the modern era to show how change occurred over time, slowly eroding the effectiveness of society's democratic components. The likelihood that governments will prioritise re-election over the development of social policies and a progressive legislative agenda, for example, is not so new, emerging from the complicated dealmaking and manoeuvring explored in *This House* in which a fluctuating majority/minority administration clings to power for five years, prioritising its own survival over its initial programme of change. Likewise, the encroachment of national party politics into local issues is the subject of *Labour of Love* that charts the business of a constituency office over more than two decades, taking in the varied personnel, political ambitions and ideological divides within the Labour Party that hold back electoral success and paralyse the organisation's development. Through detailed exploration and analysis of the pillars of democratic representation and the legitimate exercise of power the system bestows, Graham dissects and diagnoses the problems facing contemporary democracy and what may be needed to address them, all the while respecting, even advocating for those very institutions and processes when they are permitted to operate effectively.

Across Graham's work, then, several key strands emerge that explore the individual effectiveness of democratic structures and their position in a wider scheme of interlinked power bases, each with differing degrees of influence over who is selected to govern, and the mandate given to do so. From the creation of political parties that represent a particular set of interests and ideals, through the processes associated with elections such as hustings and voting, to the role of Parliament in settling (and sometimes delivering) a legislative programme, Graham considers how well each of these areas function, drawing attention to the hidden activities that sit behind and can actively undermine the illusion of democratic will. And beyond the accepted social function of democracy, the writer considers what it means to operate outside of these structures where protest and anarchic movements attempt to derail, improve or even entirely overthrow these systems to create a new kind of order. In almost all cases, individuals in these plays must subvert their needs to support the will of their party or government while those choosing to act outside of the traditional structures will become trampled by the very institutions they try to overthrow. Graham's work looks beneath the surface of the Establishment to understand the differences between democracy and power, a concept that, like Graham, Grochala sees as increasingly complex, crossing the boundaries of the nation state to create the very 'dislocation between power and politics' that Graham's work exemplifies, driven by a desire from those in power to maintain the status quo.[9]

2.1 Political Parties

The starting point for democratic organisation as a social function in Graham's work is the political party, and several plays have examined these as both established and powerful entities as well as evolving organisations responding to both changes in their own demographic make-up as well as shifting, but also very tenuous, voting patterns. The political party is the primary tool through which democracy operates in these plays, navigating the complex local powerbases in the selection of Parliamentary candidates as well as the often-obscure relationships between constituency offices, local party membership and local councils where implicit tensions exist between different and differently funded forms of political governance. But political parties also represent the charged division between regional and community needs and the demands of the central party, operating through Parliament, with often contradictory requirements. This is a prism through which Graham's political party plays can explore the trade-offs between individual ambition and career expectations at a national level as well as the consequences for constituency and community stagnation at the regional level as a direct result of the compromises democracy demands of them both, creating and sustaining the widespread social decline his work identifies. That these needs change over time is something that his work explores in detail, explaining long-term patterns of behaviour and the evolution of policy that shift the ways in which democracy simultaneously fails to represent the local and national interest as well as those of the party entity itself.

Graham's democracy plays often begin by establishing the traditional construct of national political parties for an audience, and although cliched notions of who runs for office and the party's target audience are often presented, usually with a comic flourish, Graham uses these stereotypes to reveal partial truths or define fault lines within the party that are complicated by the existence and activities of newer members as parties evolve over time. There is an inherent tension in the different vested interests which presents a number of challenges for democracy as different sides, coalitions and lobby groups from within the party attempt to exert influence if not active control over party direction, policy decisions and personnel choices that can stall development and, in some cases, actively destroy party support in very public troubles resulting in failures of confidence in the party as an effective democratic tool. *Labour of Love* is the work in which these notions are most explicitly explored, although both *This House* and the much earlier *Tory Boyz* make reference to the anatomy of political parties and its consequences for effective governance. Set in a constituency office across nearly 30-years, *Labour of Love* explains the tension between different wings of the traditional Labour Party and New Labour, and the cycles of behaviour that shapes the electability of the organisation during this period. But it also notes how this extended period also reveals an embedded, longer-term problem at the heart of the party that has affected its public life before and since. Graham's analysis in the play suggests the party has reduced its overall effectiveness in representing either traditional Labour-voting communities or the more fluid opportunistic voters that it seeks to attract. Class and party tradition underpin the distinction that the writer dramatises between different branches of the organisation, pulled between the industrial voting grounds of the north of England and the intellectual aspiration of voters in cities drawn to the socially conscious and more populist rhetoric of New Labour within the period of this play. In a scene set in 2017—the year the play was first staged—protagonist MP David Lyons summarises Labour's twenty-first-century problem early in the play:

> David: we go 'up' in university towns and cities for the same reasons we're 'down' round here. Lose the 'heartlands' for being too soft on immigration, lose the young metropolitans for being too hard. Too radical for the old, too safe for the young. Too soft-Brexit for Leavers, too hard for Remain. Too left, too right, too old, too new; do you know what they can celebrate all they fucking like, I have no actual clue where we bloody well go from here, I don't.[10]

The articulated dilemma for the Labour Party is one that still applies across the period of cyclical behaviours that Graham presents, with each scene taking the audience back in stages to 1990 by the end of Act One and forward again by the same degrees back to 2017 by the end of Act Two. *Labour of Love* unpicks that shifting demography as those two strands of party politics remain unresolved, and arguably unevolved, as the party leadership struggles to address its widening identity crisis.

Much of that comes from the perceived threat to traditional Labour values and the people it was created to represent and advocate for, a scenario Graham depicts through the dynamic between New Labour man David, perceived as an imposed central-Party figure, and born-and-bred local officers including Councillor Len, party worker Margot and David's constituency agent Jean, all representations of the traditional party, along with the unseen Terry, David's predecessor as MP before he was parachuted in:

> Len: Corporate lawyers in the Labour Party?! I recall the heady days when our membership was apprentices and craftsmen. Labourers and -[11]

In a scene set four years later in 1994, Len takes the opportunity once again to reinforce the traditional and historic values of the party by evoking its famous leaders and sulkily bemoaning the end of that era of representation:

> Len: Ah well. Moments like this, you feel the weight of history, don't you, the ghosts of – Morrison and Bevan, Attlee. Keir Hardy, even, all floating over you. All about to change now, though, of course.[12]

Against this, David explains how the party has changed and its consequences for democracy beyond the direct schism within the organisation itself:

David: And aren't you forgetting the most important people? Who are our most important people, Jean?

Jean: Easy, the members.

David: No. The public. The *electorate*. See, isn't this the problem? The, the cultish-ness of Labour. Traditional Labour. The Militant rooting out non-true believers, it… it's just another Establishment, isn't it? End of the day, only on the left. A bully-boy club of Trotskyites and unions and it intimidates people.[13]

Earlier in the same period, in a scene that Graham directly stages across the two Acts, David lays out the alternative position and hopes to be given a chance to make his party more widely palatable:

David: I'm not asking for the next couple of decades, just the next couple of weeks. I know you're sceptical, like everyone else, but I'm here to… I am here to try doing things differently. You said it, this seat is safe, so why not?

And ok, to the outside world I'm actually the centre, I only look like I'm on the right where you lot are because you're so far left here, the *centre*-left is the right to you.[14]

When the scene resumes in Act Two, David contextualises those differences through a national lens as Graham brings that wider perspective to Labour's ingrained identity problem:

David: I'm not saying it's bad, it's obvious, when you're part of a club, any club, a, a trainspotter's club, you really like and care about trains, right? Whereas most people… (*Drawing a much bigger square.*) … don't, as much. These are the people who normally vote Labour. People who don't care about the Labour constitution, are not involved in ideological war, they just think we might be best for their families. This lot (*Voters.*) are generally a teeny bit to the Right of this lot (*Members.*). But they stick with us, regardless of feeling alienated by what this lot obsess about. Then… (*Drawing a much, much larger square.*) … there are these. The rest of the country. Tories. Liberals. Southerners, the middle classes. All to the Right of *them*. (*Voters.*) And A lot to the right of *them*. (*Members.*)[15]

Graham chooses to play out the acrimonious nature of that divide across the remainder of the story, using interactions between Len and David who represent those opposing and seemingly irreconcilable viewpoints. Reordering the play chronologically, David first explains Labour's key dilemma in the play in Act Two, Scene One soon after his election in 1990 as the Party seeks renewal by implementing policy and personnel shifts that the character hopes will create a platform for government. But Graham foreshadows Labour's identity crisis through David who fears the ideological divide that separates the two incompatible directions that the party and its membership wish to take:

> David: My point is that this lot (*Members.*) for eleven years – in *opposition*, I might add – Coincidence? – have been sucked into a bubble where they're convinced they have popular support, because when they gather in their meetings and sub-committees and sub-sub-committees, and propose to, to renationalise the weather, and everyone in their small meeting cheers, they think 'oh good, look, the world agrees with us' – not realising, or not caring, that *these* others *don't* agree. At all. But these members refuse to compromise in order to get into government and actually enact 'a *version*', yes, a moderated version, of their ideas, that is palatable to everyone, in order to actually make a difference to people who really need them.[16]

Later in the same scene, David becomes even more exorcised by a backward-looking approach that he feels is keeping the party from democratic success, mocking Len's rollcall of the greats of the past:

> David: What, with Soviet-style, Marxist crap? How's that been going since 1979? Who are these 'great persuaders'? Fucking Hatton? Or Livingstone, and his, his North London, CND badge-wearing, cap-wearing 'comrades'. They aren't the Majority. It's just – *maths*. And, History. You win from the centre, always, that's it.
>
> Every time, the same bloody pattern, same lessons unlearnt – Labour loses power, the Hard Left enter, denounce the old Leadership for 'betrayal' of the 'values', and move the party to the Left, where we languish, in opposition, for years, until common sense returns, and we start edging back to power.[17]

Graham goes on to reference the leaders shuffling the party between those left and centre positions including Attlee, Bevan, Wilson and

Foot in a segment that argues Labour's inability to compromise on its demographic constituency stymies its electoral success, the answer David suggests, assuming the author's voice, is 'by setting out a platform that pleases the most amount of people, for the most amount of time. Down the middle. Or what, I believe they call, democracy.'[18]

Graham explores this relationship between the different ideological positions in more detail as the play unfolds taking this theoretical discussion and dramatising the difference between the local party membership and the elected representatives. In an increasingly irate exchange between Len and Elizabeth, David's cynical wife, she resignedly complains of the challenge that the Party structure poses to democracy:

Len: Oh well, we tried, Jean. Thank you anyway, David, for listening to our members. You did the right thing.

Elizabeth: Well, what choice does a person have, with the axe of de-selection forever hanging over their head?

David: Elizabeth...

Elizabeth: I'm sure David didn't become an elected representative to act as a mouthpiece for an unelected local clique'[19]

The substance of this scene set in 1994 focuses on the party leadership election and whether David followed membership expectations by voting for their preferred candidate rather than Tony Blair who David actually backed. The comic series of events that Graham carefully unfolds exposes a sequence of lies and deceptions that creates a significant rift between these subsets of the party that defines their relationship thereafter:

Jean: ... 'Blair.'

Len: (*hit the desk*) You treacherous... You utter and total –

David: Sod you, Len! Jean, to you, I am sorry, I'm sorry that I lied, but -

Jean: I can't believe / I fell for it.[20]

The deep ideological debates about the purpose of the Labour Party and the relationship between the holders of power within it speak directly to concerns about the nature of democracy and the extent to which the structures in which political parties operate uphold democratic independence and the mandate provided by the electorate:

> Len: Clause IV of the Labour constitution – the very soul of the party, since 1918, that links us *together* in solidarity! And you voted for the guy who'll tear it out.
>
> David: For the guy who can *win* – because I actually *care* about the people you, you 'romanticise' about, here, as a little project / I want to help them!
>
> Len: Really. David, me, you're educating me on the founding principles of this party? A Fabian scholar, who –
>
> David: Oh Len, Len –
>
> Len: Jean, it's time, no more mucking about, it's time for him to go –
>
> Elizabeth: (*returning*) Oy, that isn't your CHOICE It's the *voters*' –
>
> Len: No, it's the *party's*!
>
> Elizabeth: He increased his majority at the election, *again*, by *thousands*; how come a dozen odd members –[21]

Even seven years later in Act Two, Scene Four set in 2011, that debate continues to rage in David's constituency when Len and David lock horns once more, this time emphasising the hardened personal animosity that has characterised their relationship, widening their ideological differences further:

> Len: I mean the coup. I'm behind the coup, it isn't Margot, I want you out. I've wanted you out since the day I met you. The day you came back to this town.
>
> (*Aware of* Jean *upstairs, quietly.*) It should be me. This… should be *me*. I'm 'real', you're a – a 'nothing', always have been, this is *mine*.

David: ... You actual bastard.

Len: You Red Tory cunt.

Get out – of my party.[22]

The complex power struggle that Graham identifies at the heart of the Labour Party creates a self-destructive process that prevents individuals in the play from putting their differences aside for the sake of party unity, and Graham presents the ingrained prejudice, stubbornness and self-destructive impulses of both strands of the organisation across several years that have significant implications for the Party's viability for election and the effective operation of democracy:

> David: (*trying not to lose it, starting to pace...*) God, you could never quite bear it, could you, that I was actually part of the wave that *won*, that Got Us In, not part of your narrative, is it, the outsiders, the plucky anti-establishment protest / party, well –
>
> Len: Where you did nothing but / damage the movement, and the party that I love –
>
> David: - yes I know. (*Louder now, not caring, pacing around.*) YES, it could have been better, but why can't you be *man* enough to champion the things we – like I don't know! Lifting millions out of poverty! Record investment in hospitals, schools, police! Civil partnerships! Tax credits! Instead of you / constantly sabotaging -[23]

This divisive dynamic in Graham's play has consequences for the Labour Party's response to the local and national challenges that constituency MP David Lyons must hold in check to sustain not only his own mandate to represent his community—none of whom appear in the play—but also the demands of the formal and organised party membership who expect their views to take priority, founded in the belief that they more accurately represent the will of the community that David serves. But Graham also places his lead character in a charged position between central party (and later government) demands to support any legislation it proposes because it offers him career opportunities within the Cabinet and the personal scruples of his own conscience. And although *This House* more fully explains the compromised operation of Parliamentary politics, Graham uses *Labour of Love* to show the singular role of the MP in the centre of these different stakeholders and their influence on how David wields power, making the illusion of truly independent democracy far harder to sustain.

And these relationships of power are deeply complex. Although subsidiary roles are not explained in detail in *Labour of Love*, the attempt to hold power in different subsets of the party membership is complicated and not always exercised for reasons of loyalty to the party ideals. Of the other characters in the play, primary antagonist Len wants to use his position at the local council as a platform to launch his own claim to the role of constituency MP, while party worker Margot follows a similar trajectory in which characters begin in one position of authority but uses it to progress to a more influential role. At the beginning of the play set in 2017, David voices concerns that Margot is being lined up to replace him and use her tenure to shift the party back to the left, fulfilling the cycle of Labour self-destruction that Graham has so clear laid out. Despite the principles expressed by characters on all sides of the Labour Party spectrum in Act Two, Scene Four Len decides to stand as an independent candidate at the 2017 election, having been unable to oust David as the selected Labour candidate compromising his avowed beliefs and arguably suggesting that his desire for personal power and recognition outstripped his true devotion to the Labour Party he has spent so many years advocating and fighting with David about. Graham equally casts doubt on David's own role in the area in conversations that hope to use the position of MP in North Nottinghamshire as a stepping stone to something greater, and a place he confesses in 2001 that does not intend to stay for long:

> David: we need to be joined up, don't wanna get complacent. And after all (*Begins a kind of cheeky 'jig' towards her, semi-singing.*) Dare I say it… as a future big beast in the party… in the Brand New Cabinet… I think there might just… be cameras there this time, ra-tat-tah-tah…[24]

And while David's wife Elizabeth expresses overt contempt for this choice of constituency, David too betrays a quieter expectation that his residency will be short and personally fruitful:

David: It'll be fine, we just… we just have to *be* here. Be part of the community, we're not tourists here any more.

Elizabeth: Of course not, last tourists to visit here were the bloody Normans.

She kicks some boxes about, sits.

How can they have put you up here, I thought you were a rising – what's it?

David: They're 'put me here' because this is a safe seat. This is what safe looks like, I'm afraid…[25]

Although the practice is not specific to the Labour Party, Graham nonetheless explains the democratic consequences of selecting particular individuals for different roles in councils and constituency offices based on their personal attributes and alignment with specific party objectives rather than fitness or appropriateness for that office, with power passed almost on a hereditary basis to those deemed worthy in the next generation. An approach that is possible in safe seats, Graham suggests, does not necessarily serve community needs when during the years of the play the local quarry closes, and a data centre arrives that also eventually fails taking local voters incrementally further from their traditional occupations with little to replace them. Graham notes the economic worsening of living standards and opportunities, of the gap between the government and the governed on David's watch as a result of party in-fighting that the MP himself does not fail to notice. He speaks of his own disillusionment having spent 25 years supporting the central party direction:

David: When we had the chance, you're right, we weren't radical enough, bold enough, I wasn't…

Jean: You wanted to get in, *stay* in, it's – a fine line –

David: No it was a waste, everyone's right. CLP should de-select me.[26]

As a counterpoint to this powerplay, the personal agendas and struggles between local need and central party direction, *Labour of Love* outlines what the constituency office should be doing in order to fulfil its basic democratic function, included near the start of the play to explain David's frustration:

> David: Won't miss the 500 emails a day, about litter in the park, or the neighbours' trees. And then the other stuff, the serious, depressing stuff, going down the list, just thinking 'poor bastard, poor bastard, poor...' And the abuse, threats of violence, the worrying about you and the other staff, here, when I'm away.[27]

Graham elaborates in Act Two, Scene One when David as a newly arrived MP is given an overview of his role by Office Manager Jean and the need to prioritise constituency work over other concerns that may divide his attention:

> Jean: Most importantly – you Do Not neglect this office in favour of Westminster, I know you're there four days and here only Friday, but remember, it's *this* office and the work you do *here* that gets you re-elected back *there*.

She reinforces the expected power balance:

> Jean: Fourth and final – all major votes in the Commons, you run by the local members here; you have to listen to them first, before the chief whip or Leader or your own silly little conscience.[28]

And then explains why the work in the constituency office is so important:

> Jean: Folk come here as a last resort, having gone to every other agency and no one's helped. So *you* write a letter, to the councillor, school, GP, and it scares them into action. That's it. That's basically an MP.

And notes the expected routine:

> Jean: Constituency diary, Thursday night, Friday, Saturday if you want, we'll load it full of visits, fundraising events, press opps. We had our surgeries on a Friday, average maybe six people a week.
>
> Outside of surgeries you have to build relationships with the community, headmasters, headmistresses, police chief, hospital trust. I'll get your

started. Most important is the Leader of the District Council, that's Len Prior -[29]

Over the period of Graham's play, he shows David struggling to meet even those demands, particularly when council worker Margot descries the futility of local politics and effective process as a result of the MP's semi-absence from the area:

> Margot: I mean I've tried. Over the road, God knows, you don't feel like you're achieving much most of the time, hardly any of the time…. But you push it, you pull it, nothing happens! Just… forces, way beyond your… And yet here's you, get to hop off to Westminster, half the week, swanning around as the Big -[30]

Margot's frustration which David also stems from never feeling like progress is either possible or appreciated, but Jean feels this skims the surface of deeper-rooted social problems that constituency MPs can never expect to resolve:

> David: How come you *never*, you never ever mention the long list of – (*Counting on his fingers.*) I don't know, every school here – refurbished, rebuilt! The bloody – the two bloody city centres, regenerated! Three hospitals, / almost entirely rebuilt.
>
> Jean: Yeah, spending, good, fine, but not the actual difficult work of digging deep down, into the underlying factors woven into the rotten fabric of this unfair, fucking country.[31]

The winner of Graham's first Olivier Award and his only drama to open directly in a commercial venue, Susannah Clapp described the Noel Coward Theatre production of *Labour of Love* in her review for *The Observer* as 'a light-on-its feet canter through the past 27 years of the Labour party, it neatly encapsulates the uneasy alliance between old and New Labour.'[32] While the original production was directed by Jeremy Herrin, the American transfer in 2018 was overseen by Loera Morris and The Washington Post critic Nelson Pressley could 'see why Graham's approach succeeds: the frothy yet serious "Labour" is user-friendly.'[33] *Labour of Love* then portrays the complexity of democratic structures, how ideological divisions and cycles of behaviour threaten to undermine the electoral success of the party and how power moves between different players within the party membership, local postholders and seemingly separate entities of council and constituency office as well as the personal motives and expectations of those hoping to develop political careers by graduating through a system of hierarchical influence. How personnel are selected and expected to perform their duties, as well as commitment to central party mandates all detract from the role of the MP in representing and supporting their communities, a task that does not appeal to a career-hopeful David in the long path to power in Westminster.

Graham explored similar compromises within the two-party system with both *This House* and *Tory Boyz* also commenting on the traditional make-up of the Conservative Party as its changed position in modern politics clashes with its traditional membership and recruitment base. As with the Labour Party, characters in Graham's plays also make sweeping generalisations about Conservative Party personnel and voters, and Jean from *Labour of Love* establishes that demography in a scene set in 1990, characterising 'Tory party politics [as] Posh squirrels fighting in a bag,'[34] reflecting an underlying assumption of a right to power that repeats a key assessment in Graham's work that the Conservative Party manipulates governance structures in order to maintain the status quo and ensure power remains with them:

> Jean: What a glorious peace it must be, to be on the Right. To wake up every morning and look around and think – yeah, this is pretty much how it should be. This is fine. As opposed to knowing you'll never be finished. We'll never be done.[35]

This is a sentiment echoed by Michael Cocks, a Labour Whip in *This House*:

> Cocks: God, such a, an innate, instinctive Tory inability to, to cooperate and 'share', eh? Conservative Britain: 'As long as I'm alright, every bugger else can go hang.'[36]

Jean later bemoans the inevitability of Conservative governments and the innate confidence she presumes its members hold:

> Jean: Look, the Tories always get in eventually. Like a shitty fly; you waft it out a window, it buzzes back in through the door.[37]

Emotive though her metaphor may be, Graham explored the anatomy of the Conservative Party in greater detail in *Tory Boyz* which works in partnership with the local concerns that also shape *Labour of Love*. Graham initially sets out some demographic assumptions about Conservative Party employees and representatives who, like Labour, speak to a traditional class stereotype:

> Nicholas: Me, though, I'm true blue. Home Counties, cricket and rugger, father in the military, huzzah. That more what you'd expected?[38]

However, as with *Labour of Love*, Graham's play takes place during a period of flux in which these patterns seem to shift, and while Nicholas represents a consistent recruiting ground for Conservatism, Sam the protagonist of *Tory Boyz* is part of an altogether different and growing section of the party:

> Robbie: So. You're not your average Tory.
>
> Sam: Really.
>
> Robbie: You've got an accent.
>
> Sam: Ah. *You've* got an accent.
>
> Robbie: You've got a northern accent.[39]

And it is these traditional stereotypes of Conservatism against which Sam battles throughout the play, notably in a scene where the character engages with teenage school children to discuss changes to an Education Bill being proposed by Sam's department in his role as Parliamentary researcher. In the classroom, these cliches of Conservative membership have already been inherited by the secondary school pupils:

> Shayne: Wait, you're a Tory? Awh, man. I thought we was gonna get a Labour.
>
> Ray: Aren't Tories all posh and old, sir?
>
> Sam: No, I'm a Tory, do I sound posh or look old?[40]

When Sam explains his political affiliation in simplistic terms based on party principles, student Muznah summaries the apathy and confusion of the voter unable to distinguish between parties in a changed national landscape; 'My dad says that you're all the same now. And you're all shit.'[41] While *Tory Boyz* pre-dates *Labour of Love* by almost a decade, the complexities of demographic change in the left- and right-leaning parties continues to clash with their backwards-looking attempts to retain their traditional membership and maintain consistency in voter expectations. It is a theme Graham revisited once again in *This House* where old class distinctions between parties are starting to evolve and Conservative Party Whip Weatherill outlines these changes to the Labour Party to his opposite number, Harrison:

> Weatherill: And don't think we don't see the way the crows fly. Working class? What about Southampton Test – an Oxford law don. Lichfield and Tanworth, lecturer. Lancaster North, barrister. Must be getting you worried, I'll bet? With your 'ee by gum', northern brute shtick. All this 'middle classing', you'd better learn to genteel yourself up a bit. Classical music and fine wine. Don't want to be out of touch.[42]

And like *Labour of Love*, *Tory Boyz* also shows a Conservative Party filled with junior staff seeking and even prioritising careers as electoral representatives in which Sam, as with Margot in David Lyon's constituency, bides his time before working through an established system in order to be eventually considered for selection:

> Nicholas: (*laughs*) Oh My God, I knew it. (*Indicating the adjoining office door.*) You want to be one of them, don't you?
>
> Sam: I... (*Shrugs*) I, I don't... I'm not...
>
> Nicholas: Hey, no, listen. It's not like it wasn't obvious, even if it wasn't to you. All this... benevolent extra-curricular stuff, like with the kids and shit.'[43]

But Chief of Staff Nicholas is far more cynical about the openness to change needed within the party to support Sam's career, and Graham uses his authorial voice to expand on the state-of-the-nation implications of the deep-rooted power structures that impede fundamental changes in structure or direction:

Nicholas: You might think the country has changed, but it hasn't all that. And you might think the party's changed but you know that isn't true either. *We're* different, the new intake are different. The young 'uns. And the front bench is different. Hurrah. But behind them in the House and filling the hall of the conference are party members as rooted in the Right as they ever have been.[44]

And it soon becomes apparent that Nicholas too has a careerist agenda, seeking that same kind of recognition within his own career path:

Nicholas: Whoow! Yeah! Get in! Come on! You will never guess what, Sammy-boy, I have been put on the candidate list to be... (*drum roll*) bam bam bah! A Conservative councillor for Wandsworth. Courtesy of the local Putney Association. Booyakasha![45]

At the conclusion of *Tory Boyz*, as with *Labour of Love*, that shuffling of personnel between the central party and local offices has taken place, with Sam taking up a role as deputy fundraising and members chairman for that same Putney Association. And while this may represent a step back from Westminster, it is a brief one and in a longer and perhaps rapidly accelerated career in the party.

Across Graham's plays, political parties are complex entities that are often torn between the traditional needs of their members who, via their subscriptions, exert unelected influence but have an economically purchased stake in the role of individual MPs and the direction of public policy, with power to deflect and even undermine governmental business through disunity if they choose. This factionalism is often driven by political need as the party seeks to make itself more attractive to voters while the changing class and economic construction of members, supporters and party workers also exert an influence, all of whom have different, often contradictory, ideas about how the organisation and its exercise of power should evolve. The career-centred nature of those working for the party and the shuffling of personnel between local offices, councils, Westminster researcher roles and the ultimate prize, Member of Parliament, creates a 'closed-shop' feel in both parties, giving voters representatives who have a future in the party and are not necessarily devoted to or interested in their constituents. And while Graham does not necessarily suggest that parties are defunct democratic institutions—and in fact retains a belief in the principles behind them—equally they are presented as self-interested groups seeking power to control the country's resources.

Further, their role in representing the needs of those who vote for them is compromised by internal, unelected self-interested factions who seek to use that power to drive their own national and regional agendas based on ideological, philosophical and, sometimes, personal advancement that are often backwards-looking and reliant on tradition rather than evolving contemporary need, an ingrained problem for British democracy that Graham repeats in work set at intervals from 1978 to 2017. Having established the nature of political parties and their role in the democratic process, Graham next examines the mechanism for handing them control—elections.

2.2 Elections

Elections are the ultimate expression of democracy, at least in theory, but as Graham's work shows, the interactions between personnel and the process of voting all present challenges to the independence of the system and its effectiveness as a democratic instrument. In fact, with a play set in a Polling Station in the two hours before voting is due to end on a General Election Day, it is also the location of a smartly written farce that explores wider issues undermining the role of the ballot and the compromises it demands of staff that challenge electoral integrity. Who gets to vote and even voting itself is never in question, instead Graham probes the areas where the system fails, outlining the rules and procedures that govern the management of elections, fluid movement between the teams running services at Polling Stations, Counting Offices and local government as well as the threats to democracy that emerge when the appearance of propriety takes precedence over fairness and even the legality of the system itself. The climax of the play reveals the well-intentioned chaos of a London Polling Station within a marginal constituency where every ballot counts. In his 2016 introduction to his second volume of collected works, Graham revealed a 'geeky interest in processes – how things happen. Leaving the audience to answer the 'why.'[46] *The Vote* is a fascinating experiment in hybrid theatre, long before the practice become commonplace, staging a production onstage at the Donmar Warehouse that was simultaneously broadcast live on Channel 4 on the eve of the 2015 General Election. Performed in real time, the show ended exactly at 10 p.m. when Polling Stations across the UK officially closed. 'And though it sounds like one of those theatrical legends that verges on a lie,' Graham explained, 'we never hit 10 p.m. exactly during any preview, but come election night, with the cameras rolling… the last line was said [when] 9.59 flick[ed] to 10.00 exactly on the first bong of Big Ben.'[47]

Graham's piece makes a number of universal points about the nature of the election process and the small ways in which the most publicly accessible form of democratic expression operates in practice as well as the nature of a system that has significant margins for human error. *The Vote* begins by establishing the rules of the Polling Station and the process requirements that staff must uphold as part of their duties to safeguard the integrity of each vote and by extension the election itself. Although Graham will have his characters break most of these rules through the action of the play, throughout the drama they reinforce the parameters in which the scenario must operate. These rules are not questioned or challenged by the play, their existence accepted as fundamental to the safe operation of democracy, instead comedy emerges from trying to apply them which proves harder for the Clerks to manage as the pressure of the occasion builds and the time remaining to vote shortens.

These rules provide the structural framework in which the comedy purpose of the play will operate as well as offering contextual information to the audience to explain the limitations that the democratic system places on the characters conduct and ability to influence events—limitations that they repeatedly flout. It begins with expectation setting about Polling Station behaviours, outlining how members of the public are expected to comport themselves within the space, including a running joke about the use of mobile telephones in the room itself, an issue that staff return to repeatedly when the rule is violated by multiple voters during the two-hour period of the play:

Kirsty: I'm going to have to ask you to put your phone away, please.[48]

And later:

Stephen: I really would like you to put your phone away, sir.[49]

The increasing exasperation of staff reflects the difficulties of maintaining democratic decorum alongside the technological developments of recent years with young voters wanting to use their phones to take selfies as well as make calls, placing a minor but deliberate strain on a system that may no longer be fit for purpose:

Rochena and Alexandra *have come out of the booth, and pose for a selfie on their smartphone....*

Rochena: OK, say democra-cheese.

Kirsty: Ooh, no I'm sorry, that's not allowed.

Alexandra: It's just a selfie.

Kirsty: No, no 'selfies', not in here.[50]

These help the audience to understand the gradually weakening parameters of the play and summarise the nature of the voting process in which the Presiding Officer and the Clerks hand out ballots, keep track of numbers and prevent voters from leaving the Station with their ballot paper, generating opportunities to explore what happens when single rules are contravened in practice and as cumulative building blocks within the farce structure that Graham operates. A decisive example involves voter Alistair, a man in his 40s who wants to take his ballot paper to the pub to think about his choices, initiating a sequence of escalating activity that culminates in the play's conclusion:

Alistair: Oh, I was just going to take it away, have a quick look.

Stephen: Ah you can't leave the polling station with your ballot I'm afraid.

Alistair: ... But. It's mine. Isn't it?

Stephen: Not, erm, not technically. Your vote is yours. But the ballot paper – that, that's ours.[51]

This becomes a through-line joke running across the four parts of *The Vote*, driving the action, first when the police become involved and later when the ballot paper is returned. Graham fashions an opportunity for his Polling Station staff to misappropriate this vote to correct a counting mistake made earlier in the play, a mistake that already jeopardised the democratic independence of their ballot box. Their attempt to rectify the original error with a further anti-democratic corrective results in a classic farce moment, as the Polling Station characters blame Alistair, the voter, and thereby further misdirect the action:

> Stephen: (*to* Chika) Did he put up a struggle, the guy? If he's planning on coming back, I just have to be aware, for our staff, if he's been drinking and -.[52]

But in the high-pressure finale to the play with only a few minutes before the Station must close, Alistair returns to vote, redressing the balance and revealing that democratic fairness has been breached, a claim the audience already knows is correct, while Station staff clamber to maintain their stance:

> Alistair: Look, I just want my paper, where's my paper?
>
> Kirsty: We... we don't have it. You took it.
>
> Alistair: The copper brought it back she said.
>
> Kirsty: There's no record of that.
>
> Alistair: Oh, what? I don't believe this, what?!
>
> Alan: Is there a problem?
>
> Alistair: They're not giving me my vote.
>
> Kirsty: We don't have his vote, he took his vote.
>
> Alistair: You're... you're lying. You're a liar.[53]

It is a telling sequence in which authorised and trusted staff collude to deny an individual his electoral right and then gaslight him into believing that voting rules were followed—a significant statement about the ease with which this democratic process can be disrupted. And Graham exacerbates the original error by reapportioning blame:

> Alistair: No, I'm saying I'm sorry, you're right. I don't deserve it. My vote.[54]

Before the end of the play, the situation is clarified and the truth finally emerges, resolving the farce, yet the fragility of the electoral process has come more sharply into focus as a result.

That the electoral system is shown to be traditional, even old-fashioned is one of the facilitating factors of the farce repeated several times during the course of the play, and it is this capacity for human error that underpins almost all of the mistakes made in *The Vote*:

> Laura: Go to the booth, take a pencil, and put a cross next to the person you're voting for.
>
> Jasmin *goes to booth #1*. Carla *goes to booth #2*.
>
> Carla: Pencils?
>
> Jasmine: (*to the booth*) This is so old school. It's like the 90 s or something.[55]

Earlier in the play, another first-time voter of Russian descent makes a similar observation about the manual nature of the process in the twenty-first century:

> Alexandra: (*crossing to the booth*) So strange, one of the oldest democracies in the world and this is where you come?
>
> Tilde: (*being guided out by* Stephen) It is rather odd, isn't it? You have not upgraded to screens yet? Computers?
>
> Stephen: Nope still the HB pencils for us. They don't leave a trail.[56]

And it is this lack of a trail that allows Clerk Kirsty to cover up the issuing error and then attempt to even out the votes by using members of her family to redress the balance—a process that mirrors the Pairing notion in *This House* but taken to anti-democratic extremes. This series of process failures creates the original problem and allows staff to exacerbate the mistake, compromising the democratic process along the way:

> Kirsty: And he just voted, *again*. I saw him. But he can't have done, we didn't issue him another ballot paper.

> Laura: No, that can't, that can't have happened, because there's no way that like, yeah, bollocks, OK yeah, no I did.
>
> Kirsty: What?
>
> Laura: I gave him one.
>
> Kirsty: What? How?
>
> Laura: He gave me his name, it wasn't crossed out on the register.[57]

And from here a series of excuses pour forth, some to justify the error by blaming other personal compromises including when Kirsty complains 'but it is two people on the issue desk at all times.'[58] But when one of Kirsty's misused ballots is later required by the real voter who unexpectedly arrives, some quick thinking is required to explain the discrepancy:

> Margaret: There's a line through my name? How can that have happened? You wouldn't have marked my name off, you know me.
>
> Kirsty: Yes, I know, I can't... I literally can't think of a good enough explanation for that. Stephen?[59]

When Margaret is then issued with Alistair's ballot, returned from the pub where he had taken it, this leads to later confusion when Alistair himself comes back to vote. However, not all of the problems explored in *The Vote* stem from staff failures but other kinds of human error including confusion about the registration process between a mother and daughter with the same name who have only one vote between them and a man who arrives at the wrong Polling Station. Voters too it seems have no clearer grasp of the rules than the Clerks, and while all of this helps to shape the nature of the farce, Graham quite carefully builds the scale of the comedy from a small and entirely feasible administrative mistake exacerbated by failures of communications into a far larger democratic crisis.

In conclusion, the writer imposes a series of consequences for this electoral foul play by noting the check points that will govern the future stages of the electoral process where these mistakes will be discovered and rectified—the capacity for democracy to reassert itself against these incursions, further discussed in the next Chapter—at the Count, and its impact on the reputation of the district. Avoiding some of those effects is one of the key motivators behind the chicanery as Graham blends personal outcomes for the individuals with their potential legal ramifications within the nature of the farce and its consequences, growing the relatively minor original problem into a more serious commentary on democratic integrity that relies on small groups of trusted individuals across a network of Polling Stations. Graham frames those personal consequences as a desire for speed at all costs, a pressure characters place on themselves to beat a rival district heightening the dramatic stakes and pressing against the legitimate operation of democracy as individual ambition takes precedence:

> Stephen: I'm about halfway through counting the unused ballots, it would be great to have all the accounts done and the box in the back of my Citroen for 10.45. Charlie Russell wants to announce the count at 2 this year, finally beat Southwark.
>
> Kirsty: 'Southwark', 'booo'. S'quite nice actually, some of it.
>
> Laura: I know I keep saying it, I just still find that all a bit, I dunno, weird. This desire to count them 'fast', rather than – getting it right. Especially when we're a key marginal, need to take care, don't we?
>
> Stephen: Of course, but I don't want it to be delays at *this* station that means the count is waiting for us. If the count waits for our box, the Returning Officer waits to announce the seat, and so on and so on.[60]

The effect of these compromises is further explained at the beginning of Part Three, repeating the political dangers to the audience:

> Stephen: What we *need* to do, Kirsty, is appreciate that if a discrepancy is discovered in the box, and the box gets removed from the count, and the count gets delayed, the constituency can't be announced -
>
> Laura: Oh, that would be – that would look, *really* bad if it's us who delays –

Stephen: I'm not concerned with how it *looks*, Laura, / I'm concerned with –

Laura (*over* Stephen) – in the closest election of our life where one seat might, might, literally make the difference between majority, minority, coalition –

Stephen: Leading to instability, uncertainty, market wobbles, war, plague, disease, death, yes.[61]

This rapidly escalating scale of outcomes may feel extreme or potentially unlikely—as all farce does—but Graham uses it to draw together various thoughts on the fragility of electoral processes outlined in the play, noting the potential fallibility of a manual system run by individuals who not only have the capacity to make mistakes and cover them up, but who also have different vested interests in how effectively the electoral system is managed in practice.

Graham returns to the theme of personnel moving between different types of governance roles with the characters in *The Vote* also having a number of connections to other forms of local administration and career aspirations which hinge on the successful management of this Polling Station. The most overt of these is Presiding Officer Stephen who is presented to the audience as the epitome of good practice and compliance. But Graham gives Stephen a competitive streak in seeking to best rivals at the Southwark Station and with a core motivation explained in Part One by Poll Clerk Laura who reports Stephen's determination to provide an efficient service to voters and the 'positive noises from the council' his performance has elicited.[62]

> Kirsty: Don't mind Stephen if he seems a bit 'brusque' occasionally. (*Texting* Tilde.)
>
> Laura: Is he? Seems inhumanly calm, I thought, don't know how he does it.
>
> Kirsty: Under a bit of pressure this year – I shouldn't say, but, he's in the running. For Anita's job, Deputy Returning Officer.[63]

And the audience is given further confirmation by Stephen himself in Part Two:

Alan: So, is this true, Stephen, what I hear? You being in line for 'great things'? Anita's position, Deputy Returning?

Stephen: Yeah I'm not confident to be honest. I'm up against – you know. 'Modernists'. 'Reformers'. 'How do we get more people through the door?'

Alan (*to* Stephen) So bloody what, you're old school, I like that.[64]

Stephen's concern about the integrity of the ballot box and delays in the count are cast in a different light when it becomes clear that his fears are not only for the security of the process, but its personal consequences for his own promotional chances, an interest which manifests when Stephen himself issues a misappropriated ballot to former Councillor Margaret in order to preserve his ambitions. A few pages later, Graham reminds the audience once again that Stephen is in line for a promotion it is already widely assumed he will achieve and deserved:

Claire: Rumours are rife at the council, still. Anita's job? If it was an *actual* democracy, and we all got a say, I know who'd be a shoe in. You deserve it, Stephen.[65]

Stephen is redeemed somewhat by the end of the play by admitting the improprieties undertaken during his time in charge, but *The Vote* questions the independence and neutrality of characters appointed to manage a core democratic process when they have a resultant stake in local government and higher office.

Stephen is not the only Station employee with links to other parts of the legislature who may be potentially compromised by external interests and associations. A key exchange between Clerks Kirsty and Laura in Part One outlines both the monetary incentive they receive as well as their own roles in the council:

Kirsty: Oh well this is just a laugh, isn't it. 'Social'. And double pay. Keep your wage at the council, get a wage doing this, win-win.

Laura: I feel quite, I dunno, honoured, if that doesn't sound... to be contributing. To my community, playing my part.

> Kirsty: Not *your* community though, is it. You're up in – where are you again? North of the river. (*Sucking on a Haribo.*) Do you have aspirations of 'high office'?
>
> Laura: Me, no, I'm just – I'm the leader's press advisor, I'm not a policy –. Although, yeah, a lot of MPs were advisors at some point, so –.[66]

Graham here notes the same hankering for Parliamentary influence seen in the local council characters in *Labour of Love* where individuals treat their present role as a steppingstone to a more senior and powerful position, arguably undermining the effectiveness and investment in these lower levels of government. Kirsty also shares a family connection with someone at the next stage of the process, referring again to the financial reward it brings:

> Kirsty: Oh yeah, that's two double-times we get, from the council. And he loves counting, my husband, some reason, anything loves it; Absolutely bizarre![67]

This interconnectedness is used for comic effect in *The Vote* as Kirsty calls upon more and more of her family members to help rectify and hide her mistakes, through which Graham calls into question the independence and integrity of an electoral process managed by people who may have implicit party loyalties or individual agendas to pursue.

The Vote comments on the nature of these public processes, yet retains a degree of respect for this facet of democracy when operated correctly, arguing that the Polling Station is a 'bastion of democracy'[68] where, as Laura claims, a sense of anticipation and excitement looms, where hope and the possibility for change come together:

> Laura: Not many nights like this, where you get to wonder what 'tomorrow might be'.[69]

And while Lucas, clerk Kirsty's son, expresses contempt for the process and her role in 'propping up an outdated, undemocratic system' that he refuses to participate in,[70] Conservative candidate Adeyemi reinforces how slight the process feels, voicing the author's quiet faith in this public expression of electoral will:

Adeyemi: Funny looking at it. I'm just one of... (*counting*) eight names. Equal size, alphabetical order. Forget, don't you. Nothing stopping you putting a cross against – anyone. It looks so – fragile, here.[71]

A sentiment echoed by voter Tom in Part One who reflects on this national moment of collective expression and relative rarity of the process, making it seem an almost sacred act:

Tom: Like how many goes do you think we all get, at this? Once, every five years, so that's maybe 10 votes, in a lifetime? If you're lucky...?[72]

Maintaining trust in the election process is the key driver for characters in *The Vote*, even if, as Laura explains in Part Three, just an appearance of integrity matters. Graham believes this act has to be meaningful, noting 'I've always been something of an optimist when it comes to our democratic systems and the people running them'[73] leading Presiding Officer Stephen to echo the author's voice by wishing it mattered more, stating 'Maybe if everyone treated it a bit more carefully, if you realised how fragile it was!' Maybe if everyone didn't just step on it and then go 'oh look, it's broken, let's throw it away'.'[74] While the farcical nature of the play calls into question the fundamental sanctity of the public ballot, the writer nonetheless retains faith in the process to fulfil its core purpose—to elect a government.

2.3 Parliament

The results of an election are not always easy to understand, and as voting share and seat numbers go up or down, the complexities of the UK's First Past the Post voting system can make the formation of governments difficult. Waiting for the election count to be confirmed during the 2017 election, *Labour of Love*'s constituency agent, Jean, summarises the complex and contradictory nature of election maths:

Jean: Anyway, last count, which could be wrong, but probably not, you're trailing the Tory by just 129 votes, down from a majority of 6,063 two years ago. Except, hilariously, you've gone 'up' in actual votes cast, by 1,295, so that's a swing *to* you of – oh Christ, do the maths, channel me Carol Vorderman, 0.5 per cent. *Except*, the Tories have gained 7,000-plus votes since last time, so we're up, *and* they're up. UKIP down to nowt, but they can't all've gone Tory otherwise the Tory would be further over the line, so weirdly some of UKIP must have come *back* to us from 2015, despite us knowing on the doorstep that a lot of *our* lot went Tory.[75]

Whether the turnout changes or voting patterns shift, eventually someone wins or at least becomes the majority party and is invited to form a government, which in Graham's work proves as fragile and changeable across the five years of the Parliamentary term as every other stage of the democratic process that the writer has explored. It is in *This House* that the business of Parliamentary democracy comes under scrutiny with a period-set play examining the problematic nature of maintaining a majority, the compromises, coalitions and cajoling needed to pass legalisation, and the difficulty of removing a flailing administration when its own longevity is prioritised over the wave of change promised during the election. Part of the journey taken by this play, Graham explains, 'was to square up to that stuff and demystify it.'[76]

The action takes place during the volatile Labour administration from 1974 to 1979, and Graham charts the changing fortunes of a government in a particularly tumultuous and tenuously held Parliamentary term, using the events of *This House* to examine the broader challenges, failings and, indeed, benefits of this form of democratic governance in what Nicholas Holden has described as 'an imagination of an area of politics that has remained hidden for much of history.'[77] What is presented as a buoyant victory party at the start of the play becomes a slightly jaded leadership enmeshed in compromised politics that hinders the advancement of legislation and consequently struggles for party unity. This need to prioritise the longevity of government eventually supersedes all other business and it is a position that places the needs of the central party over other forms of democratic expression seen in *Labour of Love* and *The Vote*. Constituency MPs demand recognition for their own schemes and personal comforts, exploiting the changing fortunes of the administration as further reductions in personnel diminish the party's share of the vote and takes this government into minority with too few MPs to win legislative votes in the House of Commons without cross-party support. This engenders a new approach to collaborative coalition politics in order to retain the government's overall control of the House and their mandate to direct it. Early in the play, one of Graham's Labour Whips mirrors Jean from *Labour of Love* with some complex election calculations to explain the nature of Labour's governmental control:

Mellish: It's a mathematical problem, and one we definitely have to balance. 301, us. The Tories 297. And then we have the odds and sods. Liberals 14, the Scots 7, Irish 11, Welsh 2, others 3, meaning an Opposition total of 334…. we've got the biggest boat, but they've got more paddles.[78]

There are two General Elections in *This House*, taking place outside of the central drama which slightly alter the government's fortunes. The first at the start of the play in February 1974 puts a minority Labour government in office; the second comes at the beginning of Act One, Scene Three in October of the same year, giving the Labour Party a majority of just three. And it is this variation in the score card that drives the drama, with Graham employing a numbers game approach to help the audience understand the changed stakes as its voting ability rises and falls throughout the play, focusing the work the Labour Whips must do to maintain their administration.

The role of the Whips' office and the various practices they employ to coerce votes within their own party is the comic purpose of *This House*, sitting within a wider examination of party politics and electoral practices. Graham looks beneath the surface of Parliamentary democracy to understand how it operates in practice and how romanticised notions of MPs representing the people are compromised or challenged by the practices of national governance. 'In the theatre of politics, it is perhaps easy to overlook the extent to which political structures of power impact the lives of everyday people,' Holden explains, with Graham using the characters and storytelling in *This House* to 'understand more deeply the workings of a system that ultimately affects us all.'[79] The purpose of the Whips is a semi-secret one, their names, it is noted, unrecorded in the histories of the House, but their role involves a great deal of bargaining and coercive management of the opposition as well as members of their own party in order to ensure the sitting administration wins its votes in the Chamber and can pass legislation within the delivery timetable it sets. And this makes them a good subject for comedy-drama. To acclimatise the audience, Graham outlines the Whips' role in agreeing a schedule for legislation with their counterparts, which provides a first opportunity to disrupt the elected government. In Act One, Scene One, the newly ascendant Labour Whips host a meeting in their office to agree the diary in a swiftly managed scene with their Conservative equivalents now in opposition:

> Mellish: Alight, we were looking at this, Rates Bill to open on the 17th, Social Security 20th, Health and Safety Bill on the 21st.
>
> Atkins: Aha. (*Writing. A while.*) ... Yes, doesn't work for us, Social Security; that last week of April would be preferable...
>
> Mellish: Few days before Easter, surely you're worried about getting your members in?
>
> Weatherill: Hmm – no, actually, and it gives the Bill longer in committee, so the 26th then?
>
> Mellish: Oh wait, look, Scottish school holidays then so Scots MPs will struggle to be here.
>
> Atkins: Oh, that's shame. Still, can't revolve around seven Scottish Nationalists.[80]

Guiding that timetable becomes the key role of the Whips in this play, navigating between the party leadership and representatives to create a party unity, a notion romantically explained by Labour Whip Walter Harrison during the Prologue:

> Harrison: That's the job of the whips. The job is to transmit in a way that is undetectable to the eagles circling above, the job is to communicate the instruction '*Turn*'. 'Turn now'. 'Turn all of us, together, now, and we might make it. We might just bloody well make it.'[81]

In Graham's play that proves a less dignified activity in practice as new Whip Ann Taylor discovers during her first meeting where she is presented with a screwdriver for the practice of 'flushing':

> Harrison: Toilets. Flushing. When a vote's called and the division bell rings you've eight minutes to get members through the lobby, each whip takes a toilet, go in and try and work out if the feet in the cubicle are Labour or not. If they are, flush'em out. Everything OK?[82]

With each Whip given their own list of MPs to look after, Graham makes their early work business as usual tasks, relatively mundane and administrative, upholding the minor protocols and directives of the institution, keeping members in line while guaranteeing the minutiae of regulatory compliance and conduct:

> Atkins: If you insist on parking more than one vehicle I suggest you use the car park beneath Church House, that always has more space.
>
> Plymouth Sutton: Fine, I see, I'll just leave the house five minutes earlier every morning in order that I can park father away - wonderful![83]

But for the remainder of the play, its comedy emerges from the Whips' role in keeping the government afloat or, in the case of the Opposition Whips, trying to force a defeat that may trigger a fresh election, as Holden notes: 'The play, therefore, concentrates primarily on hierarchical relationships that exist with a controlling group, or in the context of the play, the way the Whip System functions in UK politics.'[84] This plays an integral role in the operation of democracy even when required to employ potentially anti-democratic means to ensure their party survives.

As with *Labour of Love* and *The Vote*, Graham uses characters in *This House* to examine the parameters for the drama, making new Whip Ann Taylor the audience's proxy receiving instruction in the various Parliamentary traditions that provide necessary expositional context, particularly when the withdrawal of these norms materially affects how the business of the House is conducted in the latter part of the play and provide a shorthand for the 'unequal representation of the sexes apparent in 1970s politics.'[85] The most important of these is the practice of 'Pairing,' a key custom of Parliamentary democracy, which becomes a vital dramatic device because it exists outside of the legislative process, a form of gentleman's agreement between the primary parties:

> Taylor: 'Pairing', right, and that's used when someone can't get to the House to vote, one of theirs sits out for one of ours.[86]

And soon the writer provides a live example of how this works in practice during the preamble to the first significant vote on a Social Security Amendment Bill in Act One, Scene Two in which the Labour and Conservative Whips strike a private deal to uphold this important but unofficial tradition:

Harper: (*with his*) Yes, well, as you know the Foreign Secretary is at the summit, and so courtesy dictates you take one your boys out when a minister is away.

Silvester: That's of course fine, we'll send one of our boys home.

Harper: And then another pair. For Batley. Ill at home. Any of your boys needing to slip away?

Silvester (*looks over his shoulder*) Well. Poor Batley. Fine, we'll pair him too. And may the best men win[87]

Operating efficiently in this instance, Graham includes this scene in *This House* as an exemplar of fairness and cooperation, but the practice is soon corrupted by the instability of the Labour administration when the Whips are accused of cheating to secure a vote. This simple overturning of a non-mandated tradition takes place immediately following an important recalculation of the government's tenuous numerical position, leaving them one short of commanding a majority and therefore subject to potential defeat. A comedy standoff ensues between the rival Whips, mediated by the Speaker, which directly challenges the decorum of the democratic process and eventually the reputation of the governing administration:

Speaker: (trying to get above the din) Gentlemen, *please*! Try to act like Honourable Members of this House! And not football hooligans. I've already suspended the session for twenty minutes so that everyone can calm down. I've Commons policemen pulling people apart in the lobby and fighting, *fighting*, in the House of Commons Chamber! I have never in my life.[88]

The audience is once again reminded that the practice of Paring has no official role in the operation of democracy, giving the Speaker little choice but to accept the outcome of the vote regardless of the allegations and chaos that has been caused:

Speaker: there's nothing in the Erskine May rules that recognises *pairing*. That's a gentleman's agreement between yourselves. I can't call a recount.[89]

In this situation, Graham's Labour Whips may win the battle, but the consequence of their allegedly anti-democratic actions is the withdrawal of the Pairing system entirely by their Opposition numbers as both parties move beyond 'fair play' and the prioritisation of sound Bill-making to focus more on complex tactics that seek only to retain or thwart each other's power, undermining the effectiveness of the governmental process. The outcome for the Labour Whips is immediate and wide-ranging, shrinking support among other parties who instantly lose trust in the willingness of the government to adhere to the established rules of business:

> Taylor: (*re-entering*) Chief, there's uproar among the odds and sods, The Liberals, Welsh… all of them saying they won't be voting with us again. They 'can't be associated with cheats'.
>
> Cocks: Oh brilliant, so… (*At the board, tapping away.*) All the odds and sods gone, and we can't pair, with our lot, if we *can't* pair -! Fuck it![90]

Graham creates a dramatic cliffhanger at the end of Act One that leaves the Labour Whips with a difficult problem to solve for democracy, staying in power at all costs has already replaced the optimism of a new administration with an agenda to deliver, and instead their survival by any means necessary becomes the primary driver in the rest of the play.

With Pairing no longer possible, Graham's Whips try other means of ensuring their party 'turns' together resulting in the chaotic coercion of votes by any means at their disposal:

> Cocks: Right, Defence Secretary, the member for Mansfield, he's suck in Ireland and the next flight isn't for over an hour so I've spoken to the PM, the RAF will lay on a jet.
>
> Taylor (*phone down*) No, Hunter Jet's off, but the RAF can strap on an extra fuel tank to a helicopter at the base fourteen miles from the minster, that might get him here, just.
>
> Cocks: Ann, get on the phone to the Ulster constabulary, I want all the traffic lights fixed in his favour to get him to the base, no reds, all green.[91]

Graham also constructs conversations that involve making promises to MPs from rival parties to ensure support for votes, even engaging with those who have little faith in the UK's democratic process. Here the Whips offer them anything they require in exchange for their support, or at least appear to:

> Belfast West: I mean asking us, *us*, *me*, to blindly support *you*, the British government – well you know, the 'sort of' government, bless yers – I hope you know what you're actually asking.
>
> Armagh: I'm happy to consider an arrangement, Walter, but it's got to be give and take, you know? We've got to get something back.
>
> Belfast North: Like the boundary changes.
>
> Armagh: And the pipeline –
>
> Belfast North: Ooh yeah, the pipeline.
>
> Harrison: I can promise our door will always be open, nothing is off the table to our friends.[92]

But most often, the Whips are required to respond to the demands and ambitions of their own opportunistic members to guarantee their compliance, which Graham presents as a revolving door of quick-fire scenes ahead of the first major vote:

> Ilford North: I'm just not sure it's in the interest of my constituents. Perhaps if I had… oh, I don't know, a nice easy chair in my office, that might make me feel more… 'comfortable'?
>
> Harper: An easy chair?! (*Sighs, writes it down.*) Right, easy chair.
>
> Speaker: Member for Thurrock?!
>
> Taylor: So that's one new carpet and we'll see about a place on the Science Committee. Deal?[93]

This process of bartering that Graham dramatises reminds the audience that democracy is a system where party and individual needs are frequently at odds, requiring a series of mutually advantageous deals that ensure progress on the government's agenda is made regardless of electoral and constituency need. As the Whips become more desperate to sustain their administration, the effectiveness of the government and its role in delivering its democratically elected purpose is muddied:

> Cocks: Well, some of us happen to think there's a hell of a lot more to get done, so forgive me if we don't shut up shop just yet.
>
> Atkins: 'Get done'? That's my point, you aren't *doing* anything.
>
> Cocks: We're keeping you out. That's something.[94]

Meanwhile, Graham's Conservative Whips are equally culpable for countermeasures applied to disrupt votes in order to force a motion of No Confidence in the government that would trigger a General Election:

> Atkins: Alright. New tactic. This has become a war of attrition; both sides dug into their trenches, neither making headway. To our credit, they're exhausted. After late-night debates we have no appointments until business begins at 2.30p.m. the next day, but Government ministers have to be in their departments first thing, so it's time to employ the age-old tactic of, quite simply, Wearing Them Out.
>
> Weatherill: We've crafted a rota of our chaps who will come in for what is essentially 'nightshift work', making long speeches, asking an interminable amount of questions. They'll have to hold their members back in case we call a vote, which we'll never do, thus getting their members furious at their own Whips for the incorrigible hours.[95]

Eventually, though, the system cracks under the pressure of trying to keep the governmental agenda alive under these compromised conditions. Early in Act Two, Scene Two, Labour Whip Walter Harrison talks of having 'to draw the line somewhere,'[96] although it will be another three scenes before Harrison finally admits defeat[97] and allows the government to fall by a single vote. But the writer establishes the consequences for individual MPs in Act Two, Scene Three as the Member for Newnham Northeast complains his local members are threatening personal penalties for the failures of the government and the MP to deliver the change expected of this Labour government:

Newnham North East: It's becoming intolerable, Michael. This Militant Left lot, they've infiltrated my local party, and they're close, they're this close I swear, from deselecting me, unless I – what? – start calling for revolution. The guillotine!

Cocks: Reg, I understand, we'll talk, just... not now.

Newnham North East: It's a ticking bomb, this, Michael, I'm warning you. (*Leaves, disgruntled.*)

Cocks: Exit poll in Ashfield, unbelievable. Tories are gonna take it. That and Birmingham Stetchford.

Harrison: You what? Ashfield, that's a mining town?! What they voting Tory for?![98]

This long-term debate between different factions within the Labour Party was discussed earlier in this chapter, but with changing voting patterns as a result of governmental ineffectiveness and the social decline it precipitates at a local level, Graham links the inverted power structures used to sustain the administration in *This House* to the inability of Parliamentary democracy to deliver effective representation thus straining how individual administrations unfold over time with their influence ebbing away.

Across the democracy plays, the ambition of individuals working within the system poses potential challenges for democracy. Whips are supposedly neutral forces within the party they serve, designed to support the leadership programme of whoever is chosen to head the Parliamentary party. When Harold Wilson is replaced by James Callaghan in 1976, Labour Whip Bob Mellish choses this time to 'pledge my own personal support'[99] to one of Callaghan's unnamed rivals and thereby betrays the principles of his office. It is a decision that quickly backfires when the bid fails and Bob is subsequently removed from his post at the end of the first Act. Explaining his actions to fellow Whip Cocks, Bob reveals his own desire for personal power that drove his actions:

Mellish: Backed the wrong horse, didn't I? Ebbw Vale. You play your cards...

Cocks: Why di – Why did you even *back* a horse? You always said we had to be –

Mellish: Yeah and I'm right, you should be. I ju – I just wanted... oh, I dunno Michael, I just got sick of this, being in the heart of the bloody kitchen, cleaning up the mess, doing all the... I just wanted a seat round that table. Maybe. As an equal, not the bloody whipping boy, one who makes 'em laugh with his, his... cheeky, cockney rhyming, bloody, docker's son.... You need your Whip to take a bloody bullet for you, and I stuck my neck out for the other guy. He needs someone he can trust.[100]

But the play conversely wonders whether the MPs who want to work in the Whips Office are shying away from visible power and truly fulfilling their duties as representatives of their constituency. Harrison reflects on his own role during a final exchange with rival Conservative Whip, Weatherill:

Harrison: It's all I ever wanted. You know. Other folk what came in with me. All talking about Cabinet posts, and... and the 'top job'. This is all I ever wanted. To be in the engine room. And I have... bloody *loved* it.[101]

As with the Member for Thurrock seeking a position on the Science Committee in return for his compliance with government policy, so do the Whips consider and try to protect their own career ambitions on both sides of the House. Ann Taylor at the start of Act Two voices her own intentions to colleague Cocks—'To be where you are one day. First woman Chief.[102] Even Opposition Whip Weatherill fears retribution from his leader if he agrees to a deal with Harrison that will help the government in the closing moments of the play. 'Imagine what the Lady would do to the person who didn't walk in tonight?' he explains 'Career over, that'd be it.'[103] As with personnel across the democratic institutions and structures explored in Graham's plays, serving MPs are expected to obey the party leadership and vote accordingly, regardless of their constituency support, safe seat or marginal. This applies equally to the Whips, because to do otherwise risks censure and even removal from office should they choose, like Bob Mellish, to over-reach and try to shape the agenda themselves.

As with all parts of the democratic system, Graham has faith in the process of Parliamentary governance when operated properly, and *This*

House retains an overarching optimism about its value as well as the traditions and history that it represents. 'I have a deep admiration for our democracy, Graham enthused in an introductory to the play in 2013, 'an affection for the building that houses it, a belief in what it *could* be.'[104] Reflecting on that physical expression of democratic intent, Graham feeds this into Labour Whip Bob Mellish's impassioned statement of purpose on the role:

> Mellish: It's what makes our job so hard, it's about flesh and blood at the end of the day, you vote *with* your bodies. You can't phone it in from China, can't send it through the post, can't even stay sat and raise your hand. Unless you put one foot in front of the other and pass through the lobby, you don't count. It's archaic, it's old-fashioned, it's bollocks; but somehow it works.[105]

In the same scene, the Member for Peebles makes a similar claim, valuing the work of those who came before embodied in the building itself and the connection it inspires:

> Peebles: You know this chapel is over 450 years old. I find clarity in the dignified silence of old things. Centuries' worth of human endeavour helps put one's own troubles into a kind of context. I find.[106]

In Act Two, Scene Two, Harrison expresses similar import and inspiration in the archive:

> Harrison: Over a million Parliamentary bills. Every single law of the land that was ever passed, signed by the Queen. Rolled up and stuffed in 'ere.[107]

The question of governmental effectiveness in *This House* is filtered through the importance of those upheld traditions in the face of contemporary innovation and demands for modernisation that young Conservative Whip Fred Silvester advocates for to make Parliament a more professional workplace. Yet, while his colleague Humphrey Atkins argues that muddling through is the best that can be hoped for from an imperfect but functioning system,[108] this intervention of the authorial voice expands into a far more charged discussion about the exercise of power between rival Whips, debating the concept of coalition governments and the potential for practising harmonious and stable governance in place of the bitter game-playing depicted in the play:

> Cocks: In fact I rather think we could do better as a House, a system, if we did all cooperate more. Maybe it's the way forward.

Although not everyone agrees with him:

> Atkins: It doesn't work, Michael. One party governs, and *one* party opposes. That's our system. That's *this* building. Two sides of the house, two sides of the argument, facing off against each other: the gap between the government and opposition benches the precise length of two swords drawn.
>
> Their tips, touching. We are not built for cooperation, Michael. You get a chance, we try and stop you. We get a chance, you try and stop us. That's our way.[109]

Like David Hare, Graham leaves these debates open for the audience to determine how functional Parliamentary democracy may be, whether the events of *This House* ultimately help or hinder democratic progress and if the system itself is too compromised to be salvageable.

Critic Michael Billington appreciated the play's 'startling vividness' and recreation of 'the madness of life in the Westminster village' but described it as 'an anorak's night out' in a review first published in 2012 following the premiere at the National Theatre—an opinion he maintained when the review was reprinted in Billington's 2022 anthology of reviews *Affair of the Heart*. Yet Billington's assessment of *This House* as 'a play about the daily process of politics rather than big ideas'[110] seems incomplete in a broader reading of Graham's democracy plays and their acute assessment of British political institutions. *Independent* critic Paul Taylor who countered Billington's view when the play transferred to the West End in 2016 wondering 'do political plays have a sell-by date? Not when they are as dazzling, intelligent, scrupulously well-research and as funny and moving as this one.'[111] Graham wanted his play to be 'timeless' and when it was screened for free via National Theatre at Home in 2020, Rachel Halliburton reviewing it for *The Arts Desk* wrote that it 'demonstrates anew how acute his perception is of the obsessions and motivations of our times.'[112] In the broader context of Graham's political writing outlined in this chapter, Billington underestimated not only the impact of the play which quickly becomes the benchmark against which Graham's later successes continue to be measured and the primary reason for the 'political playwright' label he bears, but also its wider state-of-the-nation analysis of the long-term decline and mismanagement of the UK political system.

Across Graham's politically focused plays, the writer unpicks the value and difficulties inherent in every aspect of Britain's democratic system, processes that allow individual ambition and careerist drivers to supersede effective governance. And while the democratic constituents themselves are rarely called into questions, these works ask where to draw the line between representing local and national needs, between the survival instincts of the governing party and the development of socially beneficial agendas, the role of membership factions in party politics and the balance between electoral will and the greater good. Democracy in Graham's work is both the culmination of centuries of tradition and practice, enshrined in legal and customary practices, and a failing system that presents plenty of scope for modernisation and responsiveness to the changing demands and demography of the electorate. In the complex interactions between local councils, party membership, constituencies, political parties and their leadership, governments, opposition and the voter, these plays note the seemingly insurmountable problems of representation, stakeholder management and expectations, and the misuse of power. Yet, somehow, the functional aspects of democracy—political parties, elections and Parliament—continue to muddle through with overall integrity, ultimately resilient to the many assaults and attacks instigated by human error and ambition. Who holds power and how that power is wielded unites Graham's work on the political system but as the Member for Merioneth warns in *This House*, 'Remember. Authority is an abstract. If you convince people you have it, then you have it.'[113]

NOTES

1. The Almeida Theatre YouTube channel. 2019. Anne Washburn and James Graham in Conversation: Writing Political Theatre. https://www.youtube.com/watch?v=OcTFetDoxqc&ab_channel=AlmeidaTheatre. Accessed: 3 January 2024.
2. Adiseshiah, Sian. 2013. The Revolution Will be Dramatized: The Problem of Meditation in Caryl Churchill's Revolutionary Plays.

Hungarian Journal of English and American Studies Fall 19:2; Price, Jason. 2016. *Modern Popular Theatre*. London: Palgrave, p.59; Edited By: Deeney, John F. and Gale, Maggie B. 2015. *Fifty Modern and Contemporary Dramatists*. London: Routledge, p.114.
3. Price, Jason. 2016. p.104 and p.23.
4. Grochala, Sarah. 2017. *The Contemporary Political Play: Rethinking Dramaturgical Structure*. London: Bloomsbury, pp.1–24.
5. Abrams, Joshua. 2010. State of the Nation: New British Theatre. *Performing Arts Journal* 32:2.
6. Graham James. Introduction. In Graham, James. 2013. *This House*. London: Methuen Drama.
7. Sierz, Aleks. 2021. *Good Nights Out: A History of Popular British Theatre Since the Second World War*. London: Methuen Drama, p.127 and 137.
8. Graham James. Introduction. In Graham, James. 2013. *This House*.
9. Grochala, Sarah. 2017. pp.1–24.
10. Graham James. 2022. *Labour of Love*. London: Methuen Drama. Act One, Scene One, p.12.
11. Ibid, Act One, Scene Four, p.48.
12. Ibid, Act Two, Scene Two, p.83.
13. Ibid, Act Two, Scene One, p.72.
14. Ibid, Act One, Scene Five, pp.66–67.
15. Ibid, Act Two, Scene One, p.73.
16. Ibid, Act Two, Scene One, pp.73–74.
17. Ibid, Act Two, Scene One, p.76.
18. Ibid, Act Two, Scene One, p.76.
19. Ibid, Act Two, Scene Two, p.84.
20. Ibid, Act Two, Scene Two, p.87.
21. Ibid, Act Two, Scene Two, pp.88–89.
22. Ibid, Act Two, Scene Four, p.106.
23. Ibid, Act Two, Scene Four, p.108.
24. Ibid, Act One, Scene Three, p.41.
25. Ibid, Act One, Scene Five, p.55.
26. Ibid, Act Two, Scene Four, p.104.
27. Ibid, Act One, Scene One, p.10.
28. Ibid, Act Two, Scene One, p.72.

29. Ibid, Act Two, Scene One, p.71.
30. Ibid, Act One, Scene Two, p.35.
31. Ibid, Act One, Scene Two, p.33.
32. Clapp, Susannah. 2017. Labour of Love Review—The Left Does the Splits Gracefully. *The Observer*, October 8, https://www.theguardian.com/stage/2017/oct/08/labour-of-love-review-james-graham-martin-freeman-tamsin-greig.
33. Pressley, Nelson. 2018. The British Political Comedy 'Labour of Love' translates well in its U.S. debut. *The Washington Post*, October 1, https://www.washingtonpost.com/entertainment/theater_dance/the-british-political-comedy-labour-of-love-translates-well-in-its-us-debut/2018/10/01/a86fee52-c574-11e8-b1ed-1d2d65b86d0c_story.html.
34. Graham, James. 2022. *Labour of Love*, Act Two, Scene One, p.70.
35. Ibid, Act Two, Scene Three, p.95.
36. Graham, James. *This House*. In Graham James. 2016. *James Graham Plays: 2*. London: Methuen Drama, Act Two, Scene Four, p.104.
37. Graham, James. 2022. *Labour of Love*, Act One, Scene One, p.8.
38. Graham, James. *Tory Boyz*. In Graham, James. 2012. *James Graham Plays: 1*. London: Methuen Drama, p.11.
39. Ibid, p.10.
40. Ibid, p.23.
41. Ibid p.24.
42. Graham, James. *This House*, Act Two, Scene Two. In Graham, James. 2016, p.87.
43. Graham, James. *Tory Boyz*. In Graham, James. 2012, p.40.
44. Ibid, p.41.
45. Ibid, p.53.
46. Graham, James. Introduction. In Graham James. 2016, p.xii.
47. Ibid, p.xiv.
48. Graham, James. *The Vote*, Part One. In Graham James. 2016, p.243.
49. Ibid, Part Two, p.267.
50. Ibid, Part One, p.242.
51. Ibid, Part One, p.242.
52. Ibid, Part Three, p.281.
53. Ibid, Part Four, p.305.
54. Ibid, Part Four, p.310.

55. Ibid, Part One, p.258.
56. Ibid, Part One, p.240–241.
57. Ibid, Part One, p.245.
58. Ibid, Part One, p.246.
59. Ibid, Part Three, p.287.
60. Ibid, Part One, p.233.
61. Ibid, Part Three, p.275–6.
62. Ibid, Part One, pp.236.
63. Ibid, Part One, pp. 244–245.
64. Ibid, Part Two, p.259.
65. Ibid, Part Three, p.292.
66. Ibid, Part One, p.238.
67. Ibid, Part One, p.249.
68. Ibid, Part One, p.237.
69. Ibid Part One, p.237.
70. Ibid, Part Two, p.263.
71. Ibid, Part Three, p.283.
72. Ibid, Part One, p.252.
73. Graham, James. Introduction. In Graham, James. 2016, p.xiv.
74. Graham, James. *The Vote*, Part Four. In Graham James. 2016, p.310.
75. Graham, James. 2022. *Labour of Love*, Act One, Scene One, p.7.
76. Graham James. Introduction. In Graham, James. 2013, p.vi.
77. Holden, Nicholas. On Graham James. 2021. *This House (Student Editions)*. London: Methuen.
78. Graham, James. *This House*, Act One, Scene One. In Graham, James. 2016, p.20.
79. Holden, Nicholas. In Graham James. 2021.
80. Graham, James. *This House*, Act One. Scene One. In Graham, James. 2016, p.26.
81. Ibid, Prologue, p.12.
82. Ibid, Act One, Scene One, p.29.
83. Ibid, Act One, Scene Three, p.44.
84. Holden, Nicholas. In Graham, James. 2021.
85. Ibid.
86. Graham, James. *This House*, Act One, Scene One. In Graham, James. 2016, p.29.
87. Ibid, Act One, Scene Two, p.37.
88. Ibid, Act One, Scene Five, p.61.

89. Ibid, Act One, Scene Five, p.64.
90. Ibid, Act One, Scene Five, p.65.
91. Ibid, Act Two, Scene One, p.70.
92. Ibid, Act One, Scene Two, pp.30–31.
93. Ibid, Act One, Scene Two, p.39.
94. Ibid, Act Two, Scene Four, p.104.
95. Ibid, Act Two, Scene Two, p.85.
96. Ibid, Act Two, Scene Two, p.78.
97. Ibid, Act Two, Scene Five, p.113.
98. Ibid, Act Two, Scene Three, p.93.
99. Ibid, Act One, Scene Four, p.55.
100. Ibid, Act One, Scene Four, pp. 56–57.
101. Ibid, Act Two, Scene Five, p.115.
102. Ibid, Act Two, Scene One, p.77.
103. Ibid, Act Two, Scene Five, p.114.
104. Graham, James. Introduction. In Graham, James. 2013, p.vi.
105. Graham, James. *This House*, Act One, Scene Two. In Graham, James. 2016, p.32.
106. Ibid, Act One, Scene Two, p.34.
107. Ibid, Act Two, Scene Two, p.87.
108. Ibid, Act One, Scene Three, p.42.
109. Ibid, Act Two, Scene Four, pp.103–104.
110. Billington, Michael. 2022. p.202.
111. Taylor, Paul. 2016. This House, Garrick Theatre, London, Review: Dazzlingly Intelligent, Scrupulously Well Researched and Funny. *Independent*, December 1, https://www.independent.co.uk/arts-entertainment/theatre-dance/reviews/this-house-garrick-theatre-review-james-graham-conservative-lib-dem-coalition-a7449831.html.
112. Halliburton, Rachel. 2020. This House, National Theatre at Home Review—Timely Revival of Brilliant House of Commons Drama. *The Arts Desk*, May 29.
113. Graham, James. *This House*, Act One, Scene Two. In Graham, James. 2016, p.33.

CHAPTER 3

Anarchy

While many of Graham's politically focused plays explore the structures of democracy and the ways in which these are subjected to human interventions that make them seem fragile, plenty of room is given in this broader analysis to dissenting voices and those who work against the established system. Graham's approach demonstrates that parts of democracy struggle to operate effectively as the clash between traditions and more contemporary forms of electoral expression, values and inclusiveness create stagnation within the legislative process or wars of attrition between factional interests within and between political parties whose stakeholders determine national policy, and sometimes legislative agendas. Yet, the writer retains an overall faith in the basic principles under which the UK's democratic structure operates and its ability to return stable government, eventually correcting course and removing obstacles that try to overturn or bypass democratic convention. Nowhere is this more apparent that in the two plays that deal with anarchic movements—*Monster Raving Loony* and *The Angry Brigade*—stories in which individuals seek to change how democracy operates through the introduction of anarchic behaviours into the system. Graham shows that while the fragility of democracy may be exposed across its many constituent parts, ultimately it proves sufficiently robust to deter and defeat those who try to challenge it.

Anarchy and democracy are usually perceived as direct opposites of one another, the first a desire to subvert and upend all established ways of

© The Author(s), under exclusive license to Springer Nature
Switzerland AG 2024
M. Philpott, *James Graham*,
https://doi.org/10.1007/978-3-031-59663-6_3

being, creating a solution without rules, while the latter seeks to impose order, compliance, cohesion and fairness through societal representation within the democratic process. But in Graham's work, these two concepts are an extension of one another rather than acting in contention, with anarchy most often the expression of discontent with the existing form of governance rather than a desire to remove governance of any kind. In fact, these plays suggest that anarchic behaviours are utilised by characters who are hoping to improve existing forms of democracy, restoring them to what they perceive as their more effective original state, one that the writer also champions without the influence of corruption and human ambition that redirect its social purpose. This idea is fundamentally in harmony with Graham's proposition that the essential structures and processes of democracy are worth upholding. Anarchy, then, is part of a public expression of discontent that looks to restore balance within a democratic system in which concepts of fairness, equality and representation have been eroded, the outcome of which is to make democratic institutions and processes better, rather than tear them down entirely.

Anarchy takes quite different forms in these plays, operating both within and outside of existing structures to effect change. Like Caryl Churchill who also borrows from 'historical narrative and myths to proffer routes to a new future',[1] Professor of Literature, Politics & Performance Siân Adiseshiah argues in her assessment of the playwright published in the *Hungarian Journal of English and American Studies*, Graham adopts a similar approach in *Monster Raving Loony* presenting a historical biographical drama about the life of Lord Sutch to explore the introduction of absurdist and anarchic concepts in the formation of political parties, policy development and electoral representation *within* the traditional boundaries of party politics. The play explores who has access to office driven by Sutch's perceived 'outsider' perspective and his attempts to enter into an otherwise bland and uniform projection of power. *The Angry Brigade* goes further in examining the anatomy of a subversive group operating *outside* usual political channels, drawing attention to the causes they espouse using violent and other extreme means to disrupt public life. But across the play, there are deep conventionalities within the Brigade resulting from the social structures in which they live that draw them back to the existing democratic forms which the group ultimately seek to champion, improve and protect through their actions. Across both plays, Graham also looks at the causal link between anarchy and youth, with ideals held onto perhaps long after the individuals themselves have become more conventional in the desire for order and social improvement. In all cases, the power of democratic organisations to fight back against anarchic incursions, results in the defeat of those acting out against a system that their behaviours only serve to reinforce.

Graham also brings anarchic concepts into the construction of these plays both in the application of dramatic devices and in determining how the presentation of these stories onstage is expected to unfold. This is an exercise in the coalescence of subject and form, sometimes in ways that will be entirely invisible to an audience, but nonetheless underpin how rules and structures in the democratic process are mirrored by those applied to the creation of these pieces of theatre themselves. The experimental application of dramatic anarchy is an interesting one, particularly in plays that may seem deceptively conventional on the surface. But Graham's quite different approaches to anarchic technique in *Monster Raving Loony* and *The Angry Brigade* adds additional layers of complexity to their performance. Both plays are complete, narrative and character-driven pieces that are the recognisable output of this author, yet they demonstrate innovative approaches to dramatic construction that enhances and comments on the themes and purposes of these works, providing a theatrical structure and order that, like democracy, can be challenged from within, without changing the system itself.

3.1 Inside the System

A rare adult lifetime biographical onstage drama from Graham, *Monster Raving Loony* follows the changing political experience of David Sutch from a young working-class man searching for purpose to a renowned, perhaps notorious, anarchic figure in late twentieth-century politics. Although the play ostensibly charts the process by which Sutch was transformed from a figure of fun, even a mistrusted representative of social subversion that members of the Establishment feared, to an accepted political institution who stood in (and lost) more elections than any other candidate in modern political history, Graham presents him as the eternal outsider who as a young man struggled to find his purpose or even a regular career. Many of Sutch's early scenes explore the limitations of his working-class upbringing, the loss of his father and closeness to his mother, a decisive character who recurs throughout the drama. That this manifests as a desire to change the world, first through music and later via politics the writer links directly to this experience and Sutch's 1960s childhood in which social and cultural change brought different opportunities for the political expression of discontent as youth issues emerged in a more public context. Early in the play, the writer aligns Sutch's desire to play music with his political aspirations, creating a culture in which his class and social position disbar him from entry to the political elite:

> Snooty: Some of the greatest Prime Ministers attended Harrow, you know, though. Stanley Baldwin, Lord Palmerston, Winston Churchill.

Confusing the town with the school, Sutch is inspired:

> Sutch: Awh. Well. Maybe *I'll* be Prime Minster one day, then.
>
> Snooty: Oh, I shouldn't think so. It isn't something one just decides.[2]

The outcome of this exchange prevents Sutch from entry into politics via traditional routes, and in the same scene Graham uses music as a metaphor for the character's determination to challenge that:

> Sutch: I'm gonna find my own instrument. There's loads o' second-hand stuff you find laying around these days. I can form my *own* orchestra, or troupe, or band!
>
> Snooty: Well if were up to me. But, like I say. It's about those who listen, those who play... (*Exits.*)
>
> Sutch: Not it isn't... oh not it isn't![3]

Sutch's motivation is to effect change inspired and facilitated by the socio-cultural changes in the 1960s including improvements to education and social mobility, initially believing anything is possible and, despite both Snooty and his mother's reservations, determinedly pursues a hope-filled course of action. The initial reality proves less golden, however, as Sutch takes a job as a window cleaner, all the while nursing his musical ambitions and plans to create a new kind of performance, one that deliberately disrupts the status quo:

> Sutch: Did I mention I was an aspiring musician?

Pauline: And here's me thinking you're a window cleaner who drove a hearse.

Sutch: Oh that. Only thing I could afford. But I am a bit into the old macabre, me. Zombies and monsters. 'Ere, you wanna know who the real Zombies are – (*at where* Mrs Nicholas *exited*) that lot. The 'living dead', just following all them what came before 'em. We're gonna break that spell. Make our own moves, find our own sound.[4]

The political associations in this speech are compounded within the descriptions of Sutch's early motivation and his clear desire to break free of social convention, escape the 'zombies' and find a new and disruptive approach. Graham combines changes in music styles in the 1960s with a similar broadening of Sutch's horizons in which his wish to subvert— and by extension to inject anarchic elements—into the system supports his development as a character and his determination to work outside of traditional and accepted routes to effect change.

Early in Part Two of *Monster Raving Loony*, Graham tells the audience that Sutch has worked for a pirate radio station which was subsequently shut down, a further example of operating in a new and unconventional space beyond traditional boundaries before he eventually alights on the possibility of a political career. Pressured to adopt a more typical lifestyle by his mother, Sutch verbalises his political stance, advocating for radical change when he exclaims 'Nobody settles now, Mother. We're in the throes of a revolution!'[5] Only a few lines later, the notion of becoming an MP is first presented to Sutch with Graham leaving the thought of revolution to linger in the minds of the audience during the formulation of Sutch's new plan. Through the remainder of the play, the writer examines the extent to which Sutch's early motivation and reliance on anarchic approaches is a symptom of a youthful fervour that he is unable to develop beyond. Referred to in Part One of the play as a 'Peter Pan' figure, the association also extends to Sutch's appeal among younger voters, whose views and contribution to democracy are dismissed as unfounded by Benny, his mother's boyfriend based entirely on their age and perceived naivety:

Sutch: Mum, people *voted* for me. Two hundred and nine votes, that's *two, zero, nine*. They actually put a cross next to my name.

Benny: I'm always cross next to *you*. Scouse, git.

Sutch: Lots of young people.

Benny: Well they would, wouldn't they, don't know their arse from their elbow. You raised a generation, Annie, don't know their arse from their elbows.[6]

This disenfranchised group, the writer suggests, find recognition in Sutch's unconventional approach to political life, reasserting a link between youth and anarchy that not only motivates Sutch but also encourages likeminded voters to support him. As the play unfolds, Graham returns once more to the notion of anarchy as an activity for the young, a state that individuals—Sutch perhaps excepted—eventually grow out of when fellow member of the Monster Raving Loony Party Stuart actively eschews the party citing youth as his primary excuse:

Stuart: I grew up! David.

I'm – sorry. But. We're not teenagers, anymore. This is the world as it is. And it's time to take that seriously. I want to be a part of it, and contribute, something, *serious*.[7]

As Sutch's career draws to a close, Graham notes the changing appeal of anarchic behaviours and their origins as the protagonist contends with an increased pressure to conform, encouraged to see his desire for radical change as a youthful folly based on unrealistic notions of how government should work. But as the play reveals, none of the problems that Sutch campaigns against are any less pertinent 40 years later.

Across his politically focused plays, Graham explores the various failings of democracy and the British State making them the foundational motivation for the drastic change that shapes Sutch's perspective. To do this, the writer first establishes the character's predisposition for change behaviours in non-political settings before considering how these were determined and incorporated into his public position as a party leader. There is a clear sense in this play that Britain is broken as a result of consistent failures in political leadership and purpose inherited by those of Sutch's era to which the Monster Raving Loony approach is a potential corrective. A multigenerational sense of decline is stark in a play that articulates both the large-scale failings of Britain's post-war approach and its personal effects on the characters. A scene set in 1966 explains the feeling of concern and uncertainty that stepfather Benny feels in this context:

> Benny: 'Change', is that a eupher-what's-it? A silly-nym for 'destruction', 'abandonment'. 'Decline'. Giving away the whole Empire that took good decent Conservatives centuries to build up.[8]

But little improves in the next two decades and shortly after Graham moves the action forward using the Falklands War in 1983 to give the play a subtle new timestamp as Sutch euphemistically summarises the state of the nation nearly 20 years later:

> Sutch: Look at this place. The same old stuff – old, tired, broke. We wipe it clean and flog it on, and still it comes back, again and again. I thought we were going to be dealing in fine antiques, not tat.[9]

A continual cycle of optimism and disappointment emerges across the play as characters put past failures behind them and hope that the next political administration will be the one to solve the nation's problems, although a resignation to the inevitability of further decline provides the subtext to such statements in the play:

> Pete: No, well, it doesn't matter does it, all going to the dogs, whatever it is. They're all the bloody same, aren't they. All in it for themselves.
>
> Dud: Who are?
>
> Pete: Well, whoever, it don't matter, that's my point. (*At his paper.*) See that, we can't even take back a canal, these days, Dud. In my day, we took whole countries. A bloody canal.
>
> Dud: Maybe we're worn out from all that taking of all the countries, Pete. Maybe it's just a small blip on our, as it were, glorious road to recovery. Now that Macmillan's in, *he* might sort it all out.[10]

A nod to *Eden's Empire* and the Suez Canal crisis of 1956, the conversation of satirical comedians Peter Cook and Dudley Moore soon turns to the nature of political leadership and the carbon copy replication of governmental ministers:

> Pete: A *story* about *Tories*. 13 of the cabinet, Dud, 13 of them went to the exact same school.
>
> Dud: Baker's dozen?
>
> Pete: To the exact same bloody school. Nothing changes, not really.[11]

It is a conversation that reinforces Snooty's comment in Part One about the number of Prime Ministers who went to Harrow, instantly reminding the audience that Sutch does not fit despite his continued aspirations to join the political elite. Britain, then, in the decades with which *Monster Raving Loony* is concerned, is perceived as a shadow of its former self managed by an unchanging—and by extension an unimaginative—class of politicians unable to conceive of a different kind of society or indeed the different kind of politics which Sutch soon presents. As Graham explained the 'idea of trying to tell his story through the popular comic styles of the time, reflected both his—and Britain's—search for a voice, an identity post-war emerged slowly.'[12]

The nature of Sutch's anarchy is ideally suited to the comic frame that Graham has created, providing repeated opportunities for the character to showcase his semi-rejection of traditional modes of political engagement as he seeks to interject absurdist and disruptive approaches into political life, and there are many examples of this throughout the text. Sutch is couched within a wider movement of subversives pitted against traditional authority figures and conceptions of power which are being challenged. Graham includes a well-known reference to a Footlights show in the 1960s that mocked Prime Minster Harold Macmillan, demonstrating society's changing relationship with government and the resurgence of centuries-old approaches to political satire for which politicians have always provided material:

> Dud: These Cambridge kids, kids from Cambridge University, taking the mickey out of him, in a theatre, our very own Prime Minister, there on the stage.[13]

That Sutch is part of a wider connection between youth and change is one of the central themes of *Monster Raving Loony*, giving purpose to the more directed approaches to anarchy that the character soon adopts, moving him away from a mere eccentric operating outside of the system to a far more interesting position as a change-maker working within a staid and unappealing political system. The first production staged at Theatre Clwyd invited 'the audience into a communal space (ostensibly a working man's club…) by creating a community between them and the live performers.'[14] And soon Sutch launches his first assault on the system, attempting to overcome the traditional nomination process by asking to stand for a constituency he does not know in the Midlands:

> Returning Office: Uh, I'm sorry, I'm just, I'm not sure what the, the protocol is. For this. We've never had anyone just, just walk in off the street, and –
>
> Sutch: Well, anyone can stand, can't they? So what do I do, just turn up on the day, then? Is it like giving blood, do I get an orange juice and a biscuit? Feel a bit faint afterwards?
>
> Returning Officer: Which part - … are you a candidate for a particular party?
>
> Sutch: I am. The National Teenage Party! (*Tapping his form.*)
>
> Returning Office: I've never heard of it.
>
> Sutch: Of course you haven't, I made it up.
>
> Returning Officer: Teenagers don't have a vote.
>
> Sutch: I know, that's why I want to represent them.[15]

Beneath the unusual entry point, Sutch nonetheless attempts to work within the existing system in order to provide representation to a group of citizens barred from electoral participation, creating a place where anarchy and democracy collide. A few lines later, Graham reiterates the failure of politics in this era through Such's entertaining inverted logic:

> Sutch: I thought the whole thing was a joke. You've been made a laughing stock of, the whole thing has. And I'd like to be a part of it, sounds fun.[16]

With traditional requirements of signatories and deposits in place, and inspired by the few hundred votes he receives at his first election, Graham's version of Sutch is encouraged to attempt further disruptive behaviours by forming a party and inspiring others to adopt his unorthodox approaches:

> Stuart: So, completely out of character, on a whim, I hopped on a train, and – here I am.
>
> Sutch: David Sutch. More the merrier. Come on then, let's start the march.
>
> Stuart: And where are you marching to, exactly?
>
> Sutch: Oh nowhere, really. Just round and round.
>
> Stuart: (*towards outside*) I can't believe you've actually got people to – to *follow* you. They're all waiting outside. Hundreds of 'em, how'd you do it?
>
> Sutch (*shrugs*) Dunno really. People have got to follow something.[17]

From holding campaign meetings in the local pub to rejecting the premise of winning, Sutch's unconventional style affects other parties who struggle to make sense of this anarchic approach to political life. Fellow Monster Raving Loony member Stuart talks of starting 'a people's revolution,' giving Sutch's elliptical reasoning an opportunity to come to the fore once again:

> Sutch: Power is the point? But what's the point in power, then, if power is the point?[18]

When the rival Labour candidate bemoans the effect of Sutch's style on his own chances of success, the play reinforces how bland the electoral choice has become with Labour choosing to adopt the same tactics and sombre styles as the Conservative candidates 'to beat them at their own game.'[19] But it is a game Sutch refuses to play at all, continually trying to reset the rules of engagement with new ways of seeing and interacting with the political system.

Sutch's next major tactic is to further defy convention by deliberately standing against the Prime Minister in their home constituency, allowing voters and the media to see two contrasting forms of government side-by-side, one the embodiment of the Establishment and the other the person attempting to inject some character into it instead:

> Sutch: You think democracy is a spectator sport, whinging from the sidelines.
>
> I want to *participate*, not just observe. Stick it straight to the man.[20]

Referencing, once again, the earlier association that Snooty made between class and entry to high office, Sutch is taken with the notion of standing next to the Prime Minister onstage as an 'equal,' resulting in an increased number of votes cast for him in the next scene, evidently tapping into a strain or receptiveness to anarchy that exists within the electorate, open to changing or disrupting how political life is conducted, an opportunity that the character of Dominic Cummings also finds appealing in Graham's television drama *Brexit: The Uncivil War* discussed in Chapter 6. Buoyed by these successes, as the decades pass, Graham's version of Sutch retains a desire to fight against the social factors affecting Britain's development:

> Sutch: I've had enough, I'm clearing out all of this stuff, I'm sick of it, it's weighing me down, I can't escape from it.[21]

And this gives the character a renewed encouragement to reform his own political party and to push the boundaries even further through additional absurdist approaches:

> Sutch: Wait. What did you say? A... a *party*...
>
> *He rummages around the junk again, pulling out different party items – party poppers, a party horn.*
>
> If they won't invite me to one of their parties. I'll just have my *own*! And *everyone* will be invited. And it will be the wildest, craziest party *EVER*![22]

Consumed by this new approach and the public profile it brings, Graham inserts a traditional conversational interview between a particularly anarchic Sutch and respected chat show host Michael Parkinson that includes squeaky toys and further examples of Sutch's satirical reasoning:

Parkinson: And this is a genuine – a *genuine* political party?

Sutch: Yes.

Parkinson: It's not a joke?

Sutch: Yes.

Parkinson: Y - ...? It *is* a joke or it *is* a political party?

Sutch: Yes it is a joke, yes it is a political party.[23]

In a segment crowded with puns and wordplay, Graham creates a quick-fire exchange that showcases Sutch's mockery of the structure of the political system and his views on how politics should be conducted:

Parkinson: Do you have any principles?

Sutch: Any principles? (*Thinks.*) No, we have a couple of caretakers, I think, and one dinner lady, but not actual principals.

Parkinson: Any *policies*? Where do you stand on unemployment?

Sutch: Well we *won't* stand for it.

Parkinson: What are your ideas for *dealing* with it?

Sutch: Well, I'm glad you asked, we've been exploring ways in which to shorten the dole queue. For a start, we're just going to make everyone stand much closer together.

Parkinson: What would you do about crime in this country?

Sutch: Ooh yes, well, prisons are very overcrowded you know. And so I came up with the idea of just releasing all of the *innocent* prisoners. And that would free up some space for the guilty ones, see?[24]

Described by Parkinson as 'a postmodern form of philosophical anarchism,' Sutch concludes the interview with a promise to 'abolish January and February. Because they're just too… they're just too cold.'[25] And it is this attempt to linguistically define, label and control his views that Sutch's character fights against, reinforcing his wider political approach to making politics more relatable and more fun.

It is a technique that also extends to his management of the Party itself which proves just as anarchic in setting policies in Part Three that include the introduction of a 99p coin, an additional Monopolies Commission to ensure fairness and a slightly more sensible plan to remove Income Tax proposed by party member Stuart, a character with broader ambitions for a political career. The consistency in Sutch's continued ethos is repeated by Graham here as his approach gains momentum:

Sutch: We're all potty. Anyone who isn't, shall be excommunicated from the party. And so to the first round of business, then, 'appointments'. A motion has been put forward by the party chairman Alan Howling Laud Hope, that Cat Mandhu here, (*lifting a cuddly cat toy onto the table*) be elected as our Shadow Secretary of State to the Treasury, for reasons being, and I quote (*with his notes*), 'he'll be the most adept at milking the taxpayer, sinking his claws into the rich, and by a whisker, he has the firmest grasp of "fish cull" policy here'.[26]

The most important criteria introduced by the party's manifesto is a rejection of the need to win, a caveat the leader soon adds to the Monster Raving Loony constitution without clear consequences:

Sutch: if anyone here present, or anyone representing the Loony Party across the country, ever, *ever*, successfully wins a seat onto a council or in Parliament… their names shall be struck off the register, and they shall not be allowed to march under the monster moniker *ever again*![27]

Graham segues from this speech directly into a Punch and Judy sequence reflecting how far Sutch's anarchic approach has expanded, reaching a pinnacle shortly after this moment when a Loony Party candidate really does win a seat on the Devon council, provoking Sutch's consternation. Making one last pitch for his disruptive ideals in the next scene, Sutch reflects again on his approach and its role in democracy:

> Sutch: (*as MERTON*) I love General Elections because it's the only day of the year when I can go into a primary school with the sole aim of bringing down the British government, and not be arrested on site. I myself as a citizen of this country have stood against the standing Prime Minister on over 10 occasions now -[28]

While Sutch's methods and attitude suggest he has never taken politics all that seriously, the juxtaposition of state-of-the-nation decline and eccentric political activities throughout *Monster Raving Loony* suggest in fact the opposite is true and is a genuine desire to create change in a broken country dominated by an exclusive system to which few gain entry. Sutch's approach works within the system by pushing it to its limits and forcing those within it to see that the rules they have established are more fluid than they might imagine. That Sutch's manifesto of anarchy appeals to enough people in Devon to elect a local councillor means subversion has become respectable enough to win influence. Yet Graham is not quite finished with Sutch's story, and as his irreverence gains greater traction, democracy itself fights back against these incursions.

From the start of the play, there are characters who do not believe in Sutch's approach, with his own mother Annie reinforcing Snooty's insistence that Sutch will never be accepted into the political world he craves. Before he seeks political life, Annie attempts to dampen his expectations:

> Annie: Trust me, love. Staring out of the window and dreaming ain't for the likes of us. It's one of the hardest things we have to learn, but learn it we must. To know our place. Why don't you get your old job back? Nothing wrong with that factory, it's where your dad worked, and his dad, and your Uncle Ben.'[29]

Later, the writer gives Annie a moment to lament the embarrassment Sutch should feel after losing his first election, wondering whether her own parenting skills are at fault: 'Did I do something wrong,' she asks, 'People say there's a few screws loose.'[30] And Annie's fears have some grounding in what follows as Graham constructs a scenario in which democratic tradition and Establishment manoeuvring try to quash Sutch's public platform in ways that both strategically protect the existing government and are part of a consensus of opinion among traditional holders of power to close ranks against Sutch's form of anarchy. His downfall begins in the middle of Part Three in a conversation that Graham dramatises behind closed doors, implying the views of then Prime Minister Margaret Thatcher, concerned about the humiliation of sharing a public platform with Sutch:

> Minister: Oh yes. This chap. Well, there's not a lot we can do is there, the law is the law.
>
> Civil Servant: Do we really have to go over this again, Minister? Yes, the law is the law. But, also, the law can be whatever you decide it to be.
>
> Minister: So what you're saying – is we should make democracy more exclusive?[31]

This manifests in the rest of the play as a series of tactics to prevent Sutch from even registering as a candidate, commuted into a brief exchange set in the town hall:

> Assistant: I'm afraid I've found a problem.
>
> Returning Officer: Oh no, a problem you say. Quelle Surprise, Marlene.
>
> Assistant: Your second nominee. They should have signed there, and there. But instead they've signed there, and there.
>
> Returning Officer: Oh yeah, you see, the form, you see. We've change it. (*Smiles.*)
>
> Sutch: Changed it?
>
> Returning Officer: Yeah. Just subtly. But we changed it.
>
> *He gives his Boycie laugh.*
>
> Sutch: But you can't do that. It's too complicated, obviously. (*At* Stuart). Even he couldn't do it, and he's got 3 GCEs.
>
> Stuart: You can't do this. He always stands, that's what he does.

Sutch: Quick, give me some more papers.

Returning Officer: (*at his watch*) Whoops, sorry, the deadline to issue new papers has passed.[32]

That this precipitates an emotional collapse for Sutch is not unexpected, and like the warm-up in *Quiz* discussed in Chapter 5, this pressure of public performance soon takes its toll. When democracy fights back, Sutch turns to alcohol and pills to sustain him. From here, Graham piles on the indignation with the betrayals coming thick and fast as long-time collaborator Stuart abandons the mission to join the Conservative Party—the ultimate model of conventionality in *Monster Raving Loony*—when the tactic of losing to overturn the system no longer appeals:

Stuart: I'm going to become a *real* MP, with *real* powers! Isn't that a good thing?

Pauline: The *Tories*! Of course you would choose the ugly, stiff, frigid ones, you'll fit right in![33]

The play concludes in 1997 when Labour's landslide ends 18 years of Conservative rule Sutch is no longer a political figure, his anarchic attempts to breach the democratic process are finally defeated when he actively chooses not to stand, noting in the process the difficulty of fighting against something far larger than himself:

Sutch: And I would normally be there, out on the stumps, I haven't missed a single one in decades, you know except when it wasn't my fault.[34]

In these final moments of the play, the writer has Sutch struggle to reconcile the effect of his career and whether it made any difference:

Sutch: Well then tell me, clever clogs, what *is* the point, because, hahaha, I'm not sure I know anymore, if I'm honest.

Pauline: David, it's OK to be sad –

Sutch: A lifetime just standing there, on stage, wearing a silly costume.

Pauline: You can drop the act.

Sutch: What act? There isn't an act. It's all an act. I am the act. Where's the act. I haven't got an act. We're *all* an act![35]

Left with uncertainty by Graham, Sutch decides that his ultimate role in the political system was to remind ordinary people of the fragility of democracy and to keep the holders of power 'grounded' as well as providing inspiration to those outside traditional political cliques—'I always thought people would think… "If *he's* bloody standing",'[36] Sutch explains. In reality, though, Sutch's anarchy is ultimately tempered by this retrospective analysis, and it is Graham himself who lands the final blow for democracy when he transforms Sutch from a comic to a serious political figure in the shaping of the play's conclusion. Only a few scenes before the character of Toksvig associates Sutch with comic actors, a non-serious and apolitical public figure:

Toksvig: You know, I was, thinking, the other day, about our friend the Lord Sutch here. Is he up there, I ask, with the greats, Tony Hancock, Kenneth Williams, John Major? What a lot of them shared is how utterly miserable they were on the inside.

A notion reinforced by Clary who denigrates Sutch's political contribution in vicious terms:

Clary: Our elections have become cheap and nasty farces, a freak show where these lunatics stand even though they have no chance of winning.[37]

Yet, in the final speech of the play, Graham chooses to make Sutch conventional in an obituary from David Frost that transforms him into a recognisably political figure:

David Frost: John F Kennedy. Lord Mountbatten. Martin Luther King. To their special club of great political titans taken from us too early… they have a gate crasher. The self-titled, self-aggrandising, self-appointed, Screaming Lord Sutch, the 3rd Earl of Harrow has died.

The linguistic connection between this and Toksvig's speech with its repetition of celebrity names is no coincidence, and Graham goes further still, making Sutch a participant in conventional democracy after all:

David Frost: Screaming Lord Sutch broke the record as being, officially, the least successful politician of all time. And yet also, at the time of his death, he became the longest-serving leader of a British political party in history. His legacy lives on.[38]

Sutch's anarchy in *Monster Raving Loony* sought to change democracy from within with unconventional and absurdist approaches that became troublesome enough to the Establishment to require retaliation. But in participating in and contributing to the system for so long, Graham makes Sutch's legacy a permanent role in that system after all. Democracy ultimately defeated David Sutch as surely as it will the next group of contenders, those working outside of the system to bring it down by any means necessary, The Angry Brigade.

3.2 Outside of the System

'How free do you think you are?'[39] is a question at the heart of Graham's work and one that motivates the four characters who set out to disrupt society through the violent targeting of democratic governance and Establishment objectives. *The Angry Brigade* explores the introduction of anarchy into social functions through a character group choosing to operate outside of the system in order to effect radical change while commenting on the legal and social conditioning that regulates individual behaviours as well as confining aspirations. This play broadens out the self-sustaining nature of political structures and presents society as something seeking only its own exact renewal with generations of young people represented within the make-up of the anarchists and the specially formed police group who are encouraged to act in ways that cohere with the example set by previous generations by replicating existing social concepts via traditional marriage, work and lawful compliance. Graham puts a strain on these notions through the unconventional beliefs and motivations of The Brigade who, at least initially, set out to disrupt and destabilise established democratic structures. The corresponding Branch section meanwhile attempts to locate the perpetrators of violent protest in the play and restore a peaceable order symbolised by the police characters. That the differences between the two halves of this drama are eventually less significant than the audience might expect, typical of Graham's writing where connections between seemingly opposite, incompatible views are often the basis for common ground, make the outcomes of this play in which order eventually assumes victory over dissent feel inevitable. In keeping with the writer's contention across these works, democracy always wins in the end.

The Angry Brigade is ultimately a story of personal and ideological betrayal in which the four-strong group of anarchists are deceived by those in their wider circle while also starting to question their own commitment to the cause. The turning point here proves to be the age-old division between using peaceful or violent means to effect change which has always come between social and political movements, stymying their progress. A moral concern that the destruction of innocent people will delegitimise their cause filters through *The Angry Brigade* and is reinforced by an official response to these violent methods that prioritises outrage and a greater determination to halt the actions of the group. Graham's play uses a series of betrayals to question the extent to which the means adopted by The Brigade obscure the political messaging behind its actions. And although the play examines the spread of both anarchic forms and the growing attraction of conventionality in the story's conclusion, the perhaps sympathetic and rational foundation of their cause is eventually destroyed by the expression of it. While the ultimate downfall of The Angry Brigade is predicated on a combination of police intelligence gathering aided by other self-interest groups including prisoners and arrested protestors looking for leniency by providing testimony, as well as effective policework that manages to establish patterns in The Brigade's activities, the writer also suggests that anarchic groups eventually betray themselves by choosing a violent course of action that ultimately distracts from their own messaging and for which democracy is not only unforgiving but able to actively reinforce its boundaries. This particular and violent demonstration of anarchy only makes democracy stronger and even less likely to change.

Like *Monster Raving Loony*, *The Angry Brigade* is an expression of youth, focusing on some key social and political divides that motivate the group's desire for change. Marriage, gender, class and education are battleground topics that Graham explores in both sections of the play—The Branch and The Brigade—that look to question the way in which society is constructed and, as Sutch discovered, the expectation that subsequent generations should live as their parents did. That divide is dramatised quite differently in each section; The Brigade discussing and mocking this social inheritance through role play, while The Branch actively embody and live out those traditional forms in their daily lives, having adopted them unquestioningly. One of the key concerns for the anarchists is marriage and the expectation of social control they believe it brings. Brigade members Anna and Jim assume the make-believe identities of Mr and Mrs Buchan as part of a game in their house, playing newlyweds moving into their first home together. In a section noting the people they could have been had they led a more conventional life, Jim sourly comments on the couple's imagined life, reflecting on the fiction in the aftermath:

> Jim: Their future together was monotony and monogamy and just convincing themselves they were happy while they wait to die.[40]

A few lines later and the cause of this delusional concept of relationships as the foundation of a conventional society is reinforced:

> Jim: But that's – it's not real, it's fantasy.
>
> Anna: It's romanticism, the corruption of real moments by projecting cliches onto them, ones we've all seen in films or read in books, star-crossed lovers, love at first sight, all that nonsense.[41]

The romance between Anna and Jim bubbles away under the surface of The Brigade section of the play and as Anna seeks that intimacy anyway with Jim despite her stated aversion, seeking the conventionality of that connection, Jim maintains his insistence that marriage is a mechanism for control, a sentiment that underpins his motivation for anarchic behaviours:

> Jim: You need the affirmation, do you, the fake affirmation of someone else telling you that you're worth something –

When Anna confirms, he continues:

> Jim: Well, I'm sorry that you need this, this crutch, because it's been drilled into you that none of us are *enough* just us on our own, we need to be in partnership to be strong, cause that's bollocks and I'm here to tell you that you are enough without me, Anna.[42]

The play here starts to explore how the personal and the political combine, an important discussion that expands notions of democracy and its effects beyond the purely political sphere of parties, elections and Parliament, and instead explores its pervasive influence on daily lives as a benign form of population control. Graham contrasts this with the embracing of marriage as a natural state in The Branch section, implying the easy happiness and contentment with self that is lacking in The Brigade characters. It also suggests a more progressive balance in contemporary marriages than either the anarchists or the older generation of characters in The Branch admit:

> The Commander: Course he's familiar, look at that white shirt, clean and pressed. Your wife's a credit to you, Smith.
>
> Smith: Well, that she is, Mister Bond, but without taking anything away from my Susan, I happen to press my own shirts.
>
> The Commander: Press your own shirts, stone me. A brave new world.[43]

The only contention in the marriage of The Commander is whether or not he should dunk biscuits into his tea, presenting the police as a picture of respectability and traditional moral values as part of the Establishment against which The Brigade are reacting.

But other forms of social control are also included as foundational reasons for The Brigade's actions that draw directly on perception of limited or encaged lives experienced by their parents from which they wish to break free. In one of the most important state-of-the-nation speeches in any Graham play, Jim suggests violence in everyday life that keeps people in their place and crushes any aspiration for more:

> Jim: I remember watching my mum doing the ironing. Ironing is not on the surface a particularly violent act but I would watch her and something would make me all, I don't know, queasy and uneasy about it. But in those, erm, rigid and repressive traditions that assign individuals ancient gender roles that saw my father sat in his armchair watching the flickering box, fat on the food that my mum had just cooked while behind him she ran an iron over his shirts, perfectly happy and unquestioning because the ant doesn't question the crumb she is lifting to take back to the farm, the fact is that it made the five-, eight-, whatever-year-old me queasy because what I was watching was one of the most violent acts I could imagine.[44]

Warming to his theme, Jim goes on to describe the north of England as an 'open prison.' This moving speech begins with a tainted nostalgia, looking back with a kind of sadness to his own personal childhood but building the emotion and sense of injustice into a political rallying cry:

> Jim: There is violence in the five-day week, and in the illusion that the weekend means you're free, but the weekend is just parole, nothing more. There is violence in the boredom and inactivity of the unemployed. There is violence in the long streets of houses – boxes for the workers, cells for the inmates, the illusion of freedom this space gives us, like the free-range chicken who wrongly equates having more soil to trample around on with escaping the axe. There is violence in the road grid of the city, in the rapid transit systems that take us to and from our prison-cell homes to the beehive. There is violence in the boy dressed in blue and the girl dressed in pink. There is violence, Anna, in the boy who is given a train set, and the girl who is given a Wendy house.[45]

This speech takes place quite early in The Brigade section of the play and sets the tone for everything that follows. Its rhythm and structure carefully shape its tonal shifts from reminiscence to polemic and from personal experience to anatomy of systemic failings in the way society operates which no amount of enfranchisement and electoral power will ever solve. What Graham does so startlingly here is to outline the limitations and inadequacies of democracy by addressing generations of decline, abuse of power and forms of control that only complete disruption can overthrow, and underlines why The Brigade's decision to apply violent means is the only way to effect change. 'Democracy in this county,' John notes, 'is a fucking illusion – here's a piece of paper, every five years. Red, or blue, or yellow, not a blind bit of difference between them. Cosmetics. Nothing more.'[46] The rest of the play may explain why Jim's conclusion about the tools of anarchy are ineffective, but the beautiful and tragic expression of his motivation is one of Graham's greatest pieces of writing.

And it introduces a notion of class distinction within The Brigade that revives similar concerns about the relationship between class, education and power included in *Monster Raving Loony*. Jim is the only working-class member of the group who dropped out of Cambridge following his dad's disapproval but it is fellow Cantabrigian John who gives voice to the association between social conformity, education and class in a discussion about the expected public school and university education of Conservative

Party members and why radical change is so difficult for ordinary people to envisage:

> John: The sound of hard shoes on the cloisters, the sight of all that ancient, immovable stone, it cannot fail but to imprint upon them the weight of the past. It represses any notion of 'another way.' Because the old ways feel so immovable and sturdy and strong.[47]

These physical and highly reverential environments, he continues, create a 'seriousness of propriety and respect from church to private school to Oxbridge, to Parliament.... There's only two types of groups in society, Jim. Those whose school had a motto, and those who didn't.' The public school system he argues instils an unbalanced form of social control, 'Walking on the left, chapel at 7.a.m., breakfast at 8, dinner at 7, sing national anthem, pray to God.'[48] A few lines later, however, John reveals he too is a product of the very same hallowed education system at Haberdasher's Aske school and then Cambridge where he met Jim who traded his original Medicine degree for economics. Here Graham subtly draws a line between the anarchists and others who emerge from the same system including the MPs and Establishment figures discussed in the Democracy chapter. Earlier in the play, Jim reveals to the audience that all of his fellow Brigade members are public school educated and expresses regret that he left Cambridge before completing his degree. This is a conversation mirrored in The Branch section of the play where the police officers reflect on the educational opportunities provided to anarchist characters and the use they have made of them:

> Henderson: All that you were given in life, such privileges, such education, all being wasted to live like, like *wasters* -[49]

The dual notion of education as both a form of social control and a place to create opportunity for development is an interesting tension in the play, providing a significant motivational role for the anarchic characters seeking to overturn notions of disparity and class distinction that education, they argue, only compounds. And although it is the Establishment figures who advocate for education as a meritocratic benefit of democracy, Graham explores the inextricable link between class, education and democracy in reinforcing the status quo.

Having explored character motivation emerging from the personal experience and background of The Brigade, the writer also explains the broader failings of democracy and society that drive anarchic behaviours. Some of these relate to the social conditioning and the claustrophobic standardisation of individuality that activities like marriage attempt to impose on forms of living. Echoing Jim's speech about his family life, Hilary expands on the suppression of self that emerges from urban planning legislation and the creation of tower block living:

> Hilary: The flicker of light from one window. And the two floors up, and three windows to the right. The same light. Flickering, changing, dancing, to the same rhythm, the same beat. And it struck me. They Are Watching The Same Thing. They all return home from the production line, enter this block, walk to their individual cells, close the doors, and they sit... watching... 'recuperating'... drawn to the light.[50]

Anna goes further a few lines later, directly referencing Jim's use of 'violence' but spreading its effects far beyond the personal in a play-acted speech addressing her 'fellow revolutionaries':

> Anna: We have sat quietly and suffered the violence of the system for too long. We are being attacked daily. Violence does not only exist in the army, the police, and the prisons. It exists in the shoddy alienating culture pushed out by TV films and magazines, it exists in the ugly sterility of urban life.[51]

A couple of pages later, and John joins in, noting the encouragement to support sports teams as further evidence of social conditioning mechanisms at work:

> John: A side to support against another side, doesn't matter who really, they try and kick this, that way, into that, they try and kick the other way, into that – stadiums, they're the new temples, footy the new religion, promotion the new heaven, relegation the new hell – so long as it occupies hearts and minds. Pick a side, any side.[52]

These are notions that Graham considered again in *Quiz* and *Best of Enemies* as well as a more detailed examination of football culture in *Dear England*, looking at popular culture in relation to democratic and state-of-the-nation principles, but the idea formulates here in *The Angry Brigade*. The purpose of this mechanism is made clear by completing

Hilary's speech about tower blocks in which deterring opportunities for conversation is a deliberate ploy, a tranquiliser that prevents action and preserves the status quo:

> Hilary: Imagine, I thought, imagine if there was a power cut, and the lights went out. Maybe they would turn to the person next to them in the room. And maybe they would talk.... and then I realised that's it. *That's* what cannot be allowed to happen. That's why the power must stay on. That's why the flickering boxes cannot break.
>
> And that's the point of the explosion. That's the point of the gunshot. It's a bang. A bang to wake everyone from their slumber. A bang to make everyone Look Up.[53]

Building on Hilary's point about the failings of democracy and the need to escape from its confines, they decide this can only be achieved through direct action. 'Everything's Victorian,' John complains, 'the attitudes, the mindset, the prejudices.' The emphatic nature of John's language anticipates the methods The Brigade will use to change society, the need to 'burn our past'[54] to create radical change. When John explains that democracy is an illusion, anarchy offers a potential middle way between the existing political parties and ideologies. 'We don't have to choose,' he argues, 'why compromise?'[55] John describes the inevitable outcomes of existing forms of democracy built into a broken system designed solely to sustain power within itself:

> John: Let me tell you something. The history of the modern United Kingdom isn't one of Labour, then Tories, then Liberals, then Tories, then Labour – it's just one of the Tories. They're the constant. They will always get back in. They don't even have to fight for it. They just have to sit back and let the passage of time roll by until it is handed to them again, wherefrom their sole principle and reason for getting up every morning will be to wherever and however possible Keep Things The Same.[56]

By demonising the anarchists, Jim later suggests, governments are able to reinforce their span of control, arguing 'there always has to be an enemy, doesn't there? Governments need there to be a threat, they have to unite people against something,'[57] even if that means turning citizens against one another like rats in a sack. Let 'em fight each other,'[58] John adds. To make the radical change required, The Brigade convince themselves that extreme measures are necessary, and having so carefully constructed their underlying cause and discontent, Anna concludes that 'the system will never collapse or capitulate by itself,'[59] they are going to have to help it along.

The personal and political motivations of the anarchist in the play are balanced by reflection on how others perceive them and why their actions are believed to threaten democracy. As with *Monster Raving Loony*, there is a close association between anarchist principles and the folly of youth with Establishment characters in The Branch section being patronising or dismissive of the Brigade regardless of the equivalent youth of the police personnel in the select investigatory group within Special Branch. Questioning Detective Sergeant Smith about his attitudes to change, The Commander makes assumptions about the link between social disaffection and age:

> The Commander: The older generation, the people in – 'power'. About what we're leaving you, as our legacy. The society we have built. Are you particularly… I don't know, disappointed?
>
> More than disappointed, would you say that you were 'cross', even?
>
> Come on, we're all friends here. It's been the prerogative of the young to tut tut at the older lot for as many generations as there have been generations.[60]

Later, Smith himself makes the same connection asking 'Who do we have as our go-to for this kind of thing? Youth activism, revolutionary anarchism, political radicalism?'[61] The association between age and political alignment recurs throughout the text, as though youth itself is the primary motivation for anarchic behaviours, yet Smith identifies some nuance in the behaviour of his antagonists:

> Smith: We believe we are the same age as the people we aim to catch, but the similarities end there. They see the world very differently to us. And have made very different choices as a result. They don't understand us, and we don't understand them. They are trying to destroy us, so we are going to have to *catch* them. And in order to catch them, we must understand them.[62]

Other characters are less willing to understand The Brigade's political and social motivations with Harris dismissively stating—'Bunch of young berks is what I'd call 'em, need a proper day's work.'[63] Ultimately, then, The Branch damagingly dismiss the motivation of the anarchists as merely violence for its own sake with colleagues Morris and Parker assuming it is, 'to cause trouble. Hooligans, vandals, thugs.'[64] Even when attempting to apply political ideology to The Brigade's motives in Scene Two, the result is to find their logic contradictory and non-sensical, further dismissing the legitimacy of the anarchists and their ideas:

> Henderson: But wait a minute let me just – (*thinks*) right, so anarchy is about no rules, isn't it? No government, or big authorities. Well that's right wing, isn't it? 'Small state', 'freedom', that's on the right. Socialism and communism, that's about government *controlling* everything. That's what anarchists are against, so they can't be left.
>
> Smith: But on the right, they wish to preserve the status quo. The left aspire to a classless society. So it is a paradox?[65]

The Establishment figures in this play treat the threat The Brigade pose seriously but only because it has violent outcomes, and it is the method that causes the police simultaneously to dismiss the political philosophy behind it, even extending to moral judgements about the communal style of living that Branch members encounter as they arrest suspects:

> Parker: All those people. And men. And women. And… women and women. And men and men.
>
> And… and the baby. Little crying baby, being looked after by a dozen different mothers. A dozen different fathers. Pretending they're like some sort of family, but that's not a family, is it, not a family I recognise and I just, I just think, I don't know, I think it's rotten if I'm honest and it's doing my head in, it's making me – I don't know, I don't know.
>
> Smith: It's alright, Parker. You're right to be… to feel that way. That's the correct response.[66]

That Graham presents both actual and perceived motivation in the two halves of *The Angry Brigade* only reinforces the anarchist group's desire to overturn a social system that cannot or will not understand them. But it also suggests how ultimately unchallenged The Branch feel by The Brigade, a minor incursion into the democratic status quo that allows them to restore stability and order quickly.

In this context, Graham begins to outline how and why particular targets are chosen and the technological process of the attacks themselves, noting how many of them initially land against democratic and Establishment targets. The Brigade set themselves up as 'other' by taking the opposite position to David Sutch and choosing to act outside of the system. 'You can't bring down the structure of something you're inside of,' John explains, 'we've gotta step out of it. Out of the system, and underground, we're doing this. Properly.'[67] This notion is explained by fellow rebel The Prophet in an interview with The Branch, emphasising the anarchists' complete withdrawal from society that will make them harder to track.

> The Prophet: These people don't have names. I don't know who they are and even if I did, it's too late. They've already gone off the map. They don't exist anymore. They've gone that one step beyond where any of us before them were willing to go.[68]

And that step is in the making of bombs which quickly becomes The Brigade's chosen weapon. 'Guns are one thing though, right,' Hilary declares, 'but guns mean you have to be there, at the target, guns require firing. Bombs don't require firing, bombs can be left.'[69] When doubts are expressed about the indiscrimination of the explosive device, John brings the point back to the state-of-the-nation vision of social control and a need to shake people out of their compliance:

> John: Who are these innocent people you speak of, do you mean politicians, do you mean the police, do you mean the, the soldiers, or the civil servants at the dole office, or the teachers in the school that lie – were the guards at the concentration camp innocent because they were just following orders unquestioningly – I'm not comparing, but I am, I sort of am, I'm -[70]

Even when their plan becomes a reality and bystanders are killed, John doubles down on his anarchist rhetoric:

> John: We don't have any choice.

Hilary: No. Shop owners aren't our enemy, post offices aren't our enemy, pubs aren't our enemy –

John: Oi, yes they are. Yes they are, Hil, they are, they're complicit, they acquiesce, they're architects of their own ignorance.[71]

The actual process of bombmaking or the planting of them is not something that Graham dramatises in the play, skipping over the period from conception of the idea to the targets themselves, only discussing their aftermath and the effect in The Branch section of the play. This is an approach that Caryl Churchill also takes in her revolutionary plays, described by Sian Adiseshiash where 'significantly, the audience does not witness these barely imaginable challenges to property, work and social relations.'[72] Likewise, to give the audience a sense of the seriousness and scale of the action taken in *The Angry Brigade*, Graham includes an expositional speech that explains how the bombs are made described by The Branch's 'Expert,' a character whose only role is to provide this contextual information:

The Expert: Crude, yes, all domestic products; mix of sugar and sodium chloride, two batteries wired to a North Sea gas lighter element, and a bog standard wrist watch you could purchase from your average Woolworths or the Co-op.[73]

The Expert outlines the flight that brought a more 'sophisticate bomb' into the country earlier that same year and its component parts emphasising the increasing skill of the anarchists. Bombs constructed, the targets are discussed simultaneously in both parts of the drama, comparing early attacks directed at democratic targets including the active Minister of State for Employment as well as senior police officer and military bases all of which have some stake in creating and maintaining social order, and, by extension, the system itself. The death of the Employment Minister is discussed in both The Branch and The Brigade sections as Graham explores cause and effect, considering why the bomb was targeted against a government official but also the bombers changing reflection in the aftermath:

> Hilary: The Right Honourable Secretary of State for Employment Robert Carr… is going to discover what is right, and what is honourable, tonight.[74]

> The Commander: That is a politician. The Minister for Employment. Last night, at his home in north London, the Minister was in his study, his 13-year-old daughter was playing the piano in the living room, and his wife was in the kitchen. At approximately twenty-two hundred hours, the back door of his house… it blew off.

> Smith: It blew off?

> The Commander: And as the family made their way through the hallway towards the front door of the house to escape via the front door… well the front door blew of as well. Two bombs. Designed to kill.[75]

But The Brigade are not as unified in this attack on democracy as their police counterparts suppose:

> Anna: The little girl was at home.

> Hilary: There are always going to be little girls, Anna, steel yourself, focus.

> Anna: A LITTLE GIRL.

> Hilary: WE KNOW!

> We're trying to wake her up. Not kill her.[76]

The focus on democratic targets, however, escalates the response resulting in the formation of the Special Branch group tasked with investigating these crimes as explained to Smith:

> The Commander: We're forming a squad, upstairs, led by DCS Habershon, entirely confidential and off the books. You will be heading up a secret sub-division within the secret squad, down here, accountable only to Habershon and myself.[77]

Before further targets are revealed, Graham also dramatises the anarchists' public demands, shown as projected images on-screen which are only included in The Branch section. And like Churchill's approach to presenting violence onstage, there are no scenes in which these communiques are formulated or discussed by The Brigade. The reason for this is character-driven, because The Brigade story asks the audience to see the individuality in members of the group, each with their own route into this organisation, the anarchic principles they apply to protest action and their very different boundaries of acceptability. Watching them prepare and undertake these collective actions would undermine the slow dismantling of the cohesion and their separation into susceptible individuals that drives this half of the play. In creating this story onstage, Graham was inspired by contemporary parallels with 'an increasingly politicized youth in the face of growing generational inequality through austerity; disillusion with established party politics; the constant looming threat of terror [which] made it a seemingly resonant time to explore.'[78] The writer finds individuality in the application of these concerns but presents an opposite impression in The Branch, where the group is perceived as a single entity with a common purpose, one that shapes the police response. Thus, it is here that these purposeful anonymous notes appear such as: 'WE ARE NO MERCENARIES. THE WAR WILL BE WON... BY THE ORGANISED WORKING CLASS.'[79] This is an attempt to self-associate with the people they wish to represent even though the audience already know or will discover (depending on the order in which the two halves of the play are presented) that three-quarters of The Brigade members are public school graduates. These missives become even more explicit about the nature of the Establishment and the need to destroy its stranglehold:

THE POLITICIANS, THE LEADERS, THE RICH, THE BIG BOSSES, ARE IN COMMAND...

THEY CONTROL.

WE, THE PEOPLE, SUFFER.[80]

That the group intend to use anarchist and violent means is signalled ahead of a wave of explosive devices unleashed on London-based targets:

THE AB IS THE MAN OR WOMAN SITTING NEXT TO YOU.

THEY HAVE GUNS IN THEIR POCKETS AND ANGER IN THEIR MINDS.

WE ARE GETTING CLOSER.[81]

Graham presents this information in a specific order, the death of the Minister followed by threats of further action and then a sequence of broader actions against socio-economic targets in a rapid campaign that is replayed differently in both parts of the drama. The writer reverses the familiarisation technique used to explore the distinctiveness of Brigade members by creating a disassociation with the consequences of the bombings in that part of the story. Three bombs are released in quick succession, mixing the illusory play-acting of The Brigade members with the political philosophies the group espouse:

Jim / John / Hilary / Anna: THE ROYAL ALBERT HALL

John: 'Miss United States of America! Look – at – that. Wowee. Give us a turn there, miss, that's it. Judges are smiling…

And here's Miss Egypt! Exotic, or what?

And on home turf, it's Miss – United – Kingdom.'

Jim / John / Hilary / Anna: BANG.

Hilary / Anna: BIBA, KENSINGTON HIGH STREET.

Hilary: 'Recuperation', that's all it is, that's capitalism's power, it holds things out of your reach so one day you think you might riot but first you need to eat so you have to work, and then suddenly through a tiny wage increase or deflation in the price of this or that, you 'obtain' one of those things – a coat, a bag, a slightly better car – and suddenly you think, 'Oh, well, actually maybe it isn't so bad' and anyway… their blouses make me look fat –

Jim / John / Hilary / Anna: BANG

John / Jim: THE POST OFFICE TOWER.[82]

The personal reality of those explosions is instead managed through The Branch section as witnesses and statements add individual detail and empathy for the victims to the sketches created in the corresponding part of the drama:

The Manager: There was, there was, there was a, a bomb –

Henderson: Yes. Can we get you anything, what do you need –

The Manager: Need? Need? I need, to, I don't know, hahaha, I feel I need to scream, actually, hahaha.

The Manager *screams, long and loud. He stops.*

The Manager: Sorry.

Henderson: That's alright.

The Manager *screams again, shorter this time.*

The Manager: Fucking, 'scuse me, fucking *fuckers*. The entire autumn line, gone up in, in smoke.[83]

And Scene Five adds further targets never dramatised but discussed by The Brigade as part of their investigation. Henderson reports that there have been 'Attacks on the Ford Motor company in Gants Hill. The Territorial Army recruitment base. Our own police computer at Tintagel. And the Post Office Tower in Central London,' guessing at the reasoning for these targets:

Henderson: Territorial Army base. Sending soldiers off to fight and die in wars they don't believe in. The police computer, containing records of criminals they probably believe to be innocent. The Post Office Tower – no idea'

Parker: Because it's ugly, I wouldn't be sad to see that go.[84]

The Angry Brigade's attempt to break social and political structures by choosing to operate outside of the system, used anarchic methods to draw attention to their cause and clarify its underpinning belief that traditional structures are no longer effective. The anonymising of targets in both parts of the play helps The Brigade and The Branch to separate themselves from the people they pursue and, importantly, to disregard opposing viewpoints on how politics, economics and society should function. But as Sutch discovered with his milder form or anarchy, democracy itself is a more robust opponent than The Angry Brigade suppose, and in the end, Graham allows it to destroy them.

When democracy eventually fights back in Graham's plays, those who oppose it have very little chance of preventing it from resuming control. The police characters are essentially the guardians of democracy and the protectors of the status quo, and Graham spends time outlining their methods of detection and reasoning to identify the perpetrators. There are 'Snitch' characters who happily betray others to ensure democracy reduces their punishment for criminal transgressions as well as 'insiders' like The Prophet who provide information to The Branch through formal interviews. But democracy's most effective tool in this play is the desire for conventionality that begins to undermine The Brigade's unity. This begins in the nascent but eventually abortive romance between Jim and Anna discussed earlier in the chapter, but Anna continues to struggle against the extremes of the anarchist ideals and the methods enacted by The Brigade as theoretical and philosophical discussions become a far murkier reality. When concepts of innocence and guilt for society's ills create conflict within the group, Anna, however, continues to crave a return to a boundaried existence and therefore becomes the first to effectively betray her team by contacting the police herself. Appearing as an anonymous 'voice' in The Branch section until they uncover her identity (after which she is named in the matching scenes), she is always labelled as Anna, reaching out to authority figures and symbols of democracy on two occasions. The first happens before the violence begins, but Smith already senses her reluctance to participate:

Voice: Look for me.

Smith: I am looking –

Voice: No, you're searching, but you're not *seeing*.[85]

But the two versions of this conversation are not quite the same, there are missing words in The Branch's report of this scene. In The Brigade part, Graham adds extra context to Anna's trajectory of disillusionment:

Anna: When the lights go out and the flicker and the buzz of all the spectacles are shut out, and you can return, almost, slightly, to a state of natural being... to a state of *you*... What do you learn about yourself in that deep, dark fall into the subconscious? What do you learn about yourself that you really, actually want...?

Smith: Tell me what *you* want.[86]

Graham uses the same technique during the second conversation between Anna and Smith which focuses on revealing Anna's identity as Smith appeals to her conventionality:

Smith: I can save you. You can live –

Anna: What makes you think I want saving?

Smith: You want a normal life, free. Family. Children. Love. I can tell –

Anna: You can't tell that.

Smith: I can

Anna: How?

Smith: Because you're the one that keeps calling me.[87]

When this scene occurs again in The Brigade section told from Anna's perspective, Graham again inserts an additional piece of text that reinforces her growing separation, something that the writer deliberately withholds from the audience in The Branch section of the play to retain the homogeneous impression of anarchy that colours The Branch's perspective:

Anna: What makes you think I want saving?

Smith: - don't let the others bring you down with them. Jim, John and Hilary.

Anna: Ha. Bring me down.

Smith: You're different from them I know it. You want out. You want a normal life, free. Family. Children. Love. I can tell -[88]

Anna's transformation occurs rapidly from here and at the conclusion of this conversation she cooks dinner for Jim, actively introducing order and normality into their previously chaotic home:

Anna: I thought we could have an evening in.

Jim: 'An evening in', what does that even mean?

Anna: I just want to talk. Please.

Jim: (*beat; sits*) What's this?

Anna: A napkin.

Jim: A... a fucking... is this... what the –

Anna: It's only a fucking napkin, Jim, in case you spill something, I get 'em cheap -[89]

In the end it is Anna's desire for order and existing democratic structures that betrays The Angry Brigade when Graham shows her posting a letter containing her own DNA traces that helps The Branch to track her down.

Smith: She's struggling to stay underground, she wants contact with the real world, *that's* how we're going to get her, she almost wants it.

Henderson: Wants what?

Smith: To be caught.

Parker: (*with the phone*) I'll send a car to retrieve the letter and match fingerprints.

Morris: Sputum, on the envelope as well![90]

As a final gesture to disruption, Graham allows some of the younger police characters to enjoy the odd moment of anarchy, smoking a 'spliff' as well as a sexual encounter between three young Branch officers, but ultimately, The Brigade's methods are overwhelmed by the strength of the system pitted against them that terminates their rebellion. Their downfall, however, comes from within because notions of how society should function and where the boundaries of public protest must lie are too ingrained to be so easily overthrown. Characters like Sutch may try to change the system from within while The Angry Brigade act from the outside, but Graham shows that democracy is ultimately inside us all and will eventually win the day. As Holly Williams noted in a review for the *Independent* in 2015 noted 'love is the one thing that cannot bend to ideology, and that human beings might just need some rules and structure after all.'[91]

3.3 Anarchy in Dramatic Form

As his Early Works have demonstrated, Graham is a writer who often plays with form, adapting structures and dramatic tools to suit the themes and nature of his drama. Nowhere is this more interestingly applied than in his anarchy plays *Monster Raving Loony* and *The Angry Brigade* which have forms of theatrical anarchy running through their very construction, allowing the plays themselves to reflect their subject matter. In their very different ways, both are an exercise in taking control away from the playwright in which Graham recognises and acknowledges himself as part of an Establishment of sorts, reinforced in the writing and publishing of his plays, as well as how they are structured and performed using the application of conventional writing tools such as Acts, Scenes and stage directions. In *Monster Raving Loony*, this goes further still to explore the tone and style in which theatre stories should be told, with Graham giving away some of his authorial power by embracing a series of styles created by others, all working outside of theatre as a medium. There is an experimental playfulness to these anarchic approaches to drama that seeks to blur the boundaries between theatre and other forms of storytelling while exploring ways to transfer the playwright's power, and potentially share it through collaborative approaches to theatre-making that will be required in the staging and performance of this play.

The Angry Brigade is the most obviously anarchic of Graham's plays however, in which the writer applies different structural devices to the two parts of his story, 'something of an experiment in form,' Graham noted, 'two separate theatrical styles applied to the two different halves of the play.'[92] The Branch section is designed to reinforce conventional forms of living including the protection and influence of established approaches to societal governance and management that the police and their actions represent. Graham structures this as a traditional drama with eight separate scenes, longer at the beginning to establish the context and purpose of the story, becoming shorter as the action moves swiftly towards its resolution. Within this, Graham includes a great deal of architecture to keep the story on track including detailed stage directions that create particular scenic design as well as indications of character activity tell to the actors where they need to stand or what music they should be listening to. All of this is imposed by the writer who has an absolute authority over how this part of the play should look and how it is to be performed. To this purpose, the writer includes an additional directive note at the beginning of the play, requesting it be performed as indicated:

> The style of THE BRANCH should feel rigid in its presentation. The detail of the text is deliberately prescriptive. It is a world of order and characters who carry themselves in a carefully considered way. It can be presented as painfully conventional as possible.[93]

The formality of this section goes further still in referring to its characters by their last names only, a practice that nods to the public school tradition that The Brigade note is replicated throughout the functions of societal authority. This breakdown of individuality in favour of more anonymised approaches to collective duty is carried into the formal ways that the actors must interpret their character's bearing and posture, instilling in these creations a self-belief that they have a mandate to impose order over others and uphold social conventions as well as potentially influencing the choice of accents, costume and physical stature of the characters. The rigidity of Graham's structure, like society itself, applies rules, order and expectations on those performing the play that limits the capacity for interpretation and simultaneously reinforces the democratic structure with which this part of the play is concerned.

In contrast, The Brigade section of the play has no such structure for a good proportion of the story—no Acts, Scenes and, crucially, no stage directions at all. This is not something an audience viewing the play would be aware of, but on the page, the text flows freely, dialogue just happens with no indication of character entrances or exits, or where changes of tone or purpose may occur in the text. Graham here actively abdicates much of his authorial power and, other than determining the words that are spoken, gives control of the play to those designing it for performance. There is a kind of anarchy in this attempt to deconstruct and abandon the structural rules of playwriting that creates considerable freedom in this section of the play and the opportunity to make directorial choices about how it should be shaped and performed. In stepping back from imposing official and largely inherited rules for how drama is structured, the writer offers up an alternative, unencumbered model of construction that proposes greater collaboration and active representation from those staging the play:

> THE BRIGADE should be an offensive, anarchic mess. The text is deliberately non-prescriptive. A bold cacophony of music, media and physicality is encouraged.[94]

Yet, a power structure is maintained within the play, the words are provided and characters have established first names that they use throughout. Most importantly, the author begins to reassert control towards the end of The Brigade section, exactly at the point when Anna herself craves conventionality and begins to engage with the established societal structures that The Angry Brigade have been protesting against by formally communicating with the police and starting to adopt socially conventional behaviours in her relationship with Jim. In the moment that Anna terminates her second call with officer Smith, Graham's control of this story reasserts itself, and the first stage directions give instructions on how to present the ensuing conversation:

> Anna *puts the phone down.*
>
> John *appears as the child psychologist, sat on tiny chairs. He gestures for* Anna *to join him...*[95]

The appeal of the existing forms of being is thereafter represented in the way the remaining pages of text are constructed, with multiple stage directions and performance notes appearing to guide the actors to where 'beats' or 'pauses' might go as well as the physical gestures or movement required. As democracy hits back against the anarchists, so too does the writer restore expectations of theatrical structure, control and his own authority. Graham's experiment with dramatic anarchy, like The Angry Brigade itself, is defeated.

Graham would also challenge his authorial voice in the construction of *Monster Raving Loony* but not in the layout of the text which retains a more formulaic 'Parts' and 'Scenes' structure. The anarchy comes from borrowing performance styles from a range of sitcoms, comedy films and humorous genres and applying a different one to almost every scene of the play. This is hugely challenging for both writer and *Monster Raving Loony's* five central performers who must adapt the style of the production every few minutes to suit whatever homage is indicated. Across the four Parts of this play, 26 separate comedy treatments or styles are applied to this story, presented in a roughly chronological order that aligns David Sutch's biography with the corresponding history of comedy. It begins with 'The Beano' and ends with 'That Was the Week that Was' passing through 'Bedroom Farce,' 'Carry On,' 'Steptoe and Son,' 'Blackadder' and 'Absolutely Fabulous' along the way. And there are two key ways in which this lends itself to theatrical anarchy.

The first is the blending of radio, television and film styles with a piece produced specifically for the stage that deliberately breaks down the boundaries between those very different forms. Theatre has been increasingly influenced by the techniques of other media, borrowing cutting, lighting and filming approaches for staging plays as well as applying cinematic concepts to the visual impact of stage shows. There have been stage adaptations of television comedy shows such as *Cleo, Camping, Emmanuelle and Dick* by Terry Johnson (1998), Victoria Wood's *Acorn Antiques: The Musical!* (2005) and *Only Fools and Horses: The Musical* (2019) by Paul Whitehouse, John Sullivan and Jim Sullivan, but Graham's application of so many very different kinds of comedy style in one play using forms he did not create, is unique and an entirely different way to think about the relationship between theatre and comedy media. Like Sutch, Graham is working inside a system created by others and using its rules to encourage his audience to see the world a little differently, taking pieces, or in this case influences, comic styles and character-based catchphrases and finding a new purpose for them just as his own character attempts to find a new use for the constituent parts of everyday democracy by introducing anarchic approaches to its application.

The second expression of anarchy as form comes within the conjunction of these styles and the biographical development of the central story in which the writer's vastly ambitious approach must also deliver a coherent and developmental line of thought through those 26 separate comedy styles. 'Graham manages to keep a body of work that largely consists of stories about middle aged men in brown suits consistently fresh by constantly shaking up form,' Time Out Theatre Critic Andrzej Lukowski noted in his four-star review of the play in 2016, describing it as 'a virtuosic technical exercise.'[96] The challenge that the writer sets here is an unusual one, upending traditional notions of biography and how these are adapted for the stage as well as the role that these other forms must play in shaping dialogue and character behaviour at any given moment. Tribute novels to celebrated writers that bring beloved characters to life in new adventures are common, tribute theatre is not, and it makes *Monster Raving Loony* quite exceptional as an exercise in dramatic and comedic storytelling that overthrows all of the usual rules by constraining the authorial voice and re-routing it through the styles and comic conventions created by other writers. In each of the scenes, Graham has found and emulated the voice and structure of scores of comedy writers responsible for the shows and styles he chooses to utilise. The 'Allo Allo' scene is a strong example of this with its highly recognisable 1980s sitcom characters as well as catchphrases such as 'Good moaning' and 'Psst! You must listen very carefully. I shall this only once,' that Graham incorporates into this scene.[97] But the same technique applies to complicated wardrobe to bed to window shenanigans detailed in the heavy stage directions of the 'Bedroom Farace' sequence. The writer is borrowing but also bending highly recognisable tropes into this work, making each referenced sitcom or style recognisable to the audience while also creating two simultaneous trajectories that outline the events of Sutch's life and the history of comedy. As a direct assault on traditional approaches to theatre-making it is anarchic stuff, with performers rapidly adopting new styles and concepts as they go.

But the most radical aspect of this is the way in which these multiple styles and tropes still produce a single, consistent story in which the writer marshals the various comedy requirements into telling both Sutch's life story and that of his anarchic entrance into the established democratic system while still offering opportunities for character and plot development. Returning, for example, to the '*Allo Allo*' sequence in Part Three in which Sutch, cast as café-owning protagonist Rene Artois, attempts to return his nomination papers to his local electoral office with station staff representing other characters from this sitcom. And the scene follows the conventions of the *Allo Allo* episode format—a piece to camera (in this case the theatre audience) outlining the context of the scene that is about to take place as the original Rene did at the beginning of every episode with all its potential for farcical misadventure, followed by the sitcom-style character behaviours and catchphrases that derail his plans as the audience already know they will:

> Assistant Officer: But sir, this is just an humble toon hall, going about its normal everyday business. You have made a bug mistook. Excuse me.
>
> *He stands and leaves.* Sutch *hovers uncertainly, a* Deputy Returning Officer *(MICHELLE) appears from underneath the table.*
>
> Deputy Officer: Psst! You must listen very carefully. I shall say this only once.
>
> *She flicks a switch and the table flips to become a registration desk.*
>
> I am the Deputy Returning Officer, and I will register you, quickly.
>
> Sutch: But, the other officer said –
>
> Deputy: They do not want you to join. It is a trap, and we must resist!
>
> *The* Chief Returning Officer *(HERR FLICK) arrives.*
>
> Chief Officer: Excuse me, I am ze Chief Returning Officer, vat is going on?[98]

The scene dramatises the latest step in Sutch's story, even referencing his close relationship with his mother in the opening sentences, yet tone, structure and writing style are all borrowed from Jimmy Perry and David Croft. And the same approach occurs across the 25 other scenes representing decades of comedy styles within the lifetime of Graham's central character. An anarchic dramatic device that limits how the writer tells the story yet fundamentally overthrows what theatre is allowed to do in its relationship with other performance media and the presentation of new work.

Graham's anarchy plays therefore combine form and content to explore the motivation behind and success of anarchic incursions into democracy. While both *Monster Raving Loony* and *The Angry Brigade* take very different approaches to style, character and the underpinning structures that help the play to operate, there is a common trajectory across these stories, in which individuals and groups attempt to reshape or entirely eradicate the existing democratic system using anarchic and deliberately unconventional methods. In both plays, Graham looks beyond surface political engagement to consider the social and cultural factors that inspire the anarchists and their desire for change as well as negative perceptions of their behaviours that drive the reactions of others and the response from democracy itself. At the heart of Graham's two plays is a desire for conventionality that comes from within in which characters like Sutch and Anna ultimately look for recognition and acceptance from the Establishment and hope to be viewed as a legitimate part of the very system they try to disrupt. Even as Graham applies anarchic methods to his own writing style, theatrical order is restored by the end of both plays. Fight the system from within or outside but the system will always fight back. Order and democracy always triumph.

Notes

1. Asiseshiah, Sian. 2013. The Revolution Will Not be Dramatized: The Problem of Mediation in Carly Churchill's Revolutionary Plays. *Hungarian Journal of English and American Studies* Fall 19:2. pp.377–393.
2. Graham, James. *Monster Raving Loony*. Part One. In Graham James. 2016. *James Graham Plays: 2*. London: Methuen Drama, p.324.
3. Ibid, Part One, p.325.
4. Ibid, Part One, p.332.
5. Ibid, Part Two, p.341.
6. Ibid, Part Two, p.351.
7. Ibid, Part Three, pp.380–381.
8. Ibid, Part Two, p.352.

9. Ibid, Part Two, p.362.
10. Ibid, Part Two, p.337.
11. Ibid, Part Two, p.338.
12. Graham, James. Introduction. In Graham, James. 2016, p.xv.
13. Graham, James. *Monster Raving Loony*. Part Two. In Graham James. 2016, p.338.
14. Graham, James. Introduction. Graham, James. 2016, p.xvi.
15. Graham, James. *Monster Raving Loony*. Part Two. In Graham James. 2016, p.344.
16. Ibid, Part Two, p.345.
17. Ibid, Part Two, p.347.
18. Ibid, Part Two, p.348.
19. Ibid, Part Two, p.349.
20. Ibid, Part Two, p.353.
21. Ibid, Part Two, p.362.
22. Ibid, Part Two, p.364.
23. Ibid Part Three, p.365.
24. Ibid, Part Three, p.366.
25. Ibid, Part Three, p.366–367.
26. Ibid, Part Three, p.368.
27. Ibid, Part Three, p.370.
28. Ibid, Part Three, p.377.
29. Ibid, Part One, pp.328–329.
30. Ibid, Part Two, p.354.
31. Ibid, Part Three, p.372.
32. Ibid, Part Three, p.379.
33. Ibid, Part Three, p.380.
34. Ibid, Part Three, p.381.
35. Ibid, Part Three, p.383.
36. Ibid, Part Three, p.385.
37. Ibid, Part Three, p.378.
38. Ibid, Part Three, p.386.
39. Graham, James. *The Angry Brigade*. The Branch, Scene Three. In Graham James. 2016, p.149.
40. Ibid, The Brigade, p.189.
41. Ibid, The Brigade, p.190.
42. Ibid, The Brigade, p.219.
43. Ibid, The Branch, Scene One, pp.131–132.
44. Ibid, The Brigade, p.183.

45. Ibid, The Brigade, pp.183–184.
46. Ibid, The Brigade, p.195.
47. Ibid, The Brigade, p.194.
48. Ibid, The Brigade, p.195.
49. Ibid, The Branch, Scene 7, p.171.
50. Ibid, The Brigade, pp.201–202.
51. Ibid, The Brigade, p.203.
52. Ibid, The Brigade, p.205.
53. Ibid, The Brigade, p.202.
54. Ibid, The Brigade, p.188.
55. Ibid, The Brigade, p.196.
56. Ibid, The Brigade, p.196.
57. Ibid, The Brigade, p.204.
58. Ibid, The Brigade, p.206.
59. Ibid, The Brigade, p.203.
60. Ibid, The Branch, Scene One, p.130.
61. Ibid, The Branch, Scene One, p.135.
62. Ibid, The Branch, Scene Two, p.138.
63. Ibid, The Branch, Scene Two, p.141.
64. Ibid, The Branch, Scene Two, p.142.
65. Ibid, The Branch, Scene Two, p.143.
66. Ibid, The Branch, Scene Four, p.160.
67. Ibid, The Brigade, p.187.
68. Ibid, The Branch, Scene Three, p.150.
69. Ibid, The Brigade, p.200.
70. Ibid The Brigade, p.201.
71. Ibid, The Brigade, pp.212–213.
72. Asiseshiah, Sian. 2013. *Hungarian Journal of English and American Studies*, pp.377–393.
73. Graham, James. *The Angry Brigade*. The Branch, Scene One. In Graham, James. 2016, p.131.
74. Ibid, The Brigade, p.204.
75. Ibid, The Branch, Scene One, p.133.
76. Ibid, The Brigade, p.207.
77. Ibid, The Branch, Scene Two, pp.135–136.
78. Graham, James. Introduction. In Graham James. 2016, p.xv.
79. Graham, James. *The Angry Brigade*. The Branch, Scene Three. In Graham James. 2016, p.148.
80. Ibid, The Branch, Scene Three, p.151.

81. Ibid, The Branch, Scene Five, p.163.
82. Ibid, The Brigade, pp.210–211.
83. Ibid, The Branch, Scene Six, p.167.
84. Ibid, The Branch, Scene Five, pp.163–164.
85. Ibid The Branch, Scene Five, p.163.
86. Ibid, The Brigade, p.212.
87. Ibid, The Branch, Scene Eight, p.174.
88. Ibid, The Brigade, p.215.
89. Ibid, The Brigade, p.218.
90. Ibid, The Branch, Scene Eight, pp.175–176.
91. Williams, Holly. 2015. The Angry Brigade, Bush Theatre, Review: A Real Play of Two Halves. *Independent*, May 7, https://www.independent.co.uk/arts-entertainment/theatre-dance/the-angry-brigade-bush-theatre-review-a-real-play-of-two-halves-10233653.html.
92. Graham, James. Introduction. In Graham, James. 2016, p.xv.
93. Graham, James. *The Angry Brigade*. In Graham, James. 2016, p.123.
94. Ibid, p.123.
95. Ibid, The Brigade, p.215.
96. Lukowski, Andrzej. 2016. Monster Raving Loony. *Time Out*, May 18, https://www.timeout.com/london/theatre/monster-raving-loony.
97. Graham, James. *Monster Raving Loony*. Part Three. In Graham, James. 2016, p.373.
98. Ibid, Part Three, p.373.

PART II

Assumed Power

CHAPTER 4

Famous Faces

Famous faces appear with considerable regularity across Graham's work providing, often comic, moments of jolting recognition for any audience suddenly able to associate and situate the drama within a context of historical and cultural understanding. But these celebrity appearances have a particular purpose within the worlds the playwright creates that go beyond the superficial enjoyment of mere namechecking. Nor is Graham particularly concerned with examining or analysing celebrity culture for its own sake, although the existence of these characters draws, to an extent, on the ongoing fascination with celebrity culture that dominates contemporary society and the playwright's examination and presentation of media outlets explored in Chapter 5. Instead, the famous face is both cameo and protagonist in Graham's work with a multi-dimensional dramatic purpose, often providing a theatrical shorthand for a particular set of political and pop culture debates as well as representing different forms of social power represented by the staging of each play. Writer Gregg Jenner defined celebrity as:

> **CELEBRITY** (noun): A unique persona made widely known to the public via media coverage, and whose life is publicly consumed as dramatic entertainment, and whose commercial brand is profitable for those who exploit their popularity, and perhaps also for themselves.[1]

Within the dramatic narratives that Graham creates, celebrity of this kind becomes a proxy for other kinds of cultural or historical discourse in which a famous face is the physical embodiment or manifestation of social tides on which the playwright is commenting. If Graham's work focuses on twentieth-century turning points resulting in novel social dynamics being created and the seeds of future power structures being sewn, then celebrity becomes the theatrical symbol for those changes, both embodying the substance of their era and, more often, presenting a direct challenge to the status quo that often drives social change within the constructed drama. If each era gets the celebrities it deserves, then Graham's work uses famous faces as a lens to scrutinise the historical significance and influence of contemporary power structures. The choice of political and pop culture icons in Graham's work acts as a beacon for their times and become the outward representation and embodiment of the complex socio-political discussions explored within each play.

As Jenner notes, celebrity is a catch-all term applied to those who actively court fame or who achieve it through the status associated with their position. The latter category incorporates politicians and those in positions of social authority such as leading churchmen, while the former captures anyone from singers and actors to television presenters, writers and newspapers magnates stepping beyond the public exposure incumbent on their role and actively embracing a concept of personality-based fame recognisable for their name as much as their specific talent. The Archbishop of Canterbury (*Tammy Faye*) is famous but holds a different kind of fame to Maureen Lipman (*The Culture*) and Andy Warhol (*Best of Enemies*). Both kinds of celebrity appear with regularity in Graham's work, often side-by-side, informally linked and distributed to varying degrees across these plays depending on the subject matter, character focus of the work and the contextual relevance to the story the writer is presenting. Indeed, the proliferation of famous faces can be divided into two categories: first Incidental-Celebrity, those appearing as adjuncts to the central narrative or as illustrative examples and comic devices in service of the wider purpose of the play. Celebrity-Protagonists form the second category including those who are a play's lead character and from whose perspective—sympathetic or not—Graham writes. There are notable differences in how and when these incidental and protagonist tropes are employed, and the inference Graham wishes the audience to draw from their existence.

Incidental-Celebrities are a form of cultural and political shorthand that Graham employs to create substance and instant understanding of contemporary society within the era of the play. These are often comic, offering moments of quick recognition for an audience, sometimes appearing in montage sequences alongside other Incidental-Celebrities with explanatory value within the drama. Their existence is a dynamic device acting in lieu of exposition about the wider world at the time of the story, yet the Incidental-Celebrity rarely has direct narrative relevance, instead acting as a technique operating in parallel to the central plot, giving it flavour, even glamour but rarely delivering vital story points or crucial information. Celebrity-Protagonists, by contrast, have distinct dramatic and narrative purpose often representing and inhabiting new kinds of social power which they usually initiate and control through their actions. The innovative or disruptive behaviours that they exhibit then affect their industry or field. As a result, it is a power that often consumes them, and in Graham's more recent works, leads to unsatisfactory or sometimes even disastrous outcomes as their brief light burns out. But there are long-term consequences of their fame, resulting often in regret-filled decline or a negative shift in the reputation of this individual that changes how they are perceived today as well as the unmanageable forces their actions have unleashed.

The ways in which Graham has employed Incidental and Celebrity-Protagonists have changed over time with the famous face becoming increasingly important to his work in the last few years, where once his plays looked to the side of celebrity to explore the structures operating beneath them, the writer's focus has expanded from political institutions to other powerful societal influences. Celebrities appear with relative rarity in Graham's earliest works with marked appearances usually by historical politicians such as Antony Eden (*Eden's Empire*) and Ted Heath (*Tory Boyz*) or are used in small roles that support the development of or insight into non-famous characters. That these creations also tend to appear in fantasy or dreamlike sequences only adds to their otherness within the drama, their separation from the central narrative which the audience charts through the lead character. Graham's use of famous faces is limited to incidental appearances through all of his early work up to and including the writing of *This House* which uses Incidental-Celebrity in tandem with references to unseen Party leaders. *Monster Raving Loony* changed that when incidental famous faces were joined, even dominated by, Celebrity-Protagonists as Graham began to write from the perspective of well-known historical and cultural figures, followed by *Ink*, *Quiz*, *Best of Enemies* and *Dear England* all of which had lead and secondary characters in the public eye. Each of those plays capture elements of biography while actively reflecting on the implications of their fame within the play's purpose. These works also continue to use Incidental-Celebrity for comic and illustrative purposes, creating those moments of audience recognition and context, but Graham's writing entered a new period of focus in which famous faces became the substance of the drama rather than a secondary feature.

4.1 Incidental-Celebrity

4.1.1 *This House*

This House was Graham's first West End play staged in 2012 which considers the fragility of governmental authority and the, often, hilarious deals and compromises politicians make to cling to power. Set during the tumultuous Labour administration of 1974–1979, when a paper-thin majority became a minority government reliant on coalition to pass legislation, the play is set in the offices of the Conservative and Labour Whips, presented side-by-side as Graham exposes and explores the engine room of Parliamentary governance. Famous faces in this context should be plentiful, recognisable politicians who would go on to become very well-known Ministers in the years ahead along with the extremely famous party leaders vying to be Prime Minister in this era—Harold Wilson, James Callaghan and Margaret Thatcher, who assumed leadership of the Conservative Party in 1974. But the temptation to write this story from the perspective of those in traditional and official positions of power, and the possibility of pastiche that this brings, are subverted by Graham who instead looks to a less visible, even secretive, corner of Westminster for his protagonists—the Whips—in a deliberate rejection of celebrity and the potentially destabilising effect that the recognition and influence of well-known political figures (and their subsequent reputation) might have on the themes and democratic questions raised in this play. In his 2016 introduction to the play, the playwright recalled having 'no desire to portray the view of the leaders at the top, I wanted the dirty, mucky, grubby world of those turning the wheels in the engine room.'[2]

Instead, the writer moves beyond these notable personalities to alternative but equally influential lead characters who are presented to the audience without historical assumption and reputation that their name suggests, leaving the viewer unencumbered by prior expectations that they bring to how the drama and its personnel will develop—a difficult balance to achieve when the historical 'facts' of this ragged administration are well-known or easy to obtain. By avoiding acknowledged celebrity in *This House*—and this is a play with no Celebrity-Protagonist—Graham returns both agency to his creations and the possibility of unexpected dramatic development to his story, allowing the audience to know and not know what the outcomes of the personal and individual dramas depicted may be, creating a necessary sense of jeopardy that motions the play. To do this, the names of the respective leaders are never directly used, distancing the audience further from any preconceptions while simultaneously acknowledging that their individual fame is sufficient for the audience to unpick the coded reference to their identity:

> Weatherill: Walter, for heaven's sake. Imagine what the Lady would do to the person who didn't walk in tonight?[3]

Graham instead disguises Incidental-Celebrity using the same euphemistic technique throughout which forces the audience to do some of the work to identify the famous faces depending on their knowledge of the era and its notorious social and pop culture scandals—some of which have since been dramatised on television. This interesting device offers a two-fold comedic opportunity, allowing some of the more outrageous incidents of this Parliament to be incorporated into the story without making them the sole focus of a political drama that looks at the consequences of the delicate numbers balance managed by the Whips. As a result, it means that Graham is able to situate the comedy of *This House* in the shape of character interactions and personalities as they react to extraordinary events as they affect the changing fortunes of the government. Incidental famous faces, then are semi-disguised and *This House* is the only major work where this happens, a technique used specifically to dampen the distorting effect of particular stories and scandals that may unbalance the behind-the-scenes drama of the Whips' office and the numerical driver as they try to keep the administration afloat against the odds. But it also allows the audience to step back from the mire of individual scandal to look at the catalogue of disasters endured, manipulated and even mastered by the non-famous protagonists in relatively quick succession.

Graham employs the theatrical equivalent of a montage sequence, a series of vignettes at two crucial points in the play. These are designed to create quick-fire bursts of energy in the pacing of the story with a series of revolving-door scenes as the Whips do deals, and their best, to avert any disasters that may see the government defeated in the House of Commons and potentially removed from office. In Act One, Scene Two having already established what is at stake and introduced key named characters to the audience that they will follow through the story, Graham introduces the first semi-disguised Incidental-Celebrity—the MP for Walsall North, John Stonehouse whose name and its associated scandal will be known to many audience members. Graham uses that knowledge to tease the fixed outcome of his story with the character appearing first as a general member of the House making a speech about a terrible dream that the Whips listen to as a recording in their office:

> Walsall North: (*off recorded*) 'I'm floating on my back down the Thames. Underneath... what? Lambeth I suppose. Lambeth Bridge... And then I.... I turn my head. And I see that... that the Houses of Parliament are on fire. And suddenly the Thames turns to... it turns to blood. Like oil in the darkness.... and then I see the bodies. Hundreds of them. I recognise the MPs. They're flowing out of a hole in the palace. Face down in the blood...'[4]

Concerned for his mental health, the Whips call Stonehouse—whose name is never used in the play—to their office where Graham again references the MP's predetermined future in a conversation about the sea:

> Walsall North: People often say that the sea makes them sad, but it's not the sea is it? It's the beach. When you're out at sea, it's actually extraordinarily peaceful, but on the beach, looking out *at* the sea... one can't help but suddenly feel so... erm... *mortal*. So aware that one only has a self-contained amount of time. Course you know why don't you? It's because the sound of the tide is the sound of *breathing*. Sucking air in... and pushing it back out. That's what we're listing to, as we strand on the edge of the world, having come as far as we can go. We're listening to our own mortality. Ebbing away. The saddest sound in the world.[5]

This is clever foreshadowing of the drama to come in which (outside the play) Stonehouse's clothes are found on a Miami beach where he was presumed drowned. Graham, however, keeps tight control of the play's numerical driver, refusing to be distracted by this potentially consuming scandal and is only concerned with the problem it creates for the Whips, and its effect is discussed from their point of view:

> Mellish: Just his clothes left. Strewn along on the bloody beach. Miami, Christ…

Prompting a connection to the public record of his time as an MP:

> Ann (*with the book*): Oh Jesus. His last question in the House. Remember? Drowning statistics.

Although Mellish is clear where the blame should lie:

> Mellish: not our fault people in this country vote in frigging lunatics, is it? We just have to make sure we don't bloody well lose any more of 'em. Christ (*Jacket on, making to go*). Just two in it. Two! No more![6]

The truth is always far stranger than any fiction that the writer could concoct and so the outcome of this building reference to Stonehouse's life comes to fruition one scene later when Graham fulfils the MP's known trajectory, which again is tied entirely to the head count required to pass whatever vote the Member for Walsall North is needed for:

> Mellish: Hah! He's alive! Ha ha… he's only a-bloody-well-live!
>
> *He runs to the board and replaces '+1' with '+2' laughing.*[7]

In a comedy side note about the desperation of the Whips' office in this period, Stonehouse returns to the drama one last time as a criminal under investigation in which the Whips have a task convincing their errant Member to support their continued calculations:

> Mellish: Oh, don't think in any other situation you wouldn't be out on your bloody bum, mate. But we *can't*. Not yet
>
> Majority's too thin. With a suspended sentence you can stay on until we're out of the danger zone and *then* piss off.

> Walsall North: No. No, I'm not staying here, I can't stay in the House. I'll resign.
>
> Mellish: Can't resign John. Only get booted out. Fact.
>
> Walsall North: Oh yes I can. The Crown Steward and Bailiff of the Chiltern Hundreds. 'An MP who accepts an office of profit *must* resign.' So there. I'm sorry. But…
>
> Mellish: (*standing, grabbing him*) You're bloody well staying right! You're staying here![8]

And then Stonehouse disappears from *This House*, his purpose as a comedic threat to the stability of the administration served, the character has no further function. But this brief appearance reinforces the compromises of democracy evident in this play when, regardless of the personalities or reputations of party members, the thin majority is protected at all costs. One of the great scandals of the 1974–1979 Parliament is therefore given no more than a few lines under the pseudonymous title of Stonehouse's constituency, but the urgency and criminality of his story is subverted and used by Graham to illustrate the chaotic series of blunders that the Incidental-Celebrities of *This House* represent.

A second Incidental-Celebrity is given far less stage time but creates drama in a similar way, added for comic effect the Labour Whips lose control as Graham only partially reveals identity details in a conversation about this character. Once again, audience members may already know Liberal Party leader Jeremy Thorpe's scandal which involved accusations of the attempted murder of his much younger homosexual lover. Graham treats this in the same way as Stonehouse, introduced as part of the same numbers game that the Whips are trying to manage, a gossipy aside in this case as falling Labour numbers require collaboration with the Conservative Whips to uphold the custom of 'pairing'—standing down an Opposition member for every government MP who cannot vote in order to create a level playing field:

> Silvester: Yeah, alright, keep your braces on. One of our trickier customers has a boat show they're trying to get to, that'll bring him on side. Say, this stuff about Thorpe, eh? Didn't come from your lot, did it? Young male lover.

Attempted assassination. All nonsense of course. Must be.

Harper: Before I came into politics, Frederick, I would have agreed with you.[9]

But Thorpe makes another appearance in *This House* and a few lines later he appears again, coincidentally just before John Stonehouse is found alive:

Mellish: And now with Thorpe on the Liberal side facing arrest. Charge of attempted murder no less. That's three new leaders in the space of months, which means our alliances are shaky at best.

Harper: A three-way changeover in one Parliament? That ever happened before? –

Mellish: What does that matter, it's happening now. (*Pointing at the board, '+1'.*) And it doesn't get more fragile than that, does it.[10]

Thorpe, though named directly, never appears in the play yet the role of his scandal, like Stonehouse, is to draw attention to the fragility of the Parliament and the difficulty of creating sufficient partnerships to support legislation as the disorder of the administration continues to spiral. With that in mind, *This House* has one final Incidental-Celebrity to share, Michael Heseltine, later to be a cabinet minister in Margaret Thatcher's subsequent government and a regular Tory leadership challenger. Heseltine appears in the script as the Member for Henley seen first brandishing the Parliamentary mace at the beginning of Act One, Scene Five—another real-life incident woven into this script—in which the Opposition believe the Labour Government has cheated to secure a vote. Only later does the audience learn that this figure is Michael Heseltine through a surname check in the dialogue. The MP is presented as an anarchic figure, driving the farcical conclusion that ends Act One as the government descends into a physical fight that the Labour Whips desperately try to mitigate in order to preserve their authority:

Henley: The song they were singing that bloody Commie song after they robbed us of the vote!

Weatherill: Heseltine, put a sock in it![11]

Incidental-Celebrity in *This House* is then a disguised dramatic device used to draw attention to the fragile leadership and extreme behaviours employed by the Whips' office to ensure Labour remains in power. While none of these stories directly drive the plot, nor are they entirely superfluous, adding more than a handful of colourful scandals that fill out the play. Instead, each one creates a problem for the protagonists to solve, a rolling issue of managing unreasonable and unpredictable human behaviour giving a flavour of the uphill battle undertaken by the Whips to keep their deteriorating and increasingly ambiguous show on the road. This is the only time that Graham actively disguises Incidental-Celebrity, and in the plays that follow some extremely recognisable famous faces appear in which Incidental-Celebrity is used in service of Celebrity-Protagonists.

4.1.2 Ink

For Graham's next major play, the focus turned from politics to the influence of media organisations and approaches to shaping national interest by influencing governments through an appetite for new forms of populist entertainment where the exposure to celebrity is far greater, although the writer carefully controls the use of famous faces in these dramas to manage the pleasure of recognition along with its social commentary. *Ink* has fewer Incidental-Celebrities than *This House* yet the device remains a useful one, providing necessary contextual information and becomes a means to convey historic shifts and developments in the period 1969 to 1970 when the play is set. Unlike *This House*, *Ink* is built around Celebrity-Protagonists, recognisable names that modern audiences are likely to already hold quite deep-rooted preconceptions about at the start of the drama which will be explored in greater detail later in the chapter. Incidental-Celebrities here are people in the same world as the primary famous faces, but they do not have a deterministic role in the plot and are used here to contribute to the play's central argument and in hastening the effect of or reflecting on the changes instigated by the Celebrity-Protagonists.

Relative to Graham's later dramas, *Ink* uses Incidental-Celebrity quite sparingly, partly as a result of having two very well-known Celebrity-Protagonists who are the focus—although *Best of Enemies* demonstrates that the balance between volumes of Celebrity-Protagonists and Incidental-Celebrities is not necessarily relative. With *Ink*, however, the writer instead uses the process of building a sensationalist newspaper to fulfil the role of Incidental-Celebrity, with many of its headlines having achieved an equivalent fame or notoriety in subsequent years. So, where *This House* had scandalous stories funnelled through the controversial MPs who created them, *Ink* has similarly salacious tales that the main characters discuss, shape, perpetuate and translate into print which in turn contribute to another kind of numbers game driver, the sales targets established at the start of the play that give purpose to the story.

Ink, like its predecessor, has a number of secondary and tertiary characters whose names may be familiar to those with specific knowledge of the late 1960s and particularly the newspaper industry at this time. From first Editor of *The Sun* Larry Lamb's wider newsroom staff to the Page Three girl who breaks boundaries, and the Fleet Street faces who manage rival newspapers, but this does not make them Incidental-Celebrities in this context, and none could be classified as a household name. The only true Incidental-Celebrity character in *Ink* is the actor Christopher Timothy, here a young performer just starting out in the business and later to become the famous name that contemporary audiences now recognise. As with the inclusion of John Stonehouse and Jeremy Thorpe in *This House*, it is not significant that Christopher Timothy is included in the drama, there is no focus on his wider life or future, nor is his appearance essential to the plot. Instead, what matters is what the character is there to do, voice the first ever television advert for a newspaper, a meeting of different kinds of media that in style and delivery proves as refreshing and innovative as the numerous developments *The Sun* offered in the focal period in Graham's drama:

> Brian: It's still a little over, slot's thirty seconds and that was forty-one, we're going to have to make some cuts.
>
> Lamb: No cuts, get him to speak faster.
>
> Christopher: Do I have to keep saying 'in the *Sun*' at the end of every line? I could just say it at the end.

Lamb: No, that's the most important bit – what's your name?

Christopher: Christopher, sir, Christopher Timothy, I'm an actor.

Lamb: Yeah, well, stop being an actor.

Christopher: Stop being an actor? I'm from the Old Vic.[12]

Like *This House*, the inclusion of this scene services the plot in synthesising and projecting the many cumulative changes Lamb and his team made to try meet the level of its readership. That Christopher Timothy voiced those adverts is fairly immaterial and that he happened to be an actor destined for greater fame is a fun by-product of this segment, one the contemporary audience momentarily enjoys, yet beyond this scene, the actor and his future are not mentioned again. For *Ink*, Christopher Timothy is only incidentally relevant, and instead the drama focuses on the role he plays in fulfilling Lamb's greater vision and the consequences it has for the role of modern media in British society.

Graham also uses Incidental-Celebrity in this play in quite another way, applying the practice in a different form than anywhere else in his work, using the newspaper's own sensational headlines to prove, as with Stonehouse and Thorpe, that once again truth is stranger than fiction. As with all Incidental-Celebrity appearances, the stories themselves are not directly important to the purpose and outcomes of *Ink*, and in the same way that Christopher Timothy's appearance is a proxy for the progress of the newspaper, so too do the doping scandals, kidnap plots and affronted outrage of the headlines reflect the pioneering approaches and inherent dangers generated within *The Sun's* first year of tabloid operation. And like Timothy, substitute them for any of the hundreds of published headlines in 1969 and it would ultimately make little directional difference to what *Ink* has to say and the longer-term social outcomes that Graham is exploring. The famous headlines then act as a device in *Ink* that gives the protagonists opportunities to discuss the moral and competitive consequences of their endeavours either within *The Sun* team or as the ramifications are felt across Fleet Street. Like Incidental-Celebrity embodied within a distinct character, these headlines have taken on a subsequent fame or notoriety that contribute to the play in several key ways. First, consider the relaunched publication's first ever headline:

Lamb: Right, front page: 'Exclusive: Racehorse dope sensation! Interview with the trainer who's giving his horses smack.

And immediately Lambs has a problem to solve:

Ray: (*entering, overalls, ink*) Er, sorry to interrupt, the type keys have arrived. Bad news. You didn't order enough of our Large Headline Font. For a start, there's only three 'E's.

Bernard: What does that mean?

Ray: Means you can't have more than three 'E's in any one paper main headline. Including front page.

Brian: (*counting the 'E's*) One, two, three, four – shit, five, six.

Bernard: Lose exclusive?

Frank: Wow wow wow –

Beverley: Change dope to smack? 'Race Horse Smack Sensation'?

Frank: Nah that just sounds like someone's been punching a horse.

Brian: Doesn't have to say *race* horse, could just be horse.

Lamb: … One, two, three, alright, fine. Good, get it off.[13]

Its role in the plot is entirely numbers driven and underpins the protocol challenge that the existence of the newspaper is shown to effect on 'the Street,' presaging a broader upending of the purpose and style of news media that followed the newspaper's launch. The characters discuss the punchy nature of the headline in the newly repurposed *The Sun's* first appearance, but it also represents a series of compromises required as a result of the few weeks that the team are given in the drama to put a first edition together. The lack of preparedness is a form of chaotic comedy in which the audience understands the pressures exerted on the team while they try to instigate their innovative approach to news generation and dissemination. Lamb here accepts a 'good enough' mentality that further separates the newspaper from the traditions and pomposity of their Fleet Street colleagues. But the writer also adds a shadow of doubt, a hint of naivety in the celebration of simplicity and the jaunty ease with which Lamb bulldozes through seemingly insurmountable problems, a very subtle warning from Graham of the far more significant events to come.

The most important example of headlines as Incidental-Celebrity in *Ink* is the appearance and coverage of Muriel McKay's abduction and subsequent murder used to both reflect on the approach and impact of *The Sun*, exploring the consequences of its consuming style and the demand it creates that the news team must continue to feed in order to meet their sales target driver. Having created a public appetite for this case, they must also maintain their exclusive reporting rights to it, thereby creating a cycle of target-driven sensation reliant on repeat custom. The McKay case is a real one, the wife of one of the newspaper's chairmen introduced fleetingly in Act One as part of a visit to the premises. When Mrs McKay is later abducted, Graham gives the paper a moral dilemma to address—whether or not to report on a story that is close to home and represents a conflict of interest:

> Lamb: We... we need to work out how to 'report'. This.
>
> Murdoch: ... Report it?
>
> Lamb: Yeah, we're a newspaper, this is news. Alick asked, I'm not just being -[14]

This problem plays out in two ways within the drama; first the writer uses it to illustrate the changing perspective and moral dependency of Larry Lamb as his colleagues—and by extension the audience—start to question his judgement on the editorial management of this story:

> Brian: Boss, maybe we should all just think about it, for a second –
>
> Lamb: There isn't *time* to think about it. We want it out there, don't we, as much information as possible. Don't we?!

And Graham uses this opportunity to remind the audience of the purpose of *The Sun's* redesign:

Lamb: We agreed! In this room, we all signed up, or have you forgotten?! Either we believe in this, or we don't! Either we're right... or we Stop Now!

The team waver, looking at one another.

You fucking hypocrites...[15]

Like the Stonehouse segments in *This House*, McKay's story plays out across a number of scenes as the period of her abduction passes and fresh information emerges. As the writer increases the complexity of the case by including personal interactions with her family members and with the police investigation, the drama uses her Incidental-Celebrity to reflect on both the push to maintain and increase sales through Lamb's determination to provide exclusive content at any cost and the ways in which the newspaper starts to transgress pre-existing boundaries to do so, that once crossed, can never be reconstructed:

Joyce: (*holding a letter*) We've received a complaint, brace yourself... from the actual fucking *kidnappers*.

Lamb: (*snatching it*) From the kidna – Complaining, to *us*?!

Joyce: They can never get through on the phone, they say, because it's always engaged. The number we gave out -

Lamb: Oh I'm sorry! Are we - ?! Is that our - ?!

Brian: And plenty more besides; hoax letters, fake ransoms, sending the police on wild goose chases, 'I think I saw Muriel McKay on the train from Ipswich to Felixstowe', we bloody ran that on page four, that's a couple of days the old bill won't get back. They're going spare, Larry –

Lamb: OK, OK, OK...[16]

Graham's use of Incidental-Celebrity here culminates in some devastating consequences for the newspaper and McKay's family, outcomes directly tied in the play to Lamb's decision to provide blanket coverage of this case:

CID Commander: I believe that if news of Mrs McKay's disappearance had not been released so early we could have established a quick line with the kidnappers. We were embarrassed by the intensity of the publicity. It could be it forced the kidnappers beyond the point of no return. That is the question that will be posed for a long time.

The headline from a rival newspaper puts that into stark relief for the audience:

Frank (*reading*) 'Did Publicity Help to Kill Muriel McKay?'

Murdoch answers that question with a further extract:

Murdoch (*snatching it from* Frank, *reading*) 'The kidnappers, kept aware of the search, every step of the way, in their own morning paper…'

Before the horrifying consequences are revealed:

Brian: They, uh, they've charged two brothers.

Murdoch: So they … (*Holding* Alick's *arm*). Have they found her?

Brian: … They think they – that they fed her to the pigs.[17]

This more unusual approach to incorporating Incidental-Celebrity works in the same way as the writer's earlier application of this device, providing parallel commentary on the central story that may not directly drive or influence the plot but does offer both character-based opportunities to reconsider the action and motivation of the leads as well as offering valuable contextual information that directly affects the play's fundamental driver. Like *This House*, *Ink* uses a numbers game structure as the characters chase a sales figure target that salacious stories and the tragedy of Muriel McKay directly contribute to.

4.1.3 Quiz

The application of Incidental-Celebrity become much more prominent in *Quiz*, an exploration of justice and public scrutiny, which confines their appearance to a tightly controlled portion of the story providing a contextual aid to summarise the history of the gameshow format and creates simultaneous opportunities to incorporate an audience participation device—a first for Graham's major work. The story of the 'Coughing Major,' a cheating scandal that engulfed ITV gameshow *Who Wants to Be a Millionaire*, *Quiz* like *Ink* before has Celebrity-Protagonist leads and is peopled by a collection of media executives and those accused of complicity in the case brought against Charles and Diana Ingram, but, like the newspaper staff in *Ink*, they are not sufficiently famous in their own right to act as Incidental-Celebrity. Instead, the writer draws on some of the most well-known names in 1970 and 1980s light entertainment to create a glitzy backdrop for this story.

Quiz has a deceptively simple justice structure; the first Act is the Case for the Prosecution and the second the Case for the Defence. Around that Graham weaves a complex set of character groups, interconnections, damning evidence and mitigating circumstances, all the while foregrounding re-enactments of pivotal scenes from *Who Wants to Be a Millionaire* that feature the protagonist's time in the 'hotseat.' Incidental-Celebrity, as ever in Graham's work, does not directly contribute to the outcomes of this story and the device cannot help the audience to decide whether the Ingrams were innocent or guilty of the deception they were accused. Rather, the technique is used to illustrate the nature of television quiz shows and the very different popular impact that this new show had for both the channel that originated the idea and its potential contestants.

The choice of Incidental-Celebrities in *Quiz* are among the most joyous that Graham has created—Des O'Connor, Jim Bowen and Leslie Crowther—legendary light-entertainment figures of their era who bring with them both instant recognition for a vast portion of the British theatre-going audience and the chance to recreate their most famous shows in an extended montage sequence that gives the audience a grounding in television history. Rather than a standalone sequence, this instead becomes a sophisticated device directly incorporated within the Case for the Prosecution, dramatically integrated within and emerging out of the evidence given by Celador CEO Paul Smith over several pages of the original 2017 script in which Graham combines flashbacks to each show within Smith's testimony that acts as an introduction to each dramatised gameshow segment:

> Paul Smith: I decided to revive the classic elements of light entertainment.

In a way, it's a return to what ITV was founded for. Commercial television. Whose only responsibility was to give people – what they *wanted*. 'Popular entertainment'[18]

The first of these is *Take Your Pick* based on a Yes/No principle, but as television audiences become overly familiar with the format that the character of Smith explains, that something new is required:

> Paul Smith: As time went on, the importance of questions and answers, is something true, or is it false, began to wane. People wanted – an 'alternative', to facts.[19]

This leads to a recreation of *Bullseye* before Smith continues:

> Paul Smith: There came a time when people, unapologetically, began to want more 'stuff'. Knowledge wasn't the prize anymore. Prizes were.[20]

Leading into a round from *The Price is Right*, this potted history of ITV quiz shows is part of Graham's toolkit, utilising Incidental-Celebrity to illustrate the evolution of this format of which *Who Wants to Be a Millionaire* was the result, a dramatic shorthand to explain how big prizes and general knowledge came together in this show at this moment. Although these scenes were excised from the tighter 2023 touring production, Graham's application of technique in the published version of the script helps to explain why a particular fan culture grew up around this programme and the competitive desire to play the system or at least maximise pre-selection opportunities to participate in the show, an argument that is integral to the Prosecution case that the writer builds. As with most examples of Incident-Celebrity in Graham's work, these illustrative choices could have been quite different without fundamentally altering the point being made, but they lay the groundwork for communicating complex histories to the audience in a dramatically recognisable and clearly accessible format.

A secondary purpose of these scenes is to create distinct opportunities for audience engagement by recreating a round from each show and calling upon members of the theatre audience—much like a TV studio—to take their place in the onstage action as contestants. An immersive addition to the plot on the one hand, it is a device that explains the style of gameshow that *Who Wants to Be a Millionaire* was to become with its lifelines and opportunities to ask other people for help which Graham feeds through the wider dramatic management of *Quiz*. Audience participation is an essential device in the original version of this play, from the Pub Quiz papers distributed to the audience before the show and answered at the start of Act Two by the Warm Up (all excised in 2023) to the chance for an Ask the Audience moment when the theatre viewer answers *Who Wants to Be a Millionaire* questions—a *Coronation Street* query during Charles Ingrams' first day on the show in Act One—by voting from their seat. This creates audience investment in the outcome of the story in the same way that the gameshow did, culminating in a crucial 50/50 poser, was Ingram innocent or guilty, a question the audience votes on at the beginning and end of the production.

The use of Incidental-Celebrity here then has a dual purpose, tightly interwoven into the interactive culture this play creates and reflecting on the nature and allure of the television quiz show as described in Smith's evidence. The *Take Your Pick* segment introduces Des O'Connor to play a round with the pre-selected members of the theatre audience:

> Des O'Connor: (*Referencing the* Audience) As usual we'll be picking our contestants from this mad lot gathered here...
>
> Des O'Connor *plays the 'Yes/No' game with two members seated in our real* Audience.[21]

Graham's text gives an example of how this semi-improvised section might play out, culminating in a prize for the winner. A similar process takes place with *Bullseye* when Jim Bowen replaces Des O'Connor:

> Jim Bowen: welcome to you viewers at home as you start your Saturday evenings on ITV, Lets meet our couple tonight!
>
> *A pre-selected* Couple *are guided up on to the stage.*[22]

Again, the script lays out different dialogue possibilities to respond to every eventuality of this largely improvised section of the play including '*Assuming its wrong-*,' '*In the unlikely event it's right -*' and '*Either way-*' again resulting in a prize for the winner. By the time Leslie Crowther appears to name the theatre audience members selected to play *The Price is Right*, the format is clear:

> Leslie Crowther: Hello! Look at you, you lovely, lovely people, all assembled, gathered here today, for what purpose – why, to win prizes of course! Get ready...[23]

Quiz then uses Incidental-Celebrity quite differently to Graham's other plays by reflecting the format and style of the drama's subject matter and involving the audience in the process of creating the show. It directly contributes to the explanatory material underpinning the Case for the Prosecution in lieu of cumbersome exposition and the result is a lively and fast-paced sequence that reflects the allure of the television quiz show and the incidental opportunity to meet their celebrity hosts. The creation of television celebrity is exactly what Graham went on to explore in his next major work, *Best of Enemies*.

4.1.4 Best of Enemies

In *Best of Enemies*, Incidental-Celebrity is applied in a number of ways to create contextual pop culture and historical audience connections as well as combining techniques that Graham has applied in other works to comment on media practices. But Incidental-Celebrity here also has a more sophisticated role to play in the moral and philosophical reflections on and by Celebrity-Protagonists, using them in a character development role for the first time. Although Incidental-Celebrity has operated in relative isolation in previous works, principally to advance the messaging and context of the story if not directly contributing to the direction of the plot, in *Best of Enemies* multiple approaches ensure that the behaviour and decisions made by the play's Celebrity-Protagonists are directly influenced and shaped in active conversation with Incidental-Celebrities to create a specific and more reflective dramatic dynamic.

First, Graham introduces a raft of very famous faces and recognisable personalities in traditional ways used as dramatic shorthand to set the social and cultural tone of the era. *Best of Enemies* takes place in 1968 at a particular moment when celebrity and television news collided, and this is mirrored in a play that allows the famous newsmen who belie their US television status to be held up as universally accepted standards of journalistic and news-presenting excellence. But alongside these characters are several pop culture celebrities mingling in their wider circle, blurring the boundaries between professional journalists, commentators, service providers and celebrities. What happens to the play's Celebrity-Protagonists, Gore Vidal and William F. Buckley, is profoundly shaped by this cultural shift and their differing connection to the various famous faces they encounter. How their own celebrity is then acknowledged, perceived and increased is driven by the extent to which both men embrace that context and, during the action of the play, allow Incidental-Celebrity to determine their own behaviour and responses.

This context first establishes their social circle surrounding Vidal peopled by many traditional celebrities that he knows and interacts with as part of a wider community of writers, artists and intellectuals that he leads. Graham depicts several party scenes at Vidal's house—famed and reputed occasions in their own right—as well as Vidal's attendance at club openings and similar occasions that place him in a position of social performance that for better or worse governs his approach to the televised political debates that he agrees to contribute to. And in doing so this helps to determine how the audience and Buckley react to Vidal as a character. These occasions are filled with entertaining encounters, most notably with Andy Warhol whose fleeting appearances situates the action in a very specific cultural context of art and artmakers who not only reflect the times they lived in but through their work and, by extension their fame, were seen to actively shape them. The inclusion of Warhol evokes a glitzy but troubled environment, where fame is aspirational but also dangerous and fickle, something that Vidal seeks to dismiss in the early part of the play:

Andy Warhol: Oh I just want everyone to be happy, really. Just…

They wait, but nothing else comes. Vidal *rolling his eyes and pushing on.*

So Warhol tries again:

Andy Warhol: I can't bear ugliness. It's so… the opposite of… you know.

He wanders again, everyone waits, and Vidal *sighs.*[24]

Other incidental appearances include Aretha Franklin whose political role in the story links her to the racial profile of the Democratic Convention at the start of Act Two where she sings the *Star-Spangled Banner*, and she notably exits the stage following the assassination of fellow Incidental-Celebrity Robert 'Bobby' Kennedy who appears in a roll call of famous assassinations in this year that frame the violent political unrest bubbling beneath this story, reinforcing this central notion about the duality of fame. What begins with an unsuccessful attempt on Warhol's life evolves into the deaths of Kennedy and Martin Luther King as well as the political profile of Enoch Powell who is also interviewed on American television. That political outrage boils over into gun violence in which the loaded televised debates depicted in *Best of Enemies* directly relates to the safety of the Celebrity-Protagonists as riots, protest and unrest unsettles the characters in the latter part of the play, directly affecting their own tense exchanges as the debates themselves become more verbally acrimonious. Incidental-Celebrity here is shown to psychologically affect the stability of the Celebrity-Protagonists.

> Vidal: What is happening? Andy shot. Martin and Bobby gone...
>
> The world feels on fire. I hadn't expected this – backdrop. When I agreed to take to the stage...[25]

Coverage of these events is woven into Graham's consideration of news media itself and the Incidental-Celebrity newscasters namechecked in this play. But their purpose is also more complicated, particularly the reference to news anchors Walter Cronkite, David Brinkley and Chet Huntley at rival stations, who are all competitors of ABC presenter Howard K. Smith who is the professional news focus and moderator of *Best of Enemies*. These characters set the standard of investigative professional journalism to which the characters aspire—at least in the early part of the story:

> Walter Cronkite: Because the business side is frankly *not* our business. We are conduits through which flows important news and –

A belief reinforced by his colleagues:

> Chet Huntley: The role of the Evening News in people's homes, and of the men who steward it, is to cement opinion, not to 'disrupt'. We don't stir the pot, we cool it down.
>
> David Brinkley: Right, we simply report, we don't express opinions. News must come from the centre. And we invite an audience of different political stripes to calmly join us there.[26]

That *Best of Enemies* also has a ratings driver, a numbers game like *This House* and *Ink*, proves significant, and Graham explores the compromises of news media as it transitions from factual reporting to driving and making the news, as well as repackaging it as entertainment. This is directly relevant to the Celebrity-Protagonists who are swept up in this shift in a drive for viewers that pushes them towards uncivilised debate to maintain ratings. Incidental-Celebrity in this instance essentially guide and counsel the perspective and development of the Celebrity-Protagonists and the forces they cannot control. The most interesting example of that new force is James Baldwin, a directly drawn Incidental-Celebrity in Graham's play who is a friend and direct interlocutor of Vidal providing advice and due warning about the growing importance of the televised debates with Buckley and their meaning in society:

> Baldwin: You're right. It shouldn't have mattered. This pageant, this pantomime. The problem is... people like blood sports, and they tuned in. And so now it does matter. Now you have to win.[27]

Baldwin's position in the play is limited in the ways that other Incidental-Celebrity tends to be, and his appearances are not of themselves sufficiently weighty or decisive to drive the plot, nor do they fundamentally alter the course of events. Like Andy Warhol and Aretha Franklin, Baldwin brings social, literary and political context to the story, vocalising Vidal's elite intellectual circle and the tides of public interest or change that the debates represent, helping the audience to understand why Vidal would be tempted to join ABC's planned broadcasts. Baldwin in this sense meets the definition of Incidental-Celebrity, but also has a prompting role to play in helping to crystallise Vidal's thinking and directly contributing to the decision-making purpose of the Celebrity-Protagonist through their direct conversation:

James Baldwin: We write our books and our plays, and don't get me wrong, I think they are vital too. For our humanity. We have our – 'debates'. But let's be honest, 'Eugene', you are a god up high on Mount Olympus, musing on the activities of Man below. As though it were an intellectual curiosity of no significance:

(*Puts his cigarette out.*) Well I'm afraid now there is. We are going to go one way, or the other. And as you say – you put yourself in that chair. And we are where we are.

And the Whole World is Watching...[28]

Baldwin is also a narrative device in *Best of Enemies*, giving shape to the story while Graham draws on Baldwin's own writing in the same way that Incidental-Celebrity has been applied in other Graham plays to convey contextual information to the audience. Yet, Baldwin, while categorised as an Incidental-Celebrity, takes on a slightly elevated status than equivalent characters in the writer's earlier work, acting as a bridge between the incidental famous faces and the Celebrity-Protagonists whose rise and fall unleashes interesting new forces in the study of social power and moments of political transition.

4.2 Celebrity-Protagonists

In Graham's major works, the Celebrity-Protagonist is a character who already has fame at the start of the play or has subsequently developed that recognition as a result of their actions within the story. In the latter case, that recognition is often born out of notoriety emanating from a change or innovation that proves to be of dubious social benefit in the long term, so the writer takes the audience back to the moment of change to examine original intention and motivation to understand how and why those expectations were derailed. Rupert Murdoch, for example, at the beginning of *Ink* in 1969 is viewed as an upstart Australian businessman by his new Fleet Street colleagues, as someone destined to fail because he lacks superior knowledge of the newspaper industry and did not then possess the fame he enjoyed by the time the play premiered in 2017 resulting from the events depicted in *Ink*. Likewise, Charles and Diana Ingram were completely unknown at the time of their appearance on *Who Wants to Be a Millionaire* in 2005 but the international news coverage that accompanied their trial meant many audience members were familiar with the story when *Quiz* appeared in 2017. Fame for Graham's Celebrity-Protagonists comes at a price even when the individual has good intentions and there are three key characteristics that link Celebrity-Protagonists across the writer's work—first they act as a deliberate or accidental innovator who exercises a soft power with important social or political consequences; second each play dramatises their last chance to make it in their field in ways that alters their behaviour, and finally the outcomes of their new fame will ultimately consume them. Where multiple Celebrity-Protagonists occur in a single play, they each look for a chance to redeem themselves by seeking this much-needed success, solving wider problems in their lives or filling a void of some kind. Although these characters often set out to do a good deed, the result tends to be far more complex than intended, creating personal consequences that shape their reputation or lives thereafter. But the Celebrity-Protagonist also unleashes populist forces that move quickly beyond their control and generate ripples that explain contemporary social structures and the influence of centres of unelected power.

4.2.1 *Create and Be the Change*

Celebrity-Protagonists in Graham's work exist at moments of change, important turning points where many of the power structures we now take for granted were created. But the Celebrity-Protagonist is not merely swept along by tides of development; they are frequently active agents in that change by creating or driving innovation in their field. This is not always a conscious act and is sometimes the by-product of their choices, but across different plays set in different time periods and on different continents, they all share a dubious honour of representing their age by setting in motion significant social change that pinpoints the holders of social power and forms of public engagement that we recognise today. The role of the innovator in Graham's plays is often a controversial one for characters who face great opposition to their work, usually from Establishment figures threatened or undermined by a populist agenda that redefines authority and influence. This fracturing of old certainties creates moments of flux from which the drama of the play is derived, and innovator characters actively seek to overturn existing customs, power structures and ways of being that have far-reaching consequences. Distinct from anarchists explored in Chapter 3, innovators do not seek to overthrow or change the Establishment but to redefine how non-traditional power bases engage with the public. These turning point moments are identified by the playwright as a chance for the conscious or unconscious innovator to change the status quo which results in the creation or solidification of their fame.

The first example of this is in *Ink* where two Celebrity-Protagonists—Rupert Murdoch and Larry Lamb—deliberately set out to disrupt the way in which newspapers are created, their terms of engagement with the reader and, ultimately, where and how power is organised within the industry. At the start of the play, Murdoch is the primary innovator frustrated by the 'closed shop' nature of Fleet Street and actively dismissive of the old boys' network that bases its interaction on codes and self-reinforcing precedent that establish a class divide in the industry:

> Murdoch: You think I'm afraid of those old bastards? I throw everything I have into this Sunday rag to 'buy my way in', finally. My first time in the Old Press Club? All the other chairmen in their leather chairs, clutching their papers, what happens? Up they go – (*Demonstrates lifting a paper over his face.*) Not one handshake. No cigar. Nothing. 'The Aussie sheep farmer'. Well not for much longer, eh?[29]

This clubbable world in which everybody else appears to know the rules is deeply divisive but also a major motivator, and Graham allows Murdoch to reflect the audience's own perspective on this restrictive enclave of powerful white men. That Murdoch wants to tear this down feels reasonable, and the playwright includes several examples of rigidity and seemingly stale tradition against which the newspaper magnate can rail:

> Murdoch: 'Signing ceremonies', photos, fuck's sake. These pompous arses.[30]

Having established a dynamic for the play and the conditions under which significant change can occur, Murdoch steps back into a secondary Celebrity-Protagonist role, leaving the operational implementation of these changes, including the detail of them, to *The Sun's* new Editor Larry Lamb, *Ink*'s primary Celebrity-Protagonist, who like Murdoch, the audience is encouraged to like, even admiring Lamb's fresh approach at first. Lamb, though, is a different kind of innovator to Murdoch, coming from within the industry and well-placed to understand the customs, traditions and expectations that he wants to overhaul, even purposefully trample over, before the story concludes. Murdoch brings the ranker of the outsider bewildered by rules, structures and processes he had no hand in making, but Lamb, until 1969 when *Ink* begins, has been part of sustaining existing power structures and is met with a far greater sense of disdain from the same men who dismissively refused to promote him and patronised his new boss:

> Cudlipp: (*hearing, turning*) Well, well. Percy, you remember Mr Lamb, used to be on the bench as a sub? He's about to try his hand at our old *Sun*.

Cudlipp goes on to condescend to Lamb again, taking the opportunity to downplay his new role:

> Cudlipp: Look at you, Larry. Taking dinner at the club, delivery of the mock-ups. You're not even going to print for a week, can't imagine what you're pretending to look at.[31]

But the character of Lamb is undeterred, unleashing a series of sweeping innovations that quickly transform the old broadsheet version of *The Sun* into something more populist and therefore more radical:

> Lamb: We're not there yet, we can't just be a cheaper imitation of theirs, well what's the point? No, we have to, to be more *honest* – we're still *censoring* ourselves, What People Want, well, what do *We* Want, we're all, aren't we, from working fucking class bloody – what do *you* want, and like, and need. Don't worry what anyone thinks, why are we ashamed?[32]

What happens to Lamb in Graham's play is consequently far more dramatic a shift than for the character of Murdoch who actively recoils from some of Lamb's innovations despite permitting them because Lamb as a former 'insider' has to overcome his class status as well as any adherence to traditional hierarchies to become the Editor he needs to be. And Graham forces Lamb to reckon with that choice, seeing through the effects of his decisions that place a continuous pressure to find new ways to surprise and shock his excited and expectant readers:

Lamb: We're trying to win. And that might by default change something.

Often my job is to convince people to do things, to say things, to tell us things, they wouldn't otherwise want to do by convincing them it might matter, and I don't want to do that with you, Ms Rahn. I think what we're doing here, is trying to sell more newspapers to people who like looking at, at tits, by showing them some, somewhere they've never seen them before.[33]

Lamb's role as an innovator is initially refreshing and, like Murdoch, *Ink* suggests these characters provide a much-needed shake-up of a restrictive industry, yet the cost of that development results in the Celebrity-Protagonist becoming trapped by their innovative nature, making their eventual success bittersweet.

Graham effects a similar proposition in *Best of Enemies* with its dual Celebrity-Protagonists Gore Vidal and William Buckley who transform the nature of television news debate in ways that are both conscious and unconscious. The two men know at the start of the play that what they are about to embark on will be a new form of televised interaction that places political events and celebrity commentators together, moving away from traditional journalism and even, to a degree, traditional politics by placing non-elected personalities at the centre of national debate as the acknowledged figureheads of opposing parties. And although they express reservations, the opportunity to innovate proves unmissable:

Buckley: You tell them, my little buttercup, that your husband is an exciting new breed of High Society. A 'public intellectual'.[34]

As their recorded bout unfolds, both Vidal and Buckley remain consciously aware of the effect they have on one another as well as on the viewing public, seeking ways to extend their fame and the debate series simultaneously. Like Lamb, both men have instant knowledge of the effect of their innovation, continuing to push boundaries in order to provoke and maintain the ratings their discussion attracts:

Buckley: Alright, feel free to drag up anything you can about him, so that we can warn America. Who the hell is he? What emotional buttons can I push? What buried trauma is there? Didn't daddy love him, is he a closeted Republican acting out of self-loathing, did he lose a cat as a child and if so – what was its name.[35]

'If you were writing from scratch, you wouldn't have chosen two people like that as a way into the story,' Graham explained in an interview with Peter Aspden for the *Financial Times* in November 2022 when *Best of Enemies* transferred to the West End. 'They spoke in this patrician, overly elaborate, verbose, semi-anglicised way. I just found it so compelling. The way they speak is almost symphonic. And the little phrases [they used]: they sound like song lyrics, I found it operatic and gorgeous.'[36] But it is also influential and at the end of the play, the writer, in the guise of a media analyst, informs the audience that these news debate pioneers altered the fabric of public discourse, changing the ways in which political debate happened across the world. Yet, like Lamb, these celebrity innovators would pay a price for their daring, quickly moving from champions of new forms to something more complex, setting off a chain of unconscious or unintended innovation outcomes that had personal and professional consequences for them both. The Celebrity-Protagonist as active innovator once again finds fame through their actions but not satisfaction.

Two other sets of innovative Celebrity-Protagonists also occur in Graham's work who less deliberately set out to create change but do so by default. The Ingrams from *Quiz* represent a cottage industry that grew up around the television gameshow *Who Wants to Be a Millionaire* advising potential contestants how to beat the system, make it past the pre-selection exercise and then onto the show itself. But the Ingrams are swept up by the exciting new gameshow which for a time became both compelling television and a commercial format that, as Paul Smith explains in Act One is sold to scores of countries. This wasn't the first time that gameshow contestants had become famous for allegedly cheating but this unique interplay of factors including the profile of the gameshow, the captive audience at the time and the vast media interest created important knock-on effects for Charles Ingram in particular who tried to improve his chances by innovatively combining the answering of questions with deliberate attempts to be entertaining, blurring the boundary between ordinary member of the public and a television personality:

> Diana Ingram: Charles, you know I love you. But… we need to talk about your 'character'.
>
> Charles Ingram: My…?

> Diana Ingram: You know your – performance. We'll need to change tactics if you're to survive; they'll want you gone. Unless you can – 'entertain' them.[37]

This arguably laid the foundations for the more reality-focused television to come, a genre that continues to evolve. What Charles Ingram learns in this scene is that innovation is the key to becoming a Celebrity-Protagonist; 'I could *pretend* I'm about to pick the wrong answer. You know, walking into enemy territory, and then-,'[38] he muses, already understanding that fame is another kind of game to be played, even by ordinary members of the public seeking a big financial prize.

Graham applies the same cycle to the experience of Celebrity-Protagonist Gareth Southgate in *Dear England*, a character also drawn from real life whose innovative approaches are a radical shift in the management of the England football team that reaps short-term rewards. But, like earlier examples of Celebrity-Protagonist characters, Gareth's motivation emerges from an earlier failure and a perceived last chance opportunity to rewrite or at least reconcile his own personal history. When Gareth ultimately abandons his own methodology, his downfall is told through the experience of the team and, although it is too soon to analyse the effects unleashed by Southgate in a story set between 2016 and 2022, there are immediate consequences for his role and the Players. But Gareth fits the profile of this character type and Graham introduces him to the audience as a man destined to change English football who, like Larry Lamb before him, is presented as someone from within the industry but not one expected to take a leadership position:

> Greg Clarke: Well, you obviously know why you're here. We need someone to man the fort, while we look for a permanent replacement for Sam.[39]

But Gareth is determined to introduce his own methods even if the position is a temporary one, setting out his radical agenda a few lines later:

> Gareth: I would obviously only be able to manage the team, even for a short time, in the way I would want to do it. And work on the things I think need to be done.'[40]

Insisting that 'I don't think sticking plasters will cut it, anymore,'[41] the threat Gareth poses to the status quo is outlined by FA Chairman Greg Clarke who advocates for existing methods:

> Greg Clarke: I think that, for right now, opening up a big old can of worms... when we're looking to just find some stability, right now. The nearest port in the storm, which is why you're, we think, perfect. For now.'[42]

The football officials are followed by a series of representational characters among the general public who also reflect negatively on Gareth's appointment:

> Fish and Chip Show Owner: That's not even scraping the barrel, that's scraping *through* the barrel, breaking the barrel into pieces, tossing those pieces into a skip, find some shit in the skip and scraping that![43]

When a Lollipop Man, Entertainer and Snooker Player join in the ribbing, Graham quickly establishes the scale of the problem facing Gareth not only in turning around the fortunes of an ailing institution, much as Lamb does with *The Sun*, but doing so under great public and media scrutiny.

Beginning his campaign of change and now confirmed as permanent England Manager, Gareth's primary aim is fan-focused, to 'get them smiling again,'[44] and while met with derision by team analyst Mike Webster and 'Physio Phil,' the Celebrity-Protagonist is determined to proceed with his new methods, 'starting with a... a psychologist.... I don't think the problem is just out there on the pitch, I think it's here. (*Taps his head.*).'[45] The introduction of Pippa Grange to the team setup begins a slew of innovative approaches that begin to reorientate how the England Players perceive one another and their relationship to the national team that they play for including taking stock of their realistic position. In a sequence that mirrors Lamb's call for populist ideas to create *The Sun's* new focus, Gareth establishes the tone for the work to come:

> Gareth: ...It's about relieving ourselves, of impossible expectations. And facing our truth.[46]

The psychological approach begins in earnest as Graham diagnoses the team's problem with taking penalties:

> Pippa: Mike, come on, this is *men*. Dealing or not dealing with *fear*. Look at what they do with their own bodies, when they miss?
>
> *We cycle through some images of penalties of old – those* Players *having missed; those* Players *watching.*
>
> Pippa: They make themselves small. Bring in their arms to their chest, or their neck, crouching. Like a foetus. Like children.[47]

This recognition takes the Players to the next stage, providing mutual support to one another as part of Gareth's tactic to build a team dynamic and trust which starts to break through the Players initial reluctance:

> Gareth: So… what we asked before. Making yourselves available to one another. Create a group, volunteers who can just – 'be there', for each other. For chats, and check-ins; doesn't have to come through us. If anyone thinks they can do that.
>
> Harry Kane: … Um, I'm happy to give that a go, yeah.
>
> Jordan Henderson: Uh, sure, I'm – yes, boss.[48]

Further innovations ensue from Gareth abandoning hierarchical and managerial titles, mixing the Players together in the canteen and even creating a culture of civility through their interactions to one another—notably countering the combative discourses unleashed by the interlocutors of *Best of Enemies*—Gareth's gentler approach reaps rewards when England reaches the semi-finals of the World Cup in Russia in 2018 and the final of the Euro 2020 competition. The Celebrity-Protagonist as innovator is a strong and consistent trope in Graham's work, each having an immediate and lasting impact on their industries, yet for those like Gareth, their determination to succeed stems from a career built on failure as each Celebrity-Protagonist seizes their last chance to make a mark.

4.2.2 Last Chances

Innovators do not spring magically into society they are made by a slow and evolving process of failure. Failed businesses, failed products, failed experiments all shape the character, purpose and knowledge of the innovator before their arrival at the right idea and are able to seize the moment to implement it. Across Graham's work, the Celebrity-Protagonist is usually someone who has experienced failure and has one last chance to achieve their goals, to become politically relevant or to be valued in ways that they expect before their career sinks into oblivion. Consistently, it is this 'nothing to lose' mentality that drives the scale of their innovative behaviours and press ahead when advised not to, precipitating an eventual notoriety or fall from grace. The Celebrity-Protagonist strives hard for recognition because, for them, the stakes are so high that failure could leave them in a worse position than they started from. In *Quiz*, Graham gives the Ingrams a financial incentive, a desperate need for money to support Diana's brother Adrian Pollock whose struggling business has left him in debt and in physical danger. Before the scandal that will engulf them following Charles's time in the hot seat, Graham dramatises both Diana and Adrian's appearances on *Who Wants to Be a Millionaire* and noting their motivation is to support his ailing company which consumes all of his eventual winnings and some of Diana's:

> Adrian Pollock: Please, please don't ask too many questions, I'm sorry, the business, it, it's a total bloody...
>
> Diana Ingram: Adrian?!
>
> Adrian Pollock: Stupid, I know, after the 32k, but I – I'm in so much debt, I've lost everything.[49]

Graham builds this context carefully, including a scene in which Adrian is recognised by the host Chris Tarrant who comments on his regular appearance during Adrian's first time in the Chair:

> Chris Tarrant: This is Adrian Pollock, a computer consultant originally from the Vale of Glamorgan. Now... you might recognise Adrian. I don't know what the odds are of this, they must actually be astronomical, but this is his fourth time on the show! But the first time he's managed to get in the hot seat.[50]

The connection is reinforced when Diana is selected:

Chris Tarrant: Diana Ingram, from Uphavon in Wiltshire, here with… and I recognise your guest here tonight, sat up there, I do believe (*through gritted teeth*), it's your brother – Adrian – Pollock.

Lights on Adrian Pollock *smiling dimly in the audience.*

Chris Tarrant: Haha. I thought we'd gotten rid of you, but here you are. Back. In the studio. For a *fifth* time.[51]

And finally, Graham has the television host repeat the connection once more when Charles first sits across from Tarrant in the hotseat:

Chris Tarrant: Welcome back. We're here with Charles Ingram, *major* in the Royal Engineers. Up there in the audience is wife Diana – now, if you recognise her, that's because she won £32,000. And her brother Adrian Pollock, he won £32,000 as well. Are you trying to get to a million between you?[52]

Graham is creating a particular context for Charles in this moment, who now aware of his brother-in-law's financial problems, consents to go on the show. When Diana suggests he participates, he reluctantly agrees when he learns that the prize money previously won by the siblings has been spent. Captured within the Case for the Defence in the second half of the play, the financial desperation of the Ingrams makes this Charles's and their last chance to secure sufficient funds to protect their family from harm, a motivation that the writer posits potentially drives Charles's innovative and unusual behaviours on the show.

Ink offers up a similar conundrum for soon-to-be Editor of *The Sun* Larry Lamb in an opening conversation with Rupert Murdoch in which Graham outlines Lamb's position within the industry, his failure to achieve the career success he hoped for and the lack of opportunity to express his ideas for change within the class-ridden editorial structure that dominates Fleet Street in this era. Lamb is well-known in the industry, a former *Mirror* worker who clashes with Editor Hugh Cudlipp in his new role at *The Sun* and offered an inferior position by his former manager.

Cudlipp: Come back, Larry. Why don't you come back on to the team. Come *home*.

Lamb: ... I can't. I'm the editor of my own newspaper now –

Cudlipp: Edit one of mine, pick one.

Lamb: You're lying, just trying to –

But when Lamb calls his bluff, Cudlipp demurs:

Lamb: ... The *Mirror*.

Cudlipp: We print more than just the *Mirror*, Larry.[53]

So, faced with no alternative for legitimate promotion, Lamb instead takes his chances with Murdoch instead, underlining the desperation of his position. Graham shows Lamb seeking staff available to work for him when many in the industry refuse to take a risk. With much at stake and a last chance to prove himself, Lamb creates positions on any terms offered by the potential employee in order to deliver the first newspaper on time:

Ray: What's your criteria?

Lamb: Anyone who says 'yes'.

Ray: Does it matter if they've been sacked, arrested, or both?

Lamb: Not in the slightest.[54]

The blaze of glory bravado that typifies Lamb's character throughout *Ink* stems from the last chance opportunity that Graham creates for him to make his mark on the industry, a scenario that, like the Ingrams, encourages his innovative behaviours. Returning to that initial conversation with Murdoch, Lamb is a character with limited choices and by extension nowhere else to go at the beginning of the play, so proving himself to his doubters becomes a key motivational driver for the character, intensifying his decision-making style and blasé attitude to this last roll of the dice.

Graham places William F. Buckley and Gore Vidal in *Best of Enemies* in a similar position with waning political influence that results in both viewing their performance in the television debates as a chance to impress the respective party leaders that they nominally represent and build their own profile as respected public commentators. Graham explains that both men sought and were denied political office, using the television debates as a platform to enhance their profile and foster a different kind of future, an approach that starts to work as they simultaneously namedrop additional Incidental-Celebrities caught up in the publicity surrounding their television appearances:

> Matt: (*with the letters*) Everyone is sending notes and leaving messages, Joan Didion. Gloria Steinham. Allen Ginsberg. Arthur Miller and Paul Newman have turned up, they'll be rooting for you on the floor of the conventional hall -[55]

It is a gamble that plagues them both as the play unfolds with Buckley shown to analyse his performance after each debate with his team, identifying successes and failures which are magnified as the debating honours are disputed. It becomes increasingly important to define who emerges as the 'winner' of each encounter, and with so much dependent on this last chance to impress his Republican contacts, how well Buckley in particular manages the pressure exerted by Vidal's discussion style becomes crucial as the stakes are raised. Both men recognise their need to perform well if they are to have any chance of developing their career within the party:

> Buckley: Please, living through it once was tedious enough. I don't see why we have to watch the tapes back again, each time –
>
> Frank Meyer: We're trying to *learn* from them, Bill. To improve.[56]

The innovative behaviours that Vidal and Buckley demonstrate during the debates thus emerge from the wider context that Graham has created for them both, using their personal circumstances and the implied notion of their last chance to achieve the career they aspire to as a driver for the drama for which their failure is inconceivable. That Graham has already pre-loaded the drama by showing the disastrous aftermath of the Buckley-Vidal clash as the pre-amble to the play only adds to the desperation to succeed. Despite taking action to prevent it, disaster is the outcome for all Celebrity-Protagonists, in Graham's writing in which a personal gamble fails, unleashing unexpected forces and leaves them facing a troubled and notoriously uncertain future.

4 FAMOUS FACES   183

In contrast, Gareth Southgate's failure is writ large in the opening scene of *Dear England*, a famous penalty miss from 1996 which sets the frame for the play as Gareth both tries to redeem his reputation and to psychologically recover from an event that cast a shadow over his subsequent career. The growing pressure, expectation and weight of the past is signalled by the writer in the stage directions all bearing down on a character yet to emerge:

Against the darkness, we hear the building sounds of a stadium full of England Fans *in full voice. The inevitable chanted singing of* 'It's coming home'...

We hear the commentary of Brian Moore echoing around us...

A whistle sounds, as the lights begin to slowly fade up....

For now – the twin towers loom over the space...

A colosseum, surrounded by the sound and sight of 70,000 fans, and the St George's Cross waving... There's a sole figure, lonely in grey. His hands around his neck in despair.

To hammer home the impact of this moment on the unnamed but still recognisable young Gareth Southgate, commentator Brian Moore in words taking directly from his television broadcast, emphasises the sense of failure and responsibility that open the play, providing a driving force for character behaviour thereafter:

Brian Moore: 'So we go into sudden death penalties. Recently forced his way into the England side, Southgate. Does everything right.'

'Let's hope he can do this right as well.'

'... Saved it! And the Germans go into the final, and England are out.'

'The dream is over for England.'[57]

When Gareth is later appointed England Manager, Graham brings the implication of the penalty miss into the contemporary character's experience, and while the play looks at the England team's broader fear of taking penalties, it is an unprocessed trauma that is also specific to the experience of Gareth throughout the play, highlighted by team psychologist Pippa Grange who asks:

Pippa: And *you* know about. Right? What *you* went through.

A moment, Gareth *not necessarily having expected to go 'here'*.

Gareth: Well. Exactly. And I don't want any of these young men to go through that.

Pippa: I am sorry, that must have been, just, huge. All those years ago.[58]

And Gareth is not the only character struggling to cope with the penalty miss as Graham includes a series of vignette conversations from members of the public who still associate the character with failure:

YouTube: What's your advice to Gareth on winning a trophy?

Shy Builder: Uh. Invent a time machine? That would help. (*Laughs*.)

Louder Fan (*grabbing the mic*) What's everyone talking about? He was a CLINICAL defender, man! He captained Palace, he captained Middlesborough!

Vicar: I still struggle to forgive him.

YouTuber: Dude, twenty years ago!

Vicar: I know, I know.[59]

The dilemma that the writer presents to Gareth in this play is whether his own problem and England's are aligned, and with so few people, even within the team and Football Association set-up that Graham presents, ready to believe in Gareth's methods, he too must acknowledge and accept his own emotional reaction to the event that dogs his career, and it is Pippa who again presses her employer to make a personal leap in order that the Players will follow or risk the failure of his entire methodology:

> Pippa: It's going to have to come from you, Gareth. You know that.
>
> Gareth: (*younger*) Left, right, up, down. Hard, soft.
>
> Do you think there's an alternative world where I picked a different spot? Where *that* England is a happier and more confident place as a result?
>
> Pippa: Dunno. Maybe. But we don't live in that England do we, we live in this one. The one where you fucking missed.[60]

Like Ingram with the financial pressures to appear on *Who Wants to Be a Millionaire* along with Buckley and Vidal searching for political relevance, Gareth eventually succumbs to Pippa's tough love approach because England are facing a last chance to make improvements to the way the team is managed, and the failure of Gareth's systems would mean a return to less Player-focused approaches that have failed to break the deadlock and created expected disappointment with the national team. In a rare soliloquy—two of which appear in this play—Gareth speaks to the Players honestly about what he felt when taking the infamous penalty and its consequences:

> Gareth: But all I was thinking was what might go *wrong*. What if I tripped, scuffed the ball. My legs were so weak. The whistle went. My head, full of the fog of negativity, and other voices... I ran up, kicked the ball softly, like – hah, so so soft. And the keeper rolled gently towards it.
>
> And I just wanted to disappear. I can't tell you... I knew I was responsible for ending millions of people's dream.
>
> No one knew what to say to me, in the changing room, and I didn't want them to say anything anyway, I couldn't bear it.
>
> I remember the pictures on TV of people *fighting*, smashing up city centres, rioting against police, in Trafalgar Square. Because of me...

The next day I avoided everybody – people who loved me. I couldn't look at them. And I wasn't offered any help. Mental health wasn't really… you know back then.

The crucial point comes a moment later, noting the last chance this Celebrity-Protagonist almost let pass him by as a result of that fear:

Gareth: It was a really, a very bad time. It just was. It nearly stopped me from saying yes to this job. Is the truth. Because I'm afraid of hurting people again, and hurting myself.[61]

The innovative behaviours that Gareth exhibits in *Dear England* stem from this broader context and the long implications of the penalty miss that shape his career as a result. But despite the empathetic substance of these revelations for all of Graham's Celebrity-Protagonists, these methods also become their eventual undoing.

4.2.3   Troubled Times

The resultant actions of the Celebrity-Protagonist is always their own fall from grace, and while their innovative approach may have been initiated with good intentions, Graham leaves the audience with ambiguous feelings about these characters and their actions by the end of the story. The activities of the play often lead to morally dubious outcomes that eventually cast the Celebrity-Protagonist in a negative light, directly resulting from their actions when a line is crossed. This may have small-scale impacts in the first instance, but they also have longer-term and permanent outcomes for public discourses and power structures in contemporary society that Graham traces back to the actions of the innovative Celebrity-Protagonist in these plays. In most cases, it is the Famous Faces themselves who are the cause of their own downfall, either through arrogance or by becoming carried away with the success of their innovative behaviours. A desire for further impact or greater exposure takes the Celebrity-Protagonist from last chance innovator to a recognisable tipping point where the opportunity exists to stop or re-route the actions, but in all cases, they go on to becoming the author of their own downfall, creating notoriety in the process.

As explored in the section on Incidental-Celebrity, in *Ink* the downfall of Larry Lamb's hinges on the morally questionable decision to print details of the Muriel McKay kidnap case in *The Sun* to drive sales. And although this comes to define Lamb's role in the play, the transition from innovator to more questionable judge of situation, is seeded by Graham far earlier in the play. For a long time, Lamb and co-Celebrity-Protagonist Rupert Murdoch are in alignment, and while it is Lamb who generates the innovative buzz that creates the success of *The Sun* in its new form, the two men are initially in unison. But in creating the very public appetite for populist journalism that Hugh Cudlipp warns Lamb about, their paths soon diverge, with Murdoch beginning to question Lamb's decision-making:

> Murdoch: I wanted to talk about some – don't get precious, just some of the choices on the themed weeks. This… the knickers thing last week. Anna didn't like it.
>
> Lamb: She didn't like 'knickers week'?

And soon, the owner reveals his own doubts:

> Murdoch: No, it's not just Anna… *I'm* not a fan of it, truth be told.[62]

That separation becomes more obvious as Murdoch steps back from the day-to-day operation of the paper, expressing greater nervousness at its extreme direction. The Lamb seen at the end of *Ink* is a man overtaken by his own vision who, through the action of the play, is prepared to stop at nothing to deliver it regardless of the warnings and concerns of others, including his own manager. When the initial backlash against Page Three creates a moral panic, Graham turns this into a moment of reflection for Lamb, and thinking about the secretive way in which Lamb puts his drastic plan into action provokes a guilty feeling of something that cannot be undone. The speech Lamb delivers to first Page Three Girl character, Stephanie Rahn, says much about the moral shift of his protagonist and his disinterest in the consequences of his actions:

> Lamb: In the fullness of time, maybe that will become important, or political, or art. I honestly don't know. Or care. And it's only fair that you know that. And that if it isn't you, it'll be someone else.[63]

Eventually, even Lamb himself recognises the effect he has had on his own career and how his influence will eventually be remembered; 'I suppose I stupidly thought I could control it. Close the box, after that one. But…' Lamb complains, before recognising the taint he has created for his own reputation:

Lamb: I'm stuck with it, aren't I?

… She was right. That'll be on *my* tombstone, My obituary, even in the *Sun*![64]

Another Celebrity-Protagonist stuck with the taint of their own actions is William Buckley in *Best of Enemies*, a man desperate to create a political name for himself, who in the picture that Graham builds, is ultimately goaded into making a homophobic slur that he could never escape the effect of. Like Lamb, until this point, Buckley has enjoyed his celebrity, almost a little too much, actively seeking ways to comically undermine his opponent. But poor performance in the early debates pushes him towards more aggressive actions despite advice from his level-headed wife to retain his temper:

Buckley: I don't care. We just have to paint his pacifism as 'weak', and our patriotism as noble strong.

Patricia Buckley: As long as you remain calm, Ducky.[65]

The moment of Buckley's disgrace happens in the most public of forums, on live television where his unanswered outburst cuts through Graham's drama, creating a shock moment that stalls the action even in the theatre while its implications reverberate in the studio simultaneously:

Buckley: (*to an assistant*) Please, can you get this off me? Please?

Elmer Lowe: What in Jesus goddamn Christ?!

William Sheehan: Boss, we know, we know, look –

Elmer Lowe: The phone calls I'm getting –

William Sheehan: Yeah ok, some, some sponsors are freaking out a bit, but –

Elmer Lowe: Spons - ... forget them, my own mother just called! Furious![66]

The outcome for Buckley is a form of infamy, one that, like Lamb has both personal and professional consequences for his reputation; 'Poor Bill, I know how much he regretted it, deep down. I saw it... in the years we spent together at home,' Patricia Buckley confirms.[67] That loss of personal control is something that the Celebrity-Protagonist fears, ultimately leading to their undoing, but it also generates a social effect that allows such unfiltered comments into the world of television as a matter of course. Buckley, like Lamb, acknowledges his own part in this, though it is Vidal who verbalises it; 'And it's why you can't forgive yourself,' he explains, leaving Buckley to admit 'I was - just so tired of life.'[68]

The Ingrams also became tired of their life when Charles's innovative performance on the gameshow led to a similar kind of public disgrace and a more obvious persecution. The downfall of the Ingrams happens quickly at first in Graham's story, a brief phone-call outlining 'irregularities' and the withdrawal of an episode that was never aired. But *Quiz* goes on to explore the very public legal fallout that ensues, reflected in the Prosecution and Defence structure of the play. The consequence of Charles's innovative behaviours is reputational, personal and professional damage that continues to plague him long after the show was filmed. In a conversation between the couple, following Charles's cross-examination, Graham records the fear and humiliation that awaits:

Charles Ingram: Oh God, I can feel the ground opening up in front of me...

They were... That policeman, he was... he was *implying* you... (*Struggling*.) Right in front of me, smiling, do you have any idea what that felt...[69]

But embarrassment is the least of the ignominies heaped on the Ingrams in Graham's play and even before the guilty verdict is received, their defence barrister summarises the abuse the family received as a result of the media coverage of their case:

Woodley QC: Someone kicked your dog to death. Shot your cat. Slashed your tyres, attacked your house, spat in your mouth when you were jogging, cough, cough, everywhere you go. You face being decommissioned from the army, and certain bankruptcy. All - for a 'game'.[70]

These Celebrity-Protagonists suffer almost more than any other in Graham's work with a fame that was created by accident and a long-lasting infamy that affected their lives. The hint of regret that the writer gives Charles when he says 'I just answered the questions correctly. Like I was supposed to. I tried to be entertaining,'[71] is telling, a steep and unpleasant fall from grace that leaves Charles as bewildered as Buckley, and Graham draws a connection between two men who experience a sudden and suddenly curtailed celebrity as a result of their television experience:

Charles Ingram: I'll have to resign my commission.

Diana Ingram: It doesn't mean anything, it doesn't matter.

Charles Ingram: It matters to me, it's who I am...[72]

Gareth Southgate's fall is less obvious in *Dear England* and given the recent setting of the play, any forces unleashed by his methods have yet to reveal their long-term implications. But the England Manager does suffer considerable set back in the final portion of the play that fulfils the Celebrity-Protagonist trajectory followed by other Graham creations. Once Gareth's innovative methods have been applied to the training and support provided to the England team, there is a short burst of match-winning form that takes the footballers to success in major tournaments. Yet, Gareth is never able to fully solve England's problems and some of their old psychological vulnerability returns when they play Italy in the Euro 2020 final and lose on penalties which go disastrously wrong:

Marcus Rashford *takes his penalty – and misses.*

Jordan Sancho steps up, and *takes his penalty – and misses.*

Bukayo Saka steps up, and *takes his penalty - and misses...*

Gary Linekar: Oohh no! No-o please, the cruelty. Yet, again, tears after a penalty shootout for England.[73]

That failure is analysed by Gareth who despairingly acknowledges his own part in the team's failure noting 'I think I may have let them down.... I thought I could spare them, but instead... Why can't we just win.' While Gareth is left to complaining about 'those old demons, I thought we were changing, but nothing is ever new, is it,'[74] Graham has already seeded the cause of this failure in Gareth's own abandonment of his approach earlier in the play, leading to the departure of team psychologist Pippa in Act Two, Scene Three when physical training starts to take precedence over the mental health work they previously championed together:

Pippa: ... Look. I feel like... you're going in this new direction, ok, and that's fine....

Pippa: But... yeah I do find it hard. This rhythm. Because... essentially my job is to care about them, isn't it. And I do, in the morsels of time we get before they're off again. Which is hard, but that's the gig, and I will do it, if I'm needed. But if I'm not needed...

Gareth: ... Of course you're needed Pippa. My God, do we - ... we just really need to press forward now, performance --

And Gareth goes on a few lines later to more forcefully insist on the results he now expects from the team, even actively betraying the consensus he and Pippa once agreed upon:

Gareth: It isn't sidelining. Look at them. They learned to be a team – great. Now that team needs to learn to win.

Pippa: 'Learn to win'? Gareth, that's not what you need to learn. You have everything you need to be able to win....

Gareth: - in the end the best defence they have against the judgement and blame that comes with it, that if they win. And if I ever misled anyone or wasn't clear about that then...[75]

The conversation ends with Pippa's resignation and from this point onwards, the team's fortunes are notably different as the real world starts to intrude on the experience of the Players with racist taunts and dismissal from equivalent elder statesmen of football sapping momentum and publicly undermining Gareth's approach:

> Matt Le Tissier: Southgate's team selection, man, come on. He's just too bloody cautious, timid....
>
> Oh, I am sure the woke Mr Southgate won't listen to anything I have to say. I wouldn't be welcome in his – safe space.
>
> What I will say is this. Real men don't kneel. To win tournaments, you need to display strength. And Gareth, I'm sorry, he's a soft lad in a hard world.'[76]

Even members of the England team set-up eventually voice bubbling concerns about the psychological methods and what they perceive as damaging and distracting consequences:

> Mike: FUCK ME. I mean JESUS. Enough, I'm sorry, boss, but that was fucking disgraceful! That's it, it's 'no more mister nice guy' time, seriously. Their heads were who knows where! School fucking meals and activism –
>
> Gareth: I will let them digest and reflect on what just took place –
>
> Mike: Gareth, for fuck's sake! Man up.[77]

While Graham does not necessarily endorse Le Tissier's and the team analyst's view, providing a more hopefully conclusion to the play, Gareth experiences the same quite sudden downfall as Ingram, Buckley, Vidal and Lamb all of whom suffer as a result of their innovative behaviours and the public backlash that follows their actions.

The experience of Celebrity-Protagonists across Graham's work is directly relevant to the writer's analysis of contemporary social power structures with each one unleashing a different social consequence that created new assumed power influences that shape the state of the nation. From the populism and hunger for scandal that now drives tabloid journalism, feeding a public appetite for more regardless of the individual cost, to the compromised legal system that allows trial-by-television to persist in which 'facts' are manipulated and misrepresented, to the binary concept of public debate where individuals are encouraged to adopt extreme positions without compromise, facilitated by the unbalanced opinions of celebrity commentators. The rise and fall of the Celebrity-Protagonists in Graham's work is a proxy for a much wider debate about how we share, discuss and interact with one another in modern society. Set at key turning point moments, Famous Faces—both Incidental-Celebrity and Celebrity-Protagonists—are both the drivers of the drama and representatives of wider changes in society that come together in particular configurations at the right time. This confluence of factors sets in motion a chain of events that result in the social and political structures of the present day, as Graham's plays reflect on where power now exists and how these changes came about. In every case that the writer explores, the Famous Face is consumed by the forces they unleash in ways that are both tragic and inevitable, arguably even deserved. And while these individuals create necessary innovation and personal success in the moment, Graham's collective works show that the existence of celebrity has facilitated the transfer of power to changed political institutions that seek their own longevity, media conglomerates that control what we see and how facts are presented and to television where entertainment trumps any other purpose and nothing is quite what it seems.

Notes

1. Jenner, Greg. 2020. *Dead Famous: An Unexpected History of Celebrity from Bronze Age to Silver Screen*. London: Weidenfeld and Nicolson.
2. Graham, James. Introduction. In Graham, James. 2016. *James Graham Plays: 2*. London: Methuen Drama, pp.x–xi.
3. Graham, James. *This House*. Act Two, Scene Five. In Graham, James. 2016, p.114.
4. Ibid, Act One, Scene Two, p.35.
5. Ibid, Act One, Scene Two, p.38.
6. Ibid, Act One, Scene Three, pp.49–50.
7. Ibid, Act One, Scene Four, p.53.
8. Ibid, Act One, Scene Four, p.54.
9. Ibid, Act One, Scene Four, p.51.
10. Ibid, Act One, Scene Four, p.52.
11. Ibid, Act One, Scene Five, p.61.

12. Graham James. 2017. *Ink*. London: Methuen Drama. Act Two, p.88.
13. Ibid, Act One, pp.60–61.
14. Ibid, Act Two, p.98.
15. Ibid, Act Two, pp.108–109.
16. Ibid, Act Two, p.105.
17. Ibid, Act Two, pp.110–111.
18. Graham, James. 2018. *Quiz*. London: Methuen Drama. Act One, p.21.
19. Ibid, Act One, p.23.
20. Ibid, Act One, p.24.
21. Ibid, Act One, p.22.
22. Ibid, Act One, p.23.
23. Ibid, Act One, p.24.
24. Graham, James. 2022. *Best of Enemies*. London: Methuen Drama. Act One, Scene One, pp.17 and 19.
25. Ibid, Act One, Scene Two, p.31.
26. Ibid, Act One, Scene One, pp.9–10.
27. Ibid, Act Two, Scene Tow, p.85.
28. Ibid, Act Two, Scene Two, p.85.
29. Graham, James. 2018. *Ink*. Act One, p.16.
30. Ibid, Act One, p.222.
31. Ibid, Act One, pp.49–50.
32. Ibid, Act One, p.53.
33. Ibid, Act Two, p.120.
34. Graham, James. 2022. *Best of Enemies*. Act One, Scene One, p.15.
35. Ibid, Act Two, Scene One, p.66.
36. Aspden, Peter. 2022. When American Ideologies Collide: James Graham on His Play Best of Enemies. *Financial Times*, November 10, https://www.ft.com/content/90a535fb-d96d-4281-818b-63f72fecbf0f.
37. Graham, James. 2018. *Quiz*. Act Two, p.78.
38. Ibid, Act Two, p.79.
39. Graham, James. 2023. *Dear England*. London: Methuen Drama. Act One, Scene One, p.7.
40. Ibid, Act One, Scene One, p.9.
41. Ibid, Act One, Scene One, p.9.
42. Ibid, Act One, Scene One, p.10.
43. Ibid, Act One, Scene Two, p.10.

44. Ibid, Act One, Scene Two, p.15.
45. Ibid, Act One, Scene Two, p.17.
46. Ibid, Act One, Scene Three, p.31.
47. Ibid, Act One, Scene Three, pp.38–39.
48. Ibid, Act One, Scene Four, p.41.
49. Graham, James. 2018. *Quiz*. Act Two, p.67.
50. Ibid, Act One, p.42.
51. Ibid, Act One, p.44.
52. Ibid, Act One, p.47.
53. Graham, James. 2017. *Ink*. Act One, p.21.
54. Ibid, Act One, p.30.
55. Graham, James.2022. *Best of Enemies*. Act Two, Scene 1, p.60.
56. Ibid, Act One, Scene 2, p.50.
57. Graham, James. 2023. *Dear England*. Prologue, p.4.
58. Ibid, Act One, Scene Two, p.19.
59. Ibid, Act One, Scene Two, p.11.
60. Ibid, Act One, Scene Four, p.40.
61. Ibid, Act One, Scene Four, p.41.
62. Graham, James. 2017. *Ink*. Act Two, pp.85–86.
63. Ibid, Act Two, pp.120–121.
64. Ibid, Act Two, p.130.
65. Graham, James. 2022. *Best of Enemies*. Act One, Scene Two, p.35.
66. Ibid, Epilogue, p. 93.
67. Ibid, Epilogue, p.95.
68. Ibid, Epilogue, p.99 and 96.
69. Graham, James. 2018. *Quiz*. Act Two, p.88.
70. Ibid, Act Two, p.97.
71. Ibid, Act Two, p.98.
72. Ibid, Act Two, p.101.
73. Graham, James. 2023. *Dear England*. Act Two, Scene Three, p.89.
74. Ibid, Act Two, Scene Three, p.89.
75. Ibid, Act Two, Scene Three, pp.75–76.
76. Ibid, Act Two, Scene Three, p.81.
77. Ibid, Act Two, Scene Three, p.82.

CHAPTER 5

Television

Television is a subject that Graham has returned to with increasing frequency, setting several of his major plays in studios and sets that examine the process of making programmes as well as the influence of the medium on our political and social interactions. Television in Graham's work is a social force that has to be taken very seriously, and although characters often dismiss it as populist or an activity associated with working-class culture, its ability to define, direct and reflect the attitudes of the day is usually decisive in these dramas. Characters may lose but television itself always wins, securing its own longevity through innovation in format and approach by the end of the story. Its influence, therefore, is not to be underestimated and while Graham's work showcases the abuses or negative forces and consequences of character interaction with the unwieldy power of television, the writer remains evenly balanced on the value of the medium itself. This fundamental point underpins Graham's reflections on television and its existence in and of itself. Instead, television is given due prominence as a tool for mass communication, popular interaction and reach appearing as the primary subject of two plays—*Quiz* and *Best of Enemies* (along with musical *Tammy Faye*)—as well as making muted but pointed appearances in others including *Ink*. The inescapable presence of television in our daily lives is immutable and Graham looks at turning point moments in the relationship between media and the public, where the power of television exponentially grew, as well as in the

© The Author(s), under exclusive license to Springer Nature Switzerland AG 2024
M. Philpott, *James Graham*,
https://doi.org/10.1007/978-3-031-59663-6_5

role of the form in defining other types of social interaction and governance, including the changing shape of news reporting and the blurring of boundaries between facts and entertainment, where the pursuit of good stories and good TV supersedes other kinds of ethical, moral and factual interactions and judgements about its value.

Television, in Graham's work, is both a tool for communicating dramatic moments projected onto the world through a camera lens and a source of dramatic content both in front and behind that same camera. These two worlds increasingly interact across character arcs and thematic choices in these plays with the pressure to perform on-screen magnifying personal failures and the tensions to which characters are subject. In constructing these televised worlds for the stage, Graham applies techniques drawn from verbatim and documentary theatre approaches to bring real events to life using some of the words spoken by his characters on television, in courtrooms and in interviews as part of the historical record, blending this with invented dialogue that the writer attributes to them in private. As Professor Mary Luckhurst notes verbatim theatre 'in its purest sense, is understood as theatre whose practitioners, if called to account, could provide interviewed sources for its dialogue, in the manner that a journalist must.'[1] It is a form applied by political writers including David Hare to draw an audience together in what Luckhurst calls 'an act of collective witness,'[2] in which Hare, in John F. Deeney's study of the play *The Permanent Way* (2003) about the privatisation of British railways, is 'juxtaposing the testimonies of a range of individuals' so a 'degree of responsibility [is] placed upon audiences to fashion a response to the origins and consequences of, in this case, a national scandal.'[3] Graham applies a similar approach to the construction of his own television-focused plays, presenting primary evidence within a dramatic framework to comment on larger state-of-the-nation concerns. As Luckhurst notes: 'documentary forms have always proved an especially effective way of putting grand narratives and received ideas under scrutiny,' in the ways that Graham's work attempts, and finds it 'not surprising that this theatre is flourishing in Britain at a time when the failing infrastructure of the civil service, the National Health Service and the justice system are constantly in the headlines.'[4] Little has changed since this 2008 assessment and Graham's work adds television to this roll call of institutions influencing state functions and the shape of public discourses. However, while individuals actively choose to appear on television with a variety of motives from financial gain to bolstering of political profiles, their decision usually backfires in this very public setting as the creation and filming process actively contributes to their downfall. Graham's work places the audience both in the studio seeing this story from the perspective of the characters understanding the factors, compromises and aspirations that have led them to this moment, but the theatre audience is also in the role of the screen viewer observing this public breakdown filtered through the camera lens. Graham's purpose is to show the audience how one distorts the other.

And that filtering is an essential component of Graham's reflection on television and truth, asking how the existence of the camera changes his characters' behaviours as well as the expectations placed on themselves and by others to utilise the opportunity that momentary exposure or even prolonged fame might bring. But the work also encourages the audience to reflect on the power that television and its creators wield, how they facilitate, edit and package programmes to create perceptions of truth and generate a surface knowledge of social and political institutions or experiences that have deep-rooted consequences for public interactions on- and off-screen. There are, then, multiple dualities that operate across Graham's reflections on television and its socio-political role. By exploring the experience in front of and behind the camera, these two strands of drama are in constant dialogue with one another, giving shape to character development and understanding. Yet there are also contrasts in these plays between television's role as a provider or creator of information and the extent to which its content is either truthful, deliberately manipulated or manufactured in the considerations of television's fundamental purpose—does it truly bring people together or create division and contention that influences contemporary modes of engagement?

Unarguably a powerful social force and one that changes over time, television is nonetheless a medium that finds new ways to sustain itself where the boundaries between the real world and entertainment are increasingly blurred. While it follows the Reithian notions of 'inform, educate and entertain,' Graham's televised worlds identify consumer patterns that programme-makers must continue to feed. Just as Larry Lamb unleashes a force he could not control in *Ink*, so too do Graham's characters experience the problematic outcomes of this alternative vehicle for the democratisation of information sharing and social engagement, where the act of communing leads to polarisation and vilification, and the public appetite for more and more entertainment shapes the approaches that programme-makers adopt. This has significant consequences for characters attempting to navigate reality and the illusion of television as well as concepts of self on- and off-screen. That is not to say that television itself is presented as the culprit or in essence a negative force in Graham's work; in fact it is often celebrated as an important mass communication art form that speaks to multiple audiences, but the writer warns of its unchecked power to affect and even sway public perceptions as well as its potential to influence what should be independent legal and political institutions.

So, who is television made for in Graham's plays? There is an initial tendency among characters to view the medium with suspicion, particularly in the works set in earlier periods of the twentieth century, who dismiss it as made for defined class groups, rejecting its relevance to the world in which they exist. Graham takes the opportunity to reflect on the snobbery or close-mindedness of characters who will soon be swept up in the possibilities of the form, such as Gore Vidal in *Best of Enemies* who is vitriolic about television and its audiences at the start of the play:

> Vidal: I gave dozens of appearances for that demonic, infantilizing little lens.[5]

As is William F. Buckley's publicist Frank Meyer who fears the negative publicity that may damage their political influence:

> Frank Meyer: I'm just saying. This is more than a magazine, it's a Movement, and we don't want to jeopardise that by cheapening it on television.[6]

In 1968 when this play is set, there remained some rejection of television as a sober medium and little recognition of its value for promotion of people or ideals. This is also noted in Rupert Murdoch's astonished response to the notion that *The Sun* advertise on-screen in *Ink* set in 1969, a first for a national newspaper:

> Lamb: I think we should be advertising on television.
>
> Murdoch: Newspapers don't advertise on television.[7]

The previous chapter considered the role of Incidental-Celebrity Christopher Timothy in this promotional experiment, but both the characters of Vidal and Buckley assume (albeit wrongly) that the people watching television are not the target markets they wish to appeal to, leading Vidal to question whether or not to adjust his rhetoric—'You're not expecting... how can I put this... me to "dumb it down", for your audience.'[8] he asks, while Lamb too shapes the content of his advert to maximise popular appeal with attention-grabbing dialogue and scandal in a style that he imagines will attract his customers:

> Lamb: Be a, be a mate down the pub, cab driver pulling up at the lights and spotting some girls, be – you know – cheeky. 'Nudge nudge, wink wink, me old darling'.[9]

Despite their cynicism about the role of television and quality-control issues associated with its creation, Vidal and Lamb ultimately embrace the opportunity that television presents to forward their personal agenda with an audience they are uncertain about, in which they eventually accept and attempt to harness the power of television to reach potential customers and voters.

Television, in the writer's work, is also an opportunity for self or product promotion in different ways and while *Ink* is largely concerned with newspaper evolution, Graham includes a single television interview conducted with Rupert Murdoch where he is able to outline his ethos while using the medium to promote his newspaper:

> Murdoch: It doesn't bother me what you think, or other people in the London media, it bothers me what normal people in the rest of the country think, and it's normal people who are buying it.
>
> Host: Well yes, if you will wallow in material that is sleazy, and downmarket –
>
> Murdoch: I don't agree that it's sleazy, I think it's fun, and I don't like this term downmarket. Who is the arbiter of whether or not something is up, or down. You?[10]

The anonymous Host here is deliberately indistinct (unlike the named newsmen of *Best of Enemies*) in order not to distract from Murdoch's own celebrity, but in staging this conversation, Graham anticipates the future of mainstream news on television both in Murdoch's own life and as journalism evolves with stage direction that anticipate the specific soundscape of the future:

> Snippets of distorted sound, which we may recognise from the future – the football stadium chants of a football game 'L- I- V- E- R- P...', the launch of the Falklands Armada to 'Land of Hope and Glory', the dialling in of a teenage girl's voicemail testimony to a Parliamentary Committee, 'the most humble day of my life...', the aggressive, shouty tones of Fox News anchors.[11]

As historian Alwyn Turner argues in *All In It Together: England in the Early 21st Century*, 'popular culture matters a great deal because it was often where battles were fought... it is certainly true that in modern times, history is made by the media.'[12] Murdoch is shown to be ahead of his time here, embracing television as a medium long before equivalent newspaper owners, but the writer is also using this interview to note the shift in social power from traditional to more populist forms and tying it to a growing role in political decision-making and social influence. 'Perceptions are shaped by entertainment as well as current-affairs shows,' Turner continues and it is no accident that Graham's version of Murdoch brings this casual interview round to politics, drawing a direct line from the consumerism he advocates to election choices, foreshadowing a future in which his media conglomerates would seek to influence the political governance of countries to which his multimedia empire extends, and even beyond:

> Murdoch: When a political party increases its vote share, that's seen as an indication of democratic intent and you place them into government. So why then is circulation not just as good a measure of the will of the people? *Better*, in fact, because the choice at the ballot box is a false choice. Two opinions, this or that. Whereas the marketplace... supply and demand, what you are willing to part with your pennies for – *that's* pure democracy. Modern democracy. Real choice.[13]

That this version of Murdoch appears on television in a discussion that pertains to 'our national narratives, the stories we tell ourselves, *about* ourselves,'[14] is essential to understanding the state-of-the-nation themes and strands of Graham's work in which assumed power forces such as television recast political debate without regulation or nuance. At the end of the interview, the writer reinforces this connection with the development of the television mogul's career and how his future influence as a social and political force is starting to take shape in this moment:

> Murdoch: It's absolutely OK to want things, in my view, even though I actually have very little desire for lots of things myself, or for being the centre of attention –
>
> Host: And yet you're here. On television...[15]

And *Ink* concludes with the fulfilment of that early promise as Murdoch ultimately leaves Lamb to pursue further opportunities in American television:

> Murdoch: I'm thinking about buying a TV network over there. TV is the future. You taught me that.[16]

Having established the universal appeal of television and its growing audience with diverse interests, Graham's later works seek to establish television as a force of considerable influence and power, where self-promotion and entertainment supersede and overshadow the other Reithian aims to inform and inspire. In fact, television grows its assumed power until it becomes a force that destabilises other areas of society, using its lens to selectively show fragments of much larger and more complicated stories. Beyond the possibility of free advertising that Murdoch embraces for his relaunched newspaper, television becomes the defining experience in the lives of Graham's later creations, shaping and ultimately facilitating their downfall. *Quiz*, *Best of Enemies* and *Tammy Faye* take a different perspective on justice, news and religion but are united in their consideration of the assumed power of the screen and how State functions are compromised by the cameras, destroying its characters along the way. Graham's work asks whether television is to blame or whether the people that make, own and appear on it misuse their direct opportunity to influence public perception?

5.1 Television Justice

Quiz is Graham's first television-set play, creating a model for drama that investigates activities both in front of and behind the camera as well as their continuing contemporary consequences. Based on the book *Bad Show* by Bob Woffinden and James Plaskett, this play combines original research with verbatim approaches, using transcripts of television appearances to inform the dialogue and action of the play. 'It is this curious overlapping of light entertainment with criminal justice that became a prominent theme for me while researching and writing *Quiz*, less than the question of the Ingrams guilt or innocent,'[17] Graham explained in a programme essay for the 2018 premier production at Chichester Festival Theatre. But this play also sets out most clearly the nature of programme-making and the technical tricks of editing that influence what the audience at home eventually sees, actively shaping perceptions of truth and reality. This exploration of television justice begins with a supposition—that the audience already knows the story of Charles Ingram's time on *Who Wants to Be a Millionaire* either in part or in full and has a predetermined assumption of Ingram's guilt. Because television told us he was guilty, this is reinforced by the audience poll taken at the start of the stage production. The 'coughing Major' moniker is well-known, even two decades later, and the first Act of *Quiz*, which covers the Case for the Prosecution, reinforces what the viewer already knows about this case by looking at activities on and off camera. Writers John Ellis and Annie van den Oever suggest there is no enduring appeal in competitive television shows in an article on storytelling in mainstream television, noting that 'popular television formats such as WHO WANTS TO BE A MILLIONAIRE (stet)… often belong to the ephemeral historical moment of their production and consumption… These forms depend on "currency" and belong within a specific historical moment.'[18] Yet, Graham's work on television suggests that even disposable television moments have a much broader cultural staying power and influence than Ellis and van den Oever suggest.

Television in this instance is an arbiter of justice so Graham constructs the first part of the play to prioritise evidence from production staff and videotaped programme recordings that make the activities of the Ingrams seem like a shameless public swindle. In Act One, television becomes the victim of the Ingrams, the medium through which the crime was recorded and the means by which order and justice can be served because the evidence is on tape. Graham here exposes the mechanics of trial by television, and at its simplest *Quiz* examines how the might and legal resources of an entire television network were leveraged against the individual, a phenomenal power imbalance that places the influential corporation in a redoubtable position, one demonstrated by the cast of television staff giving evidence against the Ingrams drawn from recorded legal testimonies, piling up the proof of their guilt with corroborating stories about how the gameshow, their production company and even television itself have been cheated.

A fictionalised version of Paul Smith, Chief Executive and co-founder of Celador, is the first to give evidence, evoking producers John de Mol and Mark Burnett, then ITV controller David Liddiment, co-creator David Briggs and an unnamed Production Manager whose role conflates various court testimony for dramatic simplicity and explains the show to the potential contestants. Already, Graham bamboozles the audience with an array of media layers all invested in the success of *Who Wants to Be a Millionaire* and determined to maintain its and their good name after the trial of the Ingrams. That same Production Manager thus gives first-hand testimony about the odd behaviours witnessed in the studio during the recording of Charles Ingram's second episode. The dramatic purpose here is not to explain how television works or what all of these people actually do, but to create a sense of scale and complexity that sits behind the making of programmes and the many people behind the camera whose influence is then distilled into and through what the audience then see on-screen. Graham's purpose is to show the theatre audience how television actively shapes the viewer's perception of what is happening, apparently spontaneously, by controlling the environment in which content is produced and how that experience is then packaged for the screen.

Quiz spends some time in Act One outlining how this particular gameshow came into existence and the manipulative tricks used to create defined reactions from contestants. Graham gives Paul Smith an extended testimony from which several different scenarios emerge, dramatised as flashback scenes that provide valuable context for the audience but also deliberately explains how individuals on-screen are manoeuvred into exhibiting certain behaviours. The consequences of failure for a production company reliant on viewing figures and format sales to maintain their business add a level of jeopardy as the format becomes more financially successful:

> Hilliard QC: How many countries have their own version of your format now?
>
> Paul Smith: It's um, gosh, it's about 160 countries, there or thereabouts.

A point later reinforced by the defence barrister:

> Woodley QC: No I'm just pointing out that the show has been personally rewarding for its creators.
>
> Paul Smith: It has.[19]

Asked specifically about how the illusion is created on television, Smith is encouraged by Prosecution Barrister Hilliard QC to elaborate on how a pub quiz becomes 'an international phenomenon'[20] which results in the parade of Incidental-Celebrity gameshow hosts and formats discussed in the previous chapter. Yet, Graham uses this testimony to instigate a discussion on the mechanics of television production and the tools used to create ratings-winning content:

> John de Mol: I invented the concept of – 'emotainment'. Emotional entertainment; taking what game shows had done for years, real people on television, but pushing it – a little further. We started to call it – 'reality' television.[21]

In this coded reference to *Big Brother*, Graham takes the audience out of the courtroom testimony and into a commissioning meeting where the character of de Mol pitches the idea to Smith who makes the connection between constructed reality and the quiz show format, simultaneously noting the deliberate unreality of television content even when presented as truth:

> John de Mol: It will be – 'constructed reality'. Blurring the lines, drama and documentary, fact, fiction. One day we will film and record and share everything, everywhere.'[22]

Graham goes on to explain that this approach created a competitive market among producers eager to master and develop the most extreme content, engineering scenarios that influenced human behaviour:

David Briggs: Drama. The human drama of it. We're watching people making – potentially making life-changing decisions in front of us. The show dangles the carrot as close to them as possible'[23]

The morality of this is something Graham uses the Case for the Defence to question:

Woodley QC: Of course, when you say 'drama', you mean by putting ordinary people under great psychological stress.

Smith: That was, whether you like it or not, the key to the show's success.[24]

Here, the writer starts to outline the tricks themselves, first referencing *Mastermind* where the player is surrounded in darkness caught in a spotlight and emotionally manipulated by music; 'the contestant can hear it, *and* feel it. We put little speakers in the chair, so the sound is constantly vibrating through them,' Smith explains.[25] Applying these approaches to *Who Wants to be a Millionaire*, constructed conditions include wrapping the studio audience around 'Greek, Roman style'[26] and altering the studio lighting when the contestant reaches a certain monetary value. Graham then explores the pressures being placed on contestants during recording and the methods used to manufacture reactions that make Celador's programming more entertaining. Given the falsity of the show's environment, the play moves the audience to wonder if what the camera thinks it saw during the recording of Ingram's episode was not quite what it seemed.

That notion is considered in Act Two when the Case for the Defence is presented, showing the extent to which the production company manipulated the 'definitive' recorded evidence. Returning for cross-examination, Paul Smith is taken through the important process of editing in which multiple perceptions of the story captured by several cameras are woven into a singular version of events:

Paul Smith: Circumstant - ... it's all there on the tape. Listen!

Woodley QC: Ah yes, the tape, let's talk about the tape.

(*Holding up a digibeta tape.*) Edited together from five separate mic tracks, is that how it works? Track one – the major's mic. Track two – Chris Tarrant's. Track Three – the *ten* fastest finger first contestants. Track four – Diana Ingram. Track five – the studio audience.

(*Holding it up.*) One – digibeta – tape. Edited by you for this trial. The jury is looking where you want them to look, hearing what you want *them* to hear.[27]

With the potential falsity of television 'evidence' now in the minds of the theatre audience, the writer sends Woodley QC into attack, noting that only nineteen of the 192 recorded coughs were enhanced in the recording to support the case made by the production company:

Woodley QC: This isn't a show, Mr Smith, and the fact is this is by definition, in television parlance, a 'clone', your 'clone', the original edits and tapes wiped and wiped again, until there is no longer any one, single, objective reality. There is only the one presented here, by you, not even an audit trail of the changes you made to this now unquestionable 'version' of events. The volume adjusted on the coughs.[28]

Building on evidence presented in Woffinden and Plaskett's *Bad Show*, Graham uses this exchange to explain the tricks that television content creators are generating for audiences, where what you think you see is constructed from several possible realities, although in this case permitted to act as evidence of individual criminal guilt, influencing the legal system and altering perceptions of the case in the following decades. 'Of course there are many cameras and microphones in a studio,' Woffinden and Plaskett explain, so 'the same events can be represented in different ways depending on which camera's pictures and which microphone's sounds are used to make up the final, edited programme,'[29] going on to emotively describe this as 'one of the most shameful episodes in the history of British television, in the history of the British press, in the history of British policing and in the history of the British criminal justice system.'[30] In Graham's version of the story, the innocence of television slowly warps across this play, reframing testimony the audience has heard in Act One and recasting narratives about the Ingrams' certain culpability to show how this piece of entertainment was deliberately designed, with contestants subjected to technological and psychological pressures that generate a desired performance, one they accept with the possibility of cash or goods-based prizes as an incentive. That things take a far darker and more serious turn with *Who Wants to Be a Millionaire* is shown to be the consequence of these tools and the money-making desires of the vast production team, amassing personal fortunes and career development opportunities from this show.

Television in Graham's work establishes itself as a purveyor of a truth that on closer inspection did not and could not exist, presenting only one of the many eye or camera-witnessed narratives that existed on the fateful day that Charles Ingram returned to the Chair. By creating an appetite for jeopardy and drama through the tension-building tricks of the show, this alters the legal arguments the media company makes in court, itself unable to distinguish between the false worlds and environment they created and the truth. Graham, in fact, has the defence lawyer say as much to Paul Smith at the close of his evidence as they discuss the coughs excluded from the tape:

> Woodley QC: You mean they weren't relevant to your version of events. Now our *only* version –

Going on to note:

> Woodley QC: And of course, we have the infamous 'no' on the Baron Haussmann question, a cough, 'no' so loud on *this* tape it made the jury howl with laughter for how seemingly obvious the fraud / committed was...

And finally landing a decisive blow:

> Woodley QC: And yet not obvious enough to you or your sound engineers to have heard it – for *eighteen months*.... You only just found it for *this* version, submitted a matter of weeks ago.[31]

This repackaging of facts for and by television, the writer suggests, even hoodwinked its own creators into believing it was real, so a jury and indeed the wider public would be unable to recognise the tricks within the tampered evidence. It all happened on cameras, so it must be true.

Having set the rules for the individual's engagement with television, Graham then explores the ways in which Charles Ingram's performance attempts to play into these tropes, to be the entertaining figure he knew he must be in order to guarantee a prolonged appearance on the show.

Looking across Graham's television plays, the first duty of any potential star is to be interesting and amusing rather than necessarily 'true'—manufactured sincerity is far better than the real thing—with a duty to make any appearance on-screen memorable for the viewer and increase ratings. The notion recurs in both *Best of Enemies* and *Tammy Faye*, and, here, Graham's version of Charles Ingram accepts the need to play to the camera, to adopt a 'personality' that will generate interest and help him to reap the financial rewards his family requires. In exploring this apparently televised crime, Graham slowly unfolds the Ingrams' intention to making Charles a more sellable contestant on camera. As a non-professional, in the Case for the Prosecution, the Ingrams' behaviour creates suspicion as the case is built against him, drawing attention to his odd behaviour as evidence of the fraud being committed, reinforced by the videotaped evidence.

Using the original transcript, first, the character of Ingram selects incorrect answers, a prevarication in answering style that perplexes host Chris Tarrant as Charles speaks his thought-process aloud:

> Charles Ingram: I think it's Paris. Yeah I think I'm going to play.
>
> Chris Tarrant: Now, wait, where are we?

The confused presenter summarises Ingram's playing style for the audience:

> Chris Tarrant: You thought it was Berlin. Berlin, Berlin, Berlin. You changed your answer to Paris.[32]

Initially reinforcing audience preconceptions, Graham depicts Charles's behaviour arousing concern among production staff, a suggestion that something must be amiss to explain the unusual activity they perceive:

> Woodley QC: Something else is going on by this point, isn't it. Behind the scenes. Something neither the cameras nor the audio tapes are picking up. Something *hidden*…
>
> *Around the studio, in the shadows, different members of the production emerge, to the sound of static, their voices picked up on mics. They're talking to one another into headsets…*

Voices: I told you – see, that was weird / Something's going on / This doesn't feel right / What is he up to? / How is he doing this?[33]

And when Ingram is later questioned by the Prosecution, his style is directly challenged as unorthodox, even unethical—and therefore surely criminal—given the radical change in performance, style and approach since the previous show where he stuttered to a small amount of money by using most of his lifelines. But Graham's second Act upends these perceptions of truth and pursues a line of defence that shows Ingram is merely trying to play by the rules of television to make himself more interesting, and thereby create entertaining viewing for the audience at home. As an amateur, this decision necessarily backfires as it will for Buckley in *Best of Enemies*, two characters playing with a power beyond their control and ultimately losing. But the writer suggests that perhaps Charles Ingram recognises the power of television far better than the show creators:

> Woodley QC: People look at that question, the Craig David question, the first example of a 'different' kind of playing, and they don't get it. What were you *doing*?
>
> Charles Ingram: I genuinely didn't know the answer. Couldn't remember any of Mr David's songs, but we had our plan. The back and forths, the suspense.[34]

With a huge and life-changing cash prize at stake, Graham's version of Ingram now in the words drawn from the court record tries to assess what makes good TV and use it to improve his chances of success—reason enough for the production team to be wary of his motives. By attempting to play to the camera and abiding by rules his character had no role in establishing, this attempt to play television at its own game is something that comes back to haunt him, and certainly for the Ingrams their 'performance' on-screen defines their lives thereafter. Graham explores these modes of presentation to reinforce the essential falsity and performative nature of television for those who create and appear on it by the blurring of multiple camera and sound perspectives to present a heightened version of individuals that is inherently deceptive even if viewers fail to recognise its artifice. Accepting that television is engineered is essential to influencing theatre audience perspectives in the play, and the writer takes their preconceptions and what the legal system proved to demonstrate the manipulation of that truth, massaged by content creators and the performer-contestant trying to win the jackpot.

As well as activities in front of and behind the camera, *Quiz* also looks through the screen itself to assess the impact of these false worlds on audience perception, pondering the extent to which the illusion of television is recognised and understood by those consuming it. Graham does this in the original 2017 published script initially by acknowledging the falsity of theatre itself, establishing a link between the television studio and the auditorium in which the production of *Quiz* takes place. The tool for this is the Warm-Up, an invented character that openly acknowledges that the real drama is yet to begin, and is tasked with breaking the fourth wall and conditioning those in the room by building a rapport and an atmosphere that facilitates the entertainment and comedy to follow:

> Warm-Up: The show's nearly ready to begin, I'm just here to get your started. I am your play fluffer. Your theatrical lube.
>
> Because we're here to have a good time are we not?! I said we're here to have a good time, ARE WE NOT?![35]

This character is a theatrical device that establishes a premise that everything audience members are about to see is a dramatic creation, a fiction based on facts that interprets truth and wrestles it into a new form. Like Charles Ingram and his fellow contestants, the theatre audience member is being treated first like a television studio viewer, an imposed fantasy about who they are in the room and the active role they play in the unfolding drama. Theatre audience behaviours are then 'managed' via similar psychological and physical measures used on gameshow contestants to demand they react on cue:

> Warm-Up: So every time you see this applause sign, guess what I'd like you to do? I'd like you to applaud – that's correct! OK, one, two, three!
>
> *'Applause' either on a light box, or projected onto screen.*
>
> And then every time you see this sign when there's an exciting prize to be won, can we have an 'oooh' – one two, three.

'Ooohs' on screen.

Good, and then laughter when you hear something utterly hilarious, this is the sign – one, two, three!

'Laughter' on screen.

Applause! (*Waits.*) Laughter. (*Waits.*) Ooohs! (*Waits.*) Applause!

Aren't you brilliant. (*Listens to his ear piece.*) We're ready to go I think, time to count us down – all together![36]

The role of audience interaction is here deliberate and purposeful, creating scenarios in which the usually passive viewer engages with the drama and learns to experience some of the exhilaration that participants in the gameshow and its environment enjoy. From completing a pub quiz sheet to answering 50/50 questions and voting on Charles Ingram's guilt, *Quiz* is designed to blur the boundaries between the action onstage, its commentary on the nature of television as a medium and the very active role of the audience in making decisions about the way in which the performance plays out, just as trial by television encourages the armchair juror to do.

Like television, Graham determines what the *Quiz* audience sees and when, a structural choice built into the play's construction which deliberately mixes the legal court case against the Ingrams with excerpts from *Who Wants to Be a Millionaire* episodes and the police investigation to demonstrate the extent to which justice and its procedures intermingled and were directly guided by televised evidence and recording protocols. *Quiz* itself is presented as two sides of an argument, for and against, through which Graham incorporates multiple perspectives that show the circumstances in which television was recorded and its aftermath, the gameshow episode itself and the personal experience of numerous characters during this time in their home, at work as well as in pursuit of leisure activities that brought them into contact with likeminded (or indeed hostile) individuals, in this case quiz fans. Graham balances these multiple narratives and scenarios, deciding what to tell the audience and when, which perspective or technique to use and how to maintain a combination of momentum, staged theatricality and dramatic entertainment. Like the makers of *Who Wants to Be a Millionaire*, the writer deliberately controls the conditions under which information is revealed and the reactions it elicits in order to sustain audience investment in the outcomes of a two Act play. In the programme accompanying the 2017 production in Chichester, Graham wonders 'what my own culpability is in this culture of blending fact with fiction for political ends. I dramatise history and real life events for "art," after all.... Version after version, filter through filter, narrative upon narratives.'[37]

There are multiple examples of this in the stage directions in which the writer anticipates audience reactions based on the controlled cues he has created for them. For example in the *Bullseye* flashback scene involving real audience participants, the character of Jim Bowen is given a set of stage directions in response to questions the host is asking contestants including '*Assuming it's wrong,*' '*In the unlikely event it's right –*' and '*Either way –*.'[38] The complex construction of this play also manages the audience in more subtle but no less purposeful ways including the deliberate withholding of the Ingrams ultimate fate until the finale of the play. Storytelling convention dictates that a play should have a beginning, middle and end, and while there will be members of the audience who may not know the outcome of this case or have not discovered it in a programme essay, Graham deliberately retains that information to ensure the play has a dramatic final flourish, just as a television creator would do, leaving a significant revelation until the play's closing moments to suit the constructed artifice of *Quiz*. Throughout the play, audiences are being asked to reconsider the evidence from different perspectives and in order to retain an openness to possibility, a firm conclusion cannot be handed down too soon despite the outcome of the trial already being an established legal fact. Thus, *Quiz* actively mirrors a legal trial, retaining its fluidity until the verdict is pronounced. The audience is even drawn into this performance process, sworn in as jurors at the start by the Prosecution Barrister:

> Hilliard QC: Members - of the *jury*. We're going to need you to take an oath. Please raise your right hand and say after me...
>
> *The* Audience *rise and raise their right hand. The oath can be projected onto the screens.*[39]

The blurring of boundaries between television and the legal process is instantaneously established in the play's Prologue with dialogue given to both Barristers blending the gameshow terminology from *Who Wants to Be a Millionaire* into their detached and formal courtroom opening statements. At this point in the story, the approach seems like a lighthearted game and only later does the writer encourage the audience to think of the characters as real people:

Hilliard QC: You are here to decide. It's a 50–50.

The options are displayed on screen.

Guilty. Or not guilty.

Woodley QC: The prize is not a million pounds. It's more valuable than that. The prize is freedom. And the decision is yours.

Chris Tarrant: OK. Let's play.[40]

Quiz has a surface two-part narrative, The Case for the Prosecution and The Case for the Defence, and the play deliberately sets out to offer different version of the story, like two camera angels capturing slightly different information. But it starts not with the first piece of testimony but a personal scene between Charles Ingram and a senior officer, wrong-footing the audience as Graham depicts the broader context from the start, situating Charles Ingram in his real life before the show existed where he is respected at work if very slightly socially awkward and not necessarily the master criminal that television has decided he must be. The playwright controls the flow of information, delaying the excitement of the courtroom to show the audience the personal stakes for this family and giving those already convinced by television's pre-established version of justice an insight they could not have previously seen. From here Graham alters perspectives and styles with considerable frequency, sometimes presenting court testimony as Prosecution Barrister Hilliard QC questions witnesses and then steps out of that narrative to dramatise personal scenes between the Ingrams and their network, as well as incorporating examples from the gameshow itself, mixing recorded evidence and creating dialogue where exact knowledge of those exchanges could not exist. As Act One unfolds, these techniques become increasingly complex as the writer starts to overlay narrative approaches and perspectives, bringing in Defence Barrister Woodley QC to object and interject in the Case for the Prosecution to manufacture the pressured feeling of the court room and link that to the equivalent conditions of the television studio during the show:

> Woodley QC: (*standing*) Objection, your honour. It is still custom in English common law that any member of our society is innocent until proven guilty.
>
> *The 'end of the show' klaxon goes.*
>
> Chris Tarrant (*pulling his standard face*). Oh no...! That's all we have time for on *this* show. But join us again, very shortly...[41]

In this sequence from Act One, Graham merges the theatre audience experience, the courtroom and the television studio simultaneously, layering realities and perspectives that explain how television justice operates. Graham massages these together, absorbing information from each of these angles to generate a new narrative entirely—much as the producers of *Who Wants to Be a Millionaire* edited the 'evidence' tape used in the trial into a composite of different camera angles and microphones. Graham does this again in Act Two during the Case for the Defence, only this time with additional scenes showing the police interviews, rolling these together to create multiple angles within the same scene showing the Ingrams', police, courtroom and media perspectives:

> DS Williamson: We will also be needing a copy of your book, Mrs Ingram.
>
> Diana Ingram: It isn't finished yet, I haven't even spell-checked it.
>
> *More commotion outside.*
>
> What's that?
>
> DS Williamson: ... it sounds like the press.
>
> Reporter *appears outside, with a Photographer. Flashbulbs popping.*
>
> Woodley QC: (*joining them*) How did you get to the Ingrams' house in time to catch them leaving in police custody? Who leaked it so quickly?

Reporter: Well, I don't wanna be thrown out of the magic circle or anything, but... there's sort of an understanding, with certain police officers, when it comes to this kind of thing...[42]

The elegance of this construction shows the audience the interwoven nature of state-influencing functions amalgamating, shaping and smoothing them into one another until it is no longer clear to the audience that these are distinct and wide-ranging testimonies occurring across multiple time periods and compressed into a quick-fire theatrical exchange. Graham, then, is using his authorial voice and the power of the dramatist to determine how information is constructed and construed, and through the agility of *Quiz*'s dramatic structure, moving rapidly between multiple viewpoints. This explains the close and distorting relationship between television and law enforcement, truth, fairness and justice with the connection between the media and the police leading to a subsequent scene in which the police present a transcript based on the first version of the edited videotape as proof of Ingram's guilt.

In the play's final moments, the influence of television on the justice system reaches its climax and Graham draws a direct connection between the modes of the gameshow and the performative nature of the courtroom:

> Woodley QC: Well, it's tradition the prosecution and defence teams go for dinner with the judge after a trial, actually. Once the 'competition' is over. Probably not what you want to hear...[43]

At sentencing a few moments later, however, the writer delivers a final revelation, a direct admission that a performance of justice is perhaps more important than the act of justice itself. Here there is a recognition of the manipulation of television that can only be corrected by how that justice is ultimately served:

> Charles Ingram: I don't understand. If we did it, why aren't we in jail? People with children go to jail all the time.
>
> Woodley QC: ... I imagine the judge is more sensible than we thought, and he sees this for what it is. Justice only has to be 'seen' to be done. More than it actually has to be...[44]

At this point, the writer exits his story and the authorial techniques used to tell it, handing control back to the audience and giving the theatregoer a chance to reflect on who to believe now—television's version of events or the theatrical one, quietly acknowledging that both are Graham's managed versions of the same truth.

Graham's explanation of television justice certainly presents a worrying picture of assumed power of television and the extent to which media evidence, and the narratives told about it, are constructed and then embedded to protect layers of executives within production companies and television channels. 'Far from putting the nails in the coughing, Graham implies there is a case to be made for the Ingrams and that there is an increasingly thin line, which he himself cunningly exploits, between courtroom justice and showbusiness,' critic Michael Billington wrote in his review for *The Guardian* in 2017,[45] a view shared by Whatsonstage critic Sarah Crompton who noted 'this is another cracking play that sheds vivid light on the state of the nation while telling an engrossing story.'[46] From Rupert Murdoch setting his sights on owning a network in America at the end of *Ink* to Paul Smith going to court to protect a format and an income stream he believed was under attack, the power of television pits the resource and influence of a major corporation against a powerless individual. Television's ability to harness public opinion—demonstrated through wider journalistic interest and the personal assaults directed at the Ingram family in the play—is shown to be a product of the composite constructed narratives designed to depict a particular version of events and label it 'definitive,' encouraging viewers to believe it. Graham both actively counters this in his presentation of alternative truth within the Ingram's story but also knowingly adds to it by creating his own perspective in *Quiz*. Ultimately, however, television actively succeeded in influencing the legal process in its case against the Ingrams using all of its tools to edit realities and create dramatic and deterministic storylines, a concerning application of unelected social power that acts as a warning within the play. Television can tell better and better-resourced stories than the individual, Graham suggests, and by creating entertaining products on-screen that spill over into everyday life these alter public perception and the independence of social institutions designed to protect the innocent. This challenge to forms of democracy, fairness and justice are heightened when an individual tries to play by television's own rules. The character of Charles Ingram discovers this to his cost, and so too do William F. Buckley and Gore Vidal when they try to revolutionise television news.

5.2 TV News

How contemporary public discourses have been shaped by the changing face of television news is the subject of Graham's 2021 play *Best of Enemies* that sets two opposing celebrity commentators against one another during the US Party leadership selection processes in 1968, a period that offered the writer considerable scope to widen the historical lens:

> Based on Morgan Neville and Robert Gordon's documentary about televised debates, it felt like such a gift to have this source material and then go off in my own direction, taking in a global picture of what was happening in 1968 – the social and political discord reminiscent of what we're living through today – and to bring in other voices from the period.[47]

Graham's play suggest that this is the point at which television changed from the factual and independent reporting of news to embrace new forms of entertainment, a process charted by *Best of Enemies* as politics, celebrity and opinion-driven ratings content replaced impartiality and public service. The story dramatises a series of acrimonious televised debates screened over several months on the ABC network in which William F. Buckley, a Conservative commentator supporting the Republican Party, and Gore Vidal, a writer and public intellectual aligned with the Democratic Party, clashed on- and off-screen. Like *Quiz*, Graham mixes verbatim testimony and documentary approaches from Robert Gordon and Morgan Neville's 2015 film of the same name with his own invented dialogue to create this story. It focuses on the effect of appearing on camera for two men with modest experience of presenting encouraged into a new public affairs format that they both use to underpin their own political credentials and enhance their public profile. As with other characters in Graham's work who attempt to use and control television as a medium to serve their own ends, neither man truly achieves their original aim, and, indeed, serve only to undermine their hopes for change. Television, as ever, emerges as the winner.

In order to understand how television news changed as a result of these debates, Graham first establishes how news was presented until this point using several of the Incidental-Celebrity newsmen who appeared in the previous chapter as a technique to explain this to the theatre audience. Graham includes a contextual scene in which they also become interview subjects, recognising both their media status but principally their role as sober and independent guardians of news, presented to the viewer as the industry standard against which subsequent events can be judged:

> TV Guide Interviewer: 1968 is an election year. All three of your networks will be covering the Conventions, in Miami Beach of the Republicans and Chicago for the Democrats. And just as those Presidential candidates will be vying for delegates, aren't you also in a kind of competition with one another? For viewers?
>
> Walter Cronkite: If you want to talk about 'competition', and 'strategy', you should speak to the network presidents, or the Marketing Men.[48]

Each news anchor character takes their responsibility seriously, a mediator between the facts and the public with a trusted service to maintain. Crucially, their role (in the words that Graham gives them) is to inform, and they actively shy away from the entertainment that overtakes the presentation of news content by the end of the play. To demonstrate this style of news presenting, they assume an expositional role announcing major events taken verbatim from original broadcast transcripts that shape the outcomes of this story in the pivotal year of 1968 and the periods leading up to it:

> Walter Cronkite: 'From Dallas, Texas, newsflash, apparently official. President Kennedy died at 1pm, Central Standard time, two o'clock Eastern Standard Time, some 38 minutes ago.'[49]

In this early section of the play, Graham also explains how news is made in this period and its distribution across multiple television networks, rivals competing for ratings who must use their content to attract the biggest audience share. A numbers arc is an important driver of *Best of Enemies*, like *Ink* and *This House*, and what happens in this narrative is shaped by the ABC news team's need to increase ratings at any cost, pushing characters to compromise their dignity and cut corners in order to achieve their goal. The writer establishes the initial problem facing the

ABC crew as the action begins with the network languishing in last place among the four main news providers:

> Howard K. Smith: 'ABC'. You know what they call us, behind our back? The *Almost* Broadcasting Company.[50]

Like *Quiz*, there is some requirement to explain how television works to the theatre audience and the layers of personnel involved in deciding on and then making television content. In the context of their struggling ratings, the ABC team immediately brainstorm a new format, a conversation involving the News President Elmer Lower, frontman of ABC News, Howard K. Smith, Master of Ceremonies for the debates and William Sheehan a news producer. But they invite a marketing executive, George Merlis to join them in the creative process, an indication in Act One, Scene One that news presentation is governed by decisions made by the leader of the division who is himself subject to pressures from sponsors and network management, but that output must also be packaged, produced and marketed. This references the shaped narratives and the distilling of perspectives that Graham began to explore in *Quiz*. Bewailing a financial investment in the news division promised by the Channel, Smith establishes the competitive parameters for ABC and *Best of Enemies* during the action of the play:

> Howard K. Smith: This is a guy from marketing and he's *laughing* at how much we're tanking. Third, out of three! If there were four networks, we'd be fifth.[51]

At this point, Graham makes the first direct link between news and entertainment, in a discussion that covers sponsorship and ratings as well as pay incentives for TV personalities:

> Elmer Lower: Here's the situation. Big year ahead for news. Haggerty understands that. But... the budget he's allocating our department is three million dollars.

> Howard K. Smith: Three million? Well that sounds like a lot. Is it? How much do Huntley and Brinkley get?

> William Sheenan... thirty three.

Howard K. Smith: God DAMMIT!

William Sheenan: Our ad revenues are down, the main entertainment shows aren't doing as well as -[52]

This necessary exposition explains to a theatre audience how television functioned in 1960s America, an important grounding in understanding the significance of the events that follow, but it also sets out both the context for the ratings and sensation-driven behaviours of ABC staff in the play, establishing the dramatic purpose of the story which is to improve the network's viewing figures by any means necessary.

Graham's characters then outline the changes being implemented to the format and timing of ABC News that have far-reaching effects on how American news is reported. With the network's limitations established, ABC's 'Unconventional Convention Coverage'[53] is required to become a budget-sensitive compression of their usual capabilities:

William Sheenan: Right; instead of rolling coverage throughout the day, we do one evening round-up show. Hosted by Howard, with his broadcasting experience.

But uh… (*clears his throat*) one new thought was that it, it might be interesting to invite real people onto the show

Howard K. Smith 'Real people'? You mean 'voters'?

William Sheenan: Oh, no I meant celebrities.

Howard K. Smith: Oh thank God.[54]

From here, Graham begins to evolve the audience's understanding of television filming conventions and processes, employing a device used in *Quiz* that stages scenes simultaneously in front of and behind the camera to show creative and technical decision-making that will influence how the debates unfold. Marketing Executive George Merlis is once again present during these meetings, helping to pitch the programme idea to selected celebrity commentators Buckley and Vidal, with the associated press benefits which television generates for cross-media coverage that raises the profile of the speakers:

> George Merlis: Uh George. Marketing. You wouldn't mind doing some press?
>
> Vidal: Hello George Marketing. And no, I don't mind.
>
> George Merlis: Great. We'd love to get people talking, about this.[55]

The play's primary theme starts to emerge here, the power of television to influence broader public discourses, further reiterated by Elmer Lower who summarises the place of television in American society long before Buckley and Vidal ever meet on-screen:

> Elmer Lower: You speak of 'trust', William. Just to reassure you. In recent years, in every poll, the institution which most Americans now place the most 'trust' in – is television.[56]

There is a self-awareness about television here and its power which is important to what follows, as both characters enter into the debates with full knowledge of the effect their appearance could have and the substantial public profile it offers. Television knows exactly what it is doing and why when these two men go head-to-head, and the audience is shown the motivational tactics and manipulation employed to bring them together.

The writer subsequently gives the audience an insight into the preparatory process ahead of the first debate as both men are taken to the make-up chair and readied to appear on-screen as a version of themselves. It is a moment for a slightly snide exchange to occur off camera and initiate a rivalry, bolstering the drama as imagined interactions are blended into original testimony amplifying the dramatic context for the on-screen encounters between two men who become antagonists off-screen as well. The location and purpose of the scene reminds the audience of the artificiality associated with factual television production, a brief insight into the respective vanity of the speakers in response to being preened for the cameras:

> Vidal: Uh, some light foundation around here, if you could, I'm fleeing blotchy today. All that late-night cramming of numbers, dates, you know.

When Buckley arrives, it is a first opportunity for Graham to compare their personalities and styles:

Vidal: And some spray for my hair as well.

Make-up: Anything for you, Mr Buckley?

Buckley: My wife will just run a brush through my hair. Thank you.[57]

Best of Enemies takes the audience through the rules of engagement and technical requirements in the moments before the live broadcast, placing the viewer in the position of Vidal and Buckley as they nervously await transmission by pre-recording statements for the advert break that reiterate the falsity of television, with the writer deliberately distinguishing between what will be 'live' and 'as live' in the recording of a show that will later also be edited by producers before it is screened in another time zone of America. Stage directions expand on that falsity as the tools of television are assembled:

They both stand and walk –

To the area of the soundstage where their seats are.

Assistant producers help them with their mic sets and earphones as they sit.

Camera shots are arranged.

Before they're finally alone together, in their seats.

Work is done in preparation by the production staff.[58]

Like *Quiz* before it, *Best of Enemies* includes long passages of dialogue taken from television transcripts, the broadcast and recorded versions of these debates taped over several months. 'Generally speaking,' Graham explained, 'the rule is that when characters are sat in front of the TV camera, we incorporated the documented words of the real-life speakers. But away from the cameras, in private, that's when I take over and try to imagine and replicate their voices.'[59] While *Best of Enemies* does not explore the veracity of these recordings as historical evidence, the ways in which Graham compresses and edits them to record their essence reflect the limits of this original debate format. Critic Sarah Crompton in her

5-star review of the premiere production at the Young Vic in 2021 notes that Graham takes the substance of the debates.

> and transform them into a play, an argument about what happens when you abandon old-style journalism and turn news into theatre and opinions into entertainment.... By the close, I was convinced they would because Graham has taken a piece of history and made it relevant to today, explained how it shaped the culture wars we are still living through, and how it made the politics that we experience.[60]

This distilled version of events thus emphasises the gladiatorial and drama-laden nature of the format, pushing the commentators to 'win' by rhetorically outmanoeuvring and belittling one another, which the writer distils into only a few minutes onstage. Notably host Howard K. Smith speaks only four times in five pages of dialogue during the first debate, two of which frame and close the discussion. During Vidal and Buckley's lively exchanges, Smith does nothing to interrupt, moderate or manage the discussion, a passive figure allowing the men to take control and in doing so shape the nature of the conversations to come. Through this Graham shows how public discourses became so fractious and even poisonous when even the architects of this new form of news media are powerless to intervene, while simultaneously its producers wonder whether it will be enough to earn the ratings they need:

> William Sheenan: Ok well, so far so good? Right?
>
> Buckley: Uh, may I comment, Mr Smith?
>
> Elmer Lower. It's uh... *interesting*? Isn't it?
>
> Howard K. Smith: Please do
>
> Buckley: Yeah...
>
> Elmer Lower: I mean... is it?[61]

Even here, then, in this first debate, the personal and political begin to merge, for which television is both the cause and the medium through which it takes place with both discussants grasping the opportunity to quip and personally attack their opponent:

> Vidal: In which case Richard Nixon might very well become the next president and I shall make my occasional trips to Europe longer.
>
> Buckley: Yes, I think a lot of people hope you will.[62]

That tension only increases as the scene draws to a close and the interlocutors patronise one another and express their increasing annoyance:

> Vidal: No, no Bill, don't step away from the record. You suggested the atom bombing of the North of Vietnam in your little magazine, which I do not read but I am told about, on February 23rd 1968.
>
> Buckley: Now, Mr Vidal, who boasts of not reading something which he is prepared to misquote in the presence of the person who edits it -
>
> Vidal: Now, Billy Buckley, the quotation is exact -[63]

The same process is repeated during the following debate with the agents of television again stepping back from the scenario they have deliberately created and allowing it to take on a momentum of its own, one that preferences entertainment over the intellectual engagement both men falsely believe they are engaged in.

In Round 2 as it is labelled by Graham in recognition of its boxing-ring style, Howard K. Smith fares no better in managing the tone or finding opportunities to interject, speaking only three times in four pages of dialogue with two of those insertions totalling only five words. And from here, the pace of the debates and their frequency only quickens with one further interaction before the end of Act One and three in Act Two that coincides with the Democratic Convention. In each, official newsman Smith is relegated to a spectator as the nature of TV news changes into entertainment without him. The interactions between the debaters become pricklier as a result of this lack of moderation despite Buckley's late assertion that news should remain independent:

> Buckley: If I may, Mr Smith, it is not the job of the news to get involved in local politics, merely report it.'[64]

Yet, Graham's management of these interactions has charted the tonal shift away from this approach across five debates in which the old rules of television and the expectations of both impartiality and reasonableness have been eroded, evidenced by the vanishing role that Smith plays in these discussions, and the increasing acrimony with which Vidal and Buckley are allowed to interact with one another unchecked, setting the scene for the dramatic finale that Graham previewed at the beginning of the play. This is a further technique to control the narrative, inserting an initial hook for the audience by staging the immediate aftermath of the final debate without revealing the reason for the consternation being expressed by the characters. This becomes the dramatic resolution to the play which, like the verdict in the Ingram trial, sustains audience investment and generates a clear narrative arc. And while Graham is not using television here to question what was said and its veracity, the outcomes for Buckley and Vidal are the same as for Charles Ingram—television won and they did not.

Television in the final part of *Best of Enemies*—the Epilogue, an usual device for Graham to employ—becomes a product to analyse, a point at which the authorial voice and the dramatist's research overtly make itself known within the play. Here this turning point moment which the play has treated as a live action event becomes historical evidence footage used to prove the change that Buckley and Vidal have instigated, much as the videotaped recordings became artefacts of justice in *Quiz*. But here, Graham uses a media analyst in lieu of his own voice as a device to reiterate the inherent falsity of television that takes characters from the make-up chair to their seats on the soundstage, and the influence of that environment on wider discourses and public reactions. This switch to a retrospective perspective means the feared national backlash prompted by Buckley's outburst instead becomes jubilation and an implicit desire for more of the same:

Howard K Smith: Quite the night? I was told the network heads – forgive me – 'shat' themselves. That kind of – 'hate', so openly displayed on live television…?

Until, that is – the ratings came in. And –

A respected newscaster completes the thought:

David Brinkley: From then on guest commentators became the norm on every network. Mr Pro versus Mrs Con, put them together, fire them up and get them going.[65]

The floodgates opened and Graham's character explains the different kind of televised public affairs broadcasting that emerges as a result with both the content and the vocabulary used to express opposing points of view forever changed:

Brooke Gladstone: Well. In terms of 'language', yelling the word queer live on television certainly broke an unbreakable taboo.

(*From her notes.*) After that, on American television we had – well, a 'motherfucker' a year later, on Dick Cavett's show. We waited eight years for a 'dirty bastard' by a Sex Pistol in the UK.[66]

Graham also returns to ideas about misconceptions of truth created by television in this Epilogue by implying that this dramatic conclusion was the final debate—that having reached a peak of dramatic entertainment, the story was over—a mythology that Graham also adds to by building his own play around their particular exchange and making it the conclusion to his own version of these events:

Brooke Gladstone: What I don't understand is that you *did* see each other again.

Vidal/Buckley: We did not.

Brooke Gladstone: You keep saying that, and you wrote that, but the memory shifts to suit the narrative, it's not the reality, the reality is there was one more debate, after that famous one that night, in Chicago?[67]

Television in Graham's work can directly affect, even rewrite, the public memory of itself, creating alternative narratives that prioritise the most exciting, convenient or entertaining version of reality, regardless of whether recordings are later manipulated as they were in *Quiz*. In this instance, Graham charts the environment in which live television was created that actively emphasised and sought to heighten the division between the men and amplified their polarised interaction. They are even reported as 'far and away the best infighters in Miami Beach.'[68] With the news professional actively stepping back from his role as a moderator, *Best of Enemies* shows how this unleashes new social forces that partially rewrote the history of how it came about. The characters of Buckley and Vidal vastly underestimated the influence of television as surely as Charles Ingram did and were unprepared for its impact as a political and populist tool.

Like *Quiz*, the play also considers the individual's experience of television, and Graham explores the naïve and failed attempt of both Vidal and Buckley to use it to enhance their personal fame and political ambitions. While Charles Ingram engaged with television in the pursuit of funds to help his family but with no desire for fame for its own sake, all three characters suffer when they attempt to assume control of the television process and present a manipulated version of themselves to the world. Vidal and Buckley's ambitions are alike, with both seeking political recognition from their respective political parties following failed bids to run for office. Vidal admits to having run for Congress in 1960 in Act One, Scene One while Smith uses his introduction to the first debate to establish Buckley's campaign for the New York mayoral race before turning to journalism. That Buckley and Vidal continue to harbour desires to return to political life becomes their core motivation for appearing on the show and is one of the many weapons they choose to use against one another:

> Frank Meyer: He grew up in D.C. No one grows up in Washington, D.C. It's a swamp you travel *to*, in order to do politics. But Gore Vidal, as I live and breathe… No wonder he's so sycophantic about Governmental Power.'[69]

Vidal is more overt in his desire for office than Buckley, using his position in the debates to solidify not only his leadership credentials but also the cultural reach he has amassed in the meantime using television to bring fame and politics together:

> Vidal: I'm afraid I have dinner with three congressmen, two senators and one soul singer. I must finish getting ready.[70]

Later, in the same scene, his lover Howard Austin explains Vidal's plans to the audience:

Vidal: Go on then, what? You men who know me so well; what has been my soul's desire. now fulfilled? Fame? I already had that.

Howard Austen: You had infamy. This is different. More than that.

(*Arms over his shoulder.*) 'Political significance'. The powerful are taking note.[71]

Vidal himself later notes a feeling of vulnerability as the pressure builds:

Vidal: I volunteered myself into that chair. Thinking it would all be a bit of fun, a nice profile booster; that Buckley would crumple under my ferocious - ... my - ...

It wasn't supposed to matter. Maybe it doesn't, maybe I'm kidding myself, as I always do...[72]

Graham uses the Epilogue to expand on the consequences of Vidal's folly, and despite having been the victim of a public homophobic slur that could have elicited sympathy for him, the political consequences for himself and his Party are clarified:

Vidal: And why the hell shouldn't I? I won, after all.

Howard Austen: Did you? I mean, Gore, I adore you. I'm just saying. Who won that election? Nixon. Then we got Reagan, which – (*at* Buckley) – to be fair this man, Bill practically invented. Conservatism, taken root in America.[73]

Vidal clings to this political disappointment once again at the end of the play bitterly referencing his failed congress run—'They wouldn't elect me, remember.'[74] Despite an offer from Mayor Daley at the height of the debates that implies a future in the party and Vidal's clear expectation, this outcome does not materialise in the aftermath of the television broadcast. Vidal's regret is palpable at the end of *Best of Enemies*, a character who thought television would be a platform he could use but failed to achieve anything significant from his appearance on it, leaving him almost where he started but with almost no possibility of resurrecting a now damaged political career. He may not suffer the legal implications heaped on Charles Ingram but nor does his attempt to control the medium result in either the personal fame or political significance he craves.

Graham applies a similar trajectory to William Buckley, taking him from television sceptic to political hopeful and to a similar shipwrecked ambition. Like Vidal, he has some prior experience of being on television and Graham includes an interview scene from another show where Buckley is in full control of the content and the mechanics of filming. Buckley barely conceals an arrogance about his possible television profile which he brags about to his wife discussed in the previous chapter on Famous Faces. But Buckley's primary motivation for appearing on television is also a return to political life although he adopts a cooler persona than his rival, at least initially, insisting on rules of engagement and a tone of civilised exchange that he thinks will give him an advantage on air:

> Buckley: Look where we are, Elmer. The political and social discord that is growing, and spreading across the globe? Do you think the framing of this new and serious mood is best served by someone as unserious as Vidal? Do you watch my show? I can't conduct such productive, calm and good-faith exchange with someone like him, he, he's -[75]

That Buckley soon waives these scruples when offered $10 million to participate along with his previous screen experience makes him overconfident, certain that he has mastered television and will be in full control of what happens when the cameras start rolling:

> Buckley: You do know this isn't my first rodeo, Ducky? And I've dispatched far tougher foe than this.

> Frank Meyer: But this is *television* Bill. I'll bet it doesn't have the order of, say, your debate with Baldwin in Cambridge.

> Buckley: Ahh... yes, Cambridge. Exactly, I must channel Cambridge. The oldest debating society in the world, the greatest minds, locking intellectual horns –

A few lines later he explains his tactic further:

> Buckley: I'm not worried about Vidal. He'll have *over*-prepared. Whereas we've just been sailing for week, resting on the open water.[76]

Graham builds Buckley up before the first debate and thus anticipates the inevitable fall to come when this new and unmanageable form of television resists Buckley's attempts to manage it. After that encounter Buckley demands changes to the format that he argues would make better television and allow him to control the debate narrative:

> Buckley: What I'm suggesting is a slight refinement of the format, that's all. No crosstalk, none of this interjecting. Smith asks a question, I get two minutes to respond, and then Vidal does the same. Like a real debating society -[77]

Again, it is significant that a marketing representative rather than a news professional tries to reassure Buckley, but he remains unconvinced by the parity of the platform he is being offered, determined that under the right conditions, he can control his image, the debate and television itself:

> George Merlis: You're both getting equally good coverage, Mr Buckley – look.
>
> Buckley: But was I getting equal *time*? It is in my contract, equal time to speak, it sure as hell felt like he was rambling on more than I was.[78]

Buckley's naivety about managing television and the way he is presented follows him through the remainder of the drama, and like Vidal, possible political influence is offered before being snatched away—television and his unmastered performance being the cause and consequence of Buckley's rise and fall. Initially, Buckley tries to learn from his mistakes, using the playback evidence to refine and improve his performance as an athlete might study his own form and the tactics of the opposition. By the end of Act One, it yields results for Buckley who receives the political recognition he craves as a result of his improved television image, receiving a call from Republican candidate Richard Nixon:

> Buckley: Oh, is that so? (*Looking at his wife.*) I hadn't realised that delegates and, and the candidates themselves were taking any notice of...
>
> Chicago? Yes, we'll be going head-to-head again. I'll certainly try my best. For you – and the. Movement. Goodbye.

He hangs up. A moment.

I don't believe it. This has actually become a thing. People are watching. The Party's... listening to me...[79]

But that recognition raises the stakes, creating additional pressure in Act Two for Buckley who must control interactions with Vidal and the evolving television format to deliver on his party's expectations to secure his future career path:

Buckley: This wasn't meant to become so... important. With someone like that, so dangerous sat opposite me, and this format, so unpredictable, and...

We have to get to work. I need to be ready in Chicago... I have to win, whatever that means, and not just narrowly, not just the 'perception', I need to completely and utterly end his tranche of reckless thought. And obliterate him.[80]

This pushes Buckley to compromise his earlier principles and formal approach, recognising that intellectual engagement and dignified debate are no longer sufficient. The demands of television slowly push Buckley to alter himself, to manipulate his image in order to present a more appealing character on-screen, just as Charles Ingram did during his second gameshow performance. It is Buckley's wife who articulates the populist developments in society as a result of the television debates, urging her husband to play to them:

Patricia Buckley: Bill, listen to me. You're too damn smart. And it is going to kill you out there. The average American as you call them cannot follow all that you're saying, they just can't. So what they are trying to work out instead, between you and Vidal – is who is the better person

And Buckley is persuaded by his wife's reasoning:

Buckley: So go on then, Ducky, do tell. How do I beat him in this disgusting popularity contest you are envisioning?[81]

And while television has rewritten its own history about the order of the debates discussed earlier in the chapter, Buckley too begins to reform his past, recasting his own eagerness for political office, even in front of his wife and friend who know him well:

Frank Meyer: He ran for Congress.

Buckley: And lost.

Patricia Buckley: You lost, when you ran for Mayor.

Buckley: Yes thank you dear, and that's different, I was running disingenuously. He was sincere.[82]

Buckley does this again when Vidal accuses him of embellishing his Second World War record, contributing to the rising tension and increasingly agitated nature of their discussion. Here the results of television pressure to change exert itself on the two men with personal insults and point scoring overtaking Buckley's planned factual focus which culminates in his dramatic outburst at the end of the show. Graham has generated this tension throughout the play as the demands of the television format overtake the two men in its glare and the debates destroy Buckley's chances of political influence, his wife noting 'the years we spent together at home, overlooking the calm waters in Connecticut' far from the Washington role this character had hoped for who then claimed never to have watched the debates again.[83] Like his opponent, Buckley tried to control television but it ended up controlling him, and Graham allows Vidal to summarise why television was too great an opponent for Buckley, preventing him from managing it:

Vidal: And it's why you can't ever forgive yourself for exploding at me, live on television, isn't it. It tears you utterly apart. The single time you *weren't* in 'control'…

Buckley (*sighs*) … I…

Vidal… of yourself, your emotions, your natural instincts on full display. It's why you're happiest, I think, when you sail, out in the open water, away from the world.[84]

At the close of *Best of Enemies*, television news and the nature of current affairs debate have expanded beyond the expectations of any of the characters, and ratings aside, unleash the same kind of consumer appetites that Murdoch and Lamb discovered in *Ink*. Graham notes that within months, even the fact-reporting newsmen from Act One, NBC's David Brinkley and Chet Huntley, have succumbed to the new ABC model of celebrity commentator making and analysing news instead of factually reporting it:

> Elmer Lower: Where *are* all these extra viewers coming from? Oh gosh, I – I sure hope we're not taking them from *you*.
>
> Chet Huntley: Said with all the characteristic grace of your political coverage, I see.
>
> Elmer Lower: Yeah, you know what I see? You two interviewing celebrities now, putting famous mouthpieces on screen. Don't seem to be laughing at our little experiment quiet so much anymore, huh.[85]

Even the Celebrity-Protagonists can retrospectively recognise the superficiality of television and their role in creating this new form of news media:

> Vidal: And, um. No reflections Mr Smith, but I do now think such debates are absolute nonsense. The way they are set up, there is almost no interchange of ideas.
>
> Buckley *might find himself looking at* Vidal *now, listening*.
>
> Vidal: Very little, even, of authentic personality. There's also the terrible thing about this medium, that hardly anyone *listens*. They sort of get an impression of somebody and they think they figure out just what he's like, by seeing him on television.[86]

Vidal goes on to point to the unhealthy influence of television on American society and, Graham suggests by extension, on our contemporary engagement with the medium:

> Vidal: The whole thing has been taken over (*pointing*) by this camera. Does television run America? There is an implicit conflict of interest,

between that which is highly viewable, and that which is highly illuminating.

So, all in all I hate to suddenly come out against the idea of 'debates' in our lives, but the way they are set up, on television… honestly I don't think I'd even bother to watch *this* one.[87]

It falls to media analyst Brooke Gladstone to represent the authorial voice, summarising for the audience the extent to which television has been the arbiter of division and dissention over time:

Brooke Gladstone: For me, watching them again… they remind me of a time when television was still a public square, where we all gathered together. More and more, we're polarised into these communities of concern. Living in our own separate realities. What can I say? It makes us less of a nation.[88]

The nature of television news changed forever in 1968, Graham's play argues, bringing with it a disbanding of traditional fact-based, impartial reporting and instead manufactured an appetite for the entertaining presentation of stories, the dilution of expertise and the polarisation of public discourses. The fears that Buckley and Vidal express at the start of the play start to realise themselves as individuals are consumed and destroyed, but as Elmer Lower's beloved ratings suggest, television only reinforced its social power.

'I think it's an unknown story that sheds light on the current state of political discourse,' director Jeremy Herrin explained in an interview accompanying the West End transfer of Best of Enemies, 'William F. Buckley Jr. and Gore Vidal are smart entertaining and contradictory characters.'[89] Graham's television plays though wide-ranging in subject matter, era and effects reveal patterns of populist appeal that leads to the repackaging and editing of facts, as well as the conflation of varied perspectives and opinions into singular narratives that purport to be definitive evidence. Graham's work reflects on what television has become across the last six decades and the extent to which it seeks to influence or even manipulate the viewer through the presentation of overly tidy and easy stories that make for simpler consumption than the messy, complicated and even contradictory realities—a new version of the truth so powerful that even those who created it start to believe their own product. As *Quiz* and *Best of Enemies* demonstrate, the nature of television represents many levels of corporate organisation from presenters and camera operators, to production company executives, marketing men, divisional controllers and media company moguls, all of whom contribute to the creation of television content, seek to protect their interests in it and wield its social and political power against any individual attempting to challenge television's version of events or to control the medium for their own ends. Even the professional cheery Warm-Up who enthuses the audience at the beginning of *Quiz* struggles to sustain themselves under the relentless pressures the camera places on them:

> *The* Warm-Up *is somewhere alone, backstage, private. Quiet.*
>
> *He is motionless, starring sadly into space.*
>
> *He slips off his wig. Stares out. Beat…*
>
> *He takes some pills from his pocket and knocks them back with a hip flash. Closes his eyes. Breathes.*[90]

It is no wonder that amateurs like Charles Ingram, William F. Buckley and Gore Vidal were trampled in television's wake. With its broad and destructive influence on the independence of the justice system and the once unimpeachable nature of news reporting, Graham's work shows that television is a mighty social force and nothing can stand it its way.

Notes

1. Luckhurst, Mary. Verbatim Theatre, Media Relations and Ethics. Edited by Holdsworth, Nadine, and Luckhurst Mary. 2008. *A Concise Companion to Contemporary British and Irish Drama.* London: Blackwell Publishing, p.201.
2. Ibid, p.210.
3. Edited by Deeney, John F., and Gale, Maggie B. 2015. *Fifty Modern and Contemporary Dramatists.* London: Routledge, p.114.
4. Luckhurst, May. In Edited by Holdsworth, Nadine, and Luckhurst, Mary. 2008, p.216.
5. Graham, James. 2022. *Best of Enemies.* Act One, Scene One, p.18.

6. Ibid, Act One, Scene One, p.21.
7. Graham, James. 2017. *Ink*. London: Methuen Drama. Act Two, p.85.
8. Graham, James. 2022. *Best of Enemies*. Act One Scene One, p.25.
9. Graham, James. 2017. *Ink*. Act Two, p.88.
10. Ibid, Act Two, p.74.
11. Ibid, Act Two, p.74.
12. Turner, Alwyn. 2021. *All In It Together: England in the 21st Century*. London: Profile Books Ltd., pp.22–23.
13. Graham, James. 2017. *Ink*. Act Two, p.75.
14. Ibid, Act Two, p.76.
15. Ibid, Act Two, p.76.
16. Ibid, Act Two, p.129.
17. Graham, James. 2018. What Happens to Trust and Truth When Justice and Entertainment Combine? In Quiz Theatre Programme, Chichester Festival Theatre.
18. Ellis, John, and van den Oever, Annie. Storytelling and Mainstream Television Today—A Dialogue. In Christie, Ian and van den Oever, Annie. 2018. *Stories: Screen Narratives in the Digital Era*. Amsterdam University Press.
19. Graham, James. 2018. *Quiz*. Act One, p.13.
20. Ibid, Act One, p.21.
21. Ibid, Act One, p.26.
22. Ibid, Act One, p.27.
23. Ibid, Act One, p.30.
24. Ibid, Act One, p.33.
25. Ibid, Act One, p.33.
26. Ibid, Act One, p.34.
27. Ibid, Act Two, p.92.
28. Ibid, Act Two, p.92.
29. Woffinden, Bob, and Plaskett, James. 2015. *Bad Show*. Bojangles Press, p.230.
30. Ibid, p.381.
31. Graham, James. 2018. *Quiz*. Act Two, pp.92–93.
32. Ibid, Act One, p.55.
33. Graham, James. 2018. *Quiz*. Act Two, p.82.
34. Ibid, Act Two, p.81.
35. Ibid, Prologue, p.5.
36. Ibid, Prologue, p.7.

37. Graham, James. 2017. What Happens to Trust and Truth When Justice and Entertainment Combine? In Quiz Theatre Programme, Chichester Festival Theatre.
38. Graham, James. 2018. *Quiz*. Act One, p.24.
39. Ibid, Prologue, p.8.
40. Ibid, Prologue, p.9.
41. Ibid, Act One, p.58.
42. Ibid, Act Two, p.86.
43. Ibid, Act Two, p.99.
44. Ibid, Act Two, p.101.
45. Billington, Michael. 2017. Quiz Review—James Graham Explores the Thin Line Between Courtroom and Showbiz. *The Guardian*, November 12, https://www.theguardian.com/stage/2017/nov/12/quiz-review-exploration-of-the-thin-line-between-courtroom-and-showbusiness.
46. Crompton, Sarah. 2017. Review Quiz (Minerva Theatre, Chichester). *Whatsonstage*, November 11, https://www.whatsonstage.com/news/review-quiz-minerva-theatre-chichester_45120/.
47. Graham James. 2022. In Best of Enemies Theatre Programme, Noel Coward Theatre.
48. Graham, James. 2022. *Best of Enemies*, Act One, Scene One, p.9.
49. Ibid, Act One, Scene One, p.9.
50. Ibid, Act One, Scene One, p.11.
51. Ibid, Act One, Scene One, p.11.
52. Ibid, Act One, Scene One, p.12.
53. Ibid, Act One, Scene One, p.13.
54. Ibid, Act One, Scene One, pp. 13–14.
55. Ibid, Act One, Scene One, p.26.
56. Ibid, Act One, Scene One, p.24.
57. Ibid, Act One, Scene Two, p.38.
58. Ibid, Act One, Scene Two, p.39.
59. Graham, James. 2022. In Best of Enemies Theatre Programme, Noel Coward Theatre.
60. Crompton, Sarah. 2021. Best of Enemies Review—James Graham Is Back, Doing What He Does Best. *Whatsonstage*, December 10, https://www.whatsonstage.com/news/best-of-enemies-review-james-graham-is-back-doing-what-he-does-best_55516/.
61. Graham, James. 2022. *Best of Enemies*. Act One, Scene Two, p.42.
62. Ibid, Act One, Scene Two, p.44.

63. Ibid, Act One, Scene Two, p.45.
64. Ibid, Act Two, Scene Two, p.83.
65. Ibid, Epilogue, p.94.
66. Ibid, Epilogue, pp.95–96.
67. Ibid, Epilogue, p.97.
68. Ibid, Act One, Scene Two, p.46.
69. Ibid, Act Two, Scene One, p.67.
70. Ibid, Act Two, Scene One, p.62.
71. Ibid, Act Two, Scene One, p.63.
72. Ibid, Act Two, Scene Two, p.85.
73. Ibid, Epilogue, p.95.
74. Ibid, Epilogue, p.98.
75. Ibid, Act One Scene Two, p.28.
76. Ibid, Act One, Scene Two, p.32.
77. Ibid, Act One, Scene Two, p.47.
78. Ibid, Act One, Scene Two, p.48.
79. Ibid, Act One, Scene Two, p.57.
80. Ibid, Act One, Scene Two, p.57.
81. Ibid, Act Two, Scene One, p.65.
82. Ibid, Act Two, Scene One, p.67.
83. Ibid, Epilogue, p.95.
84. Ibid, Epilogue, p.99.
85. Ibid, Act Two, Scene Two, p.80.
86. Ibid, Epilogue, p.100.
87. Ibid, Epilogue, p.101.
88. Ibid, Epilogue, p.96.
89. Herrin, Jeremy. 2022. In Best of Enemies Theatre Programme, Noel Coward Theatre.
90. Graham, James. 2018. *Quiz*. Act Two, p.59.

PART III

The State of the Nation

CHAPTER 6

Writing for Television

As well as writing about television, Graham has also written for it including *Coalition* (Channel 4, March 2015), a film-length television drama for Channel 4 about the relationship between Nick Clegg, David Cameron and Gordon Brown during the formation of the Conservative-Liberal coalition in 2010, a three-part ITV adaptation of his own play *Quiz* (April 2020) and an episode of Netflix drama *The Crown* (November 2019) from Season Three exploring the Prince of Wales investiture in 1972. A brief survey of this work notes a series of cross-cutting themes that appear consistently across the writer's output. These are relevant to Graham's evolving engagement with state-of-the-nation debates and challenges including the effectiveness of political functions and their ability to withstand the pressures of twenty-first-century society as well as the persuasive influence of media organisations on both electoral behaviour and the national mood. Graham's work for television employs many of the same themes and narrative approaches used in his stage work including Celebrity-Protagonists and Incidental-Celebrity characters to explore approaches to innovation and public scrutiny as well as charting periods of decline and disengagement resulting from the failures of national policy to alleviate local concerns and economic deprivation. By setting work at different points in Britain's post-war history and presenting a snapshot of the time within a wider continuum of state failure. Graham's television work is concerned with the consequences of national policy on local communities and collective beliefs about the nation, referencing many of the same failures to address the loss of industries and community purpose outlined in *Labour of Love* and the ways in which the short-termist approaches to governance explored in *This House* have exacerbated these issues to create further social division. That this sets the traditional, even 'old-fashioned' nature of British structures and institutions in a context of media innovations and rapid social development is significant, emphasising one of Graham's central concerns that a country with one foot in the past struggles to manage its present or effectively plan for its future, entering instead into cycles of decline. This chapter examines two of the writer's recent television dramas to explore the detailed state-of-the-nation analysis they provide and the ways in which they reinforce ideas emerging from Graham's stage drama.

Brexit: The Uncivil War, screened on Channel 4 in January 2018, focuses on the campaign and vote to leave the European Union in 2016 and, like much of Graham's stage work, even-handedly examines the Leave and Remain campaign offices and the techniques both sides used to convince the electorate. This detailed analysis of a specific electoral process links to Graham's wider collection of democracy plays analysed in Part One exploring different aspects of government process, selection and management. It sits as a companion piece to *The Vote* exploring how a political campaign is run by contrasting traditional approaches with the innovative and highly persuasive tools developed and employed by the Leave campaign led by Celebrity-Protagonist Dominic Cummings played by Benedict Cumberbatch. This is in large part a highly technological story looking at the use of social media adverts and quizzes to project highly controlled and targeted messaging that was applied in new ways to this campaign. But the idea of narratives being shaped and disseminated in controlled ways by media companies is a common one in Graham's work and those employed here are an evolution of the cutting and editing techniques explored in *Quiz* that shape notions of truth, as well as the selection of information that determines what is and is not classified and reported as news. What makes *Brexit: The Uncivil War* different is the exposure of false claims presented as facts as well as the rejection of expertise in favour of an emotional connection to ideas of Britain and reclamation of a mythological position of independence and influence incited by the campaign. Graham develops his notions of information control, thinking not only about how the management and timing of its release to create political and emotional responses in contemporary society, but how media organisations are able to fabricate similar reactions by planting false or manipulated claims that drive voter behaviour and the resultant public discourses. This repositioning of facts as malleable or subject to interpretation has significant ramifications for the effective functioning of modern Britain, population control and notions of identity which the writer argues are directly informed by the production and distribution of this information.

The ability of organisations with assumed societal power to influence those with delegated power is thus blended in *Brexit: The Uncivil War* in which Graham demonstrates how a democratic function—essentially a 'party' running an election campaign—uses the assumed power of media organisations to influence the public democratic process. The active recognition of the role of soft-power services to sway the outcomes of official governance processes is highly significant in the picture of modern Britain that Graham presents, especially when that power is applied within and between democratic constituents who use it to influence other related parts of the electoral process—in this case a public referendum. This 90-minute film takes the concept of a binary choice between Leave and Remain and attempts to reverse the simplistic messaging advocated by the character of Dominic Cummings that shrinks the public response to emotional and straightforward reactions. Instead, Graham restores the complex underpinning approaches to these two campaigns and situates their consequences within broader state-of-the-nation debates. In doing so, it combines different themes across Graham's work that comment on reactions to traditional politics and politicians along with the embedded feelings of disenfranchisement and loss of personal control that the Leave campaign utilised to encourage votes.

The film opens with a montage of news and archive footage summarising key moments in Britain's relationship with Europe since 1940, speaking to the context of disconnected thinking and separation between the government and the governed that forms the backdrop to all of Graham's work. *Brexit: The Uncivil War* considers this in some detail, noting the contrasting campaign approaches distilled into another binary choice of head versus heart, with the Remain team representing traditional politics staffed by formal-sounding people focused on facts, while the Leave group is masterminded by a character variously described as 'a geeky anarchist' and 'an egotist with a wrecking ball.' Like *Monster Raving Loony*, *Brexit: The Uncivil War* is concerned with anarchic actions undertaken within the existing system to create 'a new politics.'[1] Although many may baulk at the comparison, Graham suggests a thematic similarity between the actions of David Sutch and Dominic Cummings in his work as they both react against a stale and sober version of the Establishment into which they attempt to insert a different approach to the electoral process to create fresh voter appeal. Crucially, the backdrop of British decline and the existence of communities left behind by contemporary society is a mutually motivating factor with both Sutch and Cummings emerging from non-traditional backgrounds and launching themselves into a creaking Westminster system.

The challenge for Cummings in this film is to overcome similar scepticism from those who hire him to oversee the Leave campaign approach and who initially default to standard and accepted political behaviours, mistrusting the assumed technological power that Cummings claims and instead attempts to assert their own officially delegated authority to determine what happens. Graham portrays the rising influence of non-democratic forces led by someone with no elected authority to decide how a major act of public participation should be carried out. But Cummings utilises the clothes of traditional democracy to do it, deliberately distancing the campaign from the comedy caricatures of political influencers Nigel Farage, the leader of the UK Independence Party (UKIP) at the time of the Vote and co-founder of the campaign, businessman Arron Banks who appear as Incidental-Celebrities, and in their place offering a credible alternative to the extreme right. The same thing happens in *Monster Raving Loony* when the Labour candidate is mocked for adopting the physical expression of Conservative Party MPs in order to appeal to the electorate, and Graham's version of Cummings does exactly the same thing here. The target is the 'persuadeables,' a middle group of floating voters who are not yet convinced by either the Leave or Remain positions but can be manipulated into registering to vote and then casting a ballot in favour of Leave. Graham's characters here call on many of the systematic failings that the writer has long considered, including the lack of public trust in traditional democratic and social governance institutions while still using them to legitimise the campaign. Cummings notes that influential MPs like Boris Johnson, then MP for Harrow, and Michael Gove, MP for Surrey Heath—also treated here as Incidental-Celebrity—must be the public face of the campaign bringing with them delegated authority and status to represent political issues, but it is clear that Cummings believes the assumed power of media has the real authority to determine how the referendum is won. The language that the character of Cummings employs is often combat-based, speaking of 'an insurgence against the Establishment'[2] which uses the campaign as an entry point to overturn existing political rules.

Several different things happen across this drama that Graham believes have significant consequences for modern Britain; the first and most obvious is the questionable means by which an official electoral campaign was able to create a voter database through the targeted planting of adverts and clickbait tailored to individual social media accounts that use entertaining or deceptive packaging to obtain personal data. The character of Cummings, who reports having no access to voter profiles stored by traditional political parties, insists that the collection, management and use of data are crucial to winning the referendum. In *Sketching*, Graham's co-written 2018 anthology play based on a Dickens-style interleaving of London narratives, his own villainous character Peter Piper also sets out to obtain personal data, because it gives great power to the holder and can cause potential chaos:

> *We see an animated, visual representation of all the data that has been absorbed into their possession – some of it relating to our own characters. Hozan's Snapchat, for example. Mo's bank account?*
>
> Nico: It worked. OH MY GOD, IT WORKED! This is the biggest treasure trove anyone has ever seen, something from Everyone, the whole of London! Private messages! Passwords! *Bank accounts*! Jesus Christ oh my god so what's the next part of the plan – no don't tell me? Blackmail? Like you did to us? Stealing?! Fake identities?!
>
> Peter: ... delete it.
>
> Nico: ... mmm?
>
> Peter: Delete it. All of it. 'Reset.'

And a few lines later, the hope for chaos ensues:

> Mayor: Tom, my God! I've got City traders going nuts, saying their portfolios have been wiped! Heathrow traffic control is paralysed, contactless cards aren't working anywhere and my daughter's having an eppy because her Spotify account's deleted?![3]

Cummings may not have such an elaborate plan in mind, but in a more targeted way the character recognises the value of personal data harnessed from social media and other public platforms to effect another kind of social control, and he sets out to shift narratives about the European Union in the referendum away from facts and economics by narrowing the choice being offered to voters to two simple messages, cost and control. This has important effects on public discourses, and it not only completes a process Graham began in *Ink* where the very concept of public interest is determined by the media, but Cummings here actively instigates simplistic but polarised national debates that actively remove nuance and balance from public discussion around the election. It is a thought Graham returned to a few years later with *Best of Enemies* set in 1968, but here, in 2016, the consequences of this long-gestating shift occur leading to violent altercations and dissent in the weeks before the referendum vote dramatised towards the end of the film. Whether this was incitement or a process that gave people a voice is one of the piece's key questions, but its effect on modern Britain in the control and use (or misuse) of personal data in a democratic process as well as the effects on the nature of national debate are of considerable importance Graham argues. 'I think what's more interesting is to get behind the curtain and interrogate the strategies and the people who came up with ideas and messages and how a campaign works in the 21st Century,' he told Channel 4 in an interview accompanying the show's release, 'It's really important to talk about data and particularly how it allows messages to be targeted and distributed. It's clearly affecting our politics. It's affecting how we think and talk to each other and our political discourse.'[4]

Although Dominic Cummings is presented as an anarchic character whose actions have wide-ranging consequences for political activity and national conversations in contemporary society, he ultimately suffers the same fate as disruptive characters in Graham's other anarchy-focused plays, *Monster Raving Loony* and *The Angry Brigade* in which established forms of democracy fight back against Cummings's incursions. This leaves an unusual final statement in Graham's work where Cummings is shown to have changed everything and nothing at the same time, or perhaps has failed to change the one thing he attempted to reform—the political system itself—and instead unleashes forces beyond his control. Remain campaign leader and Cummings's counterpart in this drama, Craig Oliver (Rory Kinnear) joins Hugh Cudlipp from *Ink* in issuing a warning to Cummings about the effect his tactics will have, but it is only in the final scenes of the film that this unsatisfactory outcome is realised, leaving Cummings unsettled by the victory celebrations taking place in his office, and then in a scene set at an inquiry into the conduct of the Leave campaign two years later. Graham is deliberately opaque in outlining the failures to deliver the promised political upheaval that Cummings hoped for but gives the character an opportunity to reflect in hindsight. A closing speech by the character of Cummings references the author's ongoing emphasis on the human failings that prevent democracy from functioning effectively while also deterring any lasting change in the political life of the country. A moping Cummings responds to the questions by complaining the existing modes of political engagement have resumed since the vote to leave the European Union and the opportunity to seize the moment and change how politics takes place has been lost, bringing his vision for a new politics down with it. Placed in the same position as both Sutch and The Angry Brigade, this outcome only emphasises and reinforces the power of existing democratic structures exacerbated by a lack of courage to really change them, a frequent theme across the writer's work. In *Brexit: The Uncivil War*, Graham shows once again that current forms of politics are not fit for the purpose of governing so complex a national picture but that the assumed power of media is only increasing the ways in which it both harnesses and rouses public emotion. Graham reflects here on a broader feeling of powerless pervading the country and a deliberate attempt to harness that by creating a tribalism that is given only momentary relief by the Brexit vote in this drama. Graham shows the Leave campaign using questions of sovereignty and national identity, emotively described as a fight for the 'soul of our country'[5] to subvert the accepted idea of the status quo, promising a return to a better time that never comes. This enduring belief in Britain's semi-mythological past is one that Graham's work has frequently countermanded, demonstrating the long failures to reconcile the country's role in the world and its social purpose since the Second World War, but *Brexit: The Uncivil War* speaks to continued beliefs that a golden age has been lost, fed by media messaging, and of the failure of successive administrations to govern and heal the wounds of modern society.

Some of these deep-seated wounds have created decades of community division and resentment and this is the focus of Graham's television drama, *Sherwood*, a six-part story for the BBC exploring the deeply entwined tensions resulting from government failures to address the changing industrial face of post-war Britain. Broadcast in June and July

2022 and set in a former mining community 30 years after their closure, the social and economic consequences of the 1984 strikes are the basis for a multi-character piece taking place in a Midlands village still bitterly divided by the choices made by different mining unions during this period. Ostensibly a police drama framed by a double murder with a cast including David Morrissey, Adeel Akhtar and Lesley Manville, Graham creates the much wider context in which these crimes take place, with a dual narrative structure following events in the present day and an equivalent track involving younger versions of the same characters in 1984. The impression of a Britain unchanged in decades is given a very human face through the hostile interactions of members in the local Miner's Welfare Club, a place where old resentments between the strikers and those who continued to work still provoke vocal skirmishes in the bar. Graham frames this with news and archival footage at the start of Episode One depicting picket lines, altercations and a charged relationship with the police, all of which provide a visual shorthand for the context in which the ensuing drama takes place. Summarised by the female Conservative Party candidate as people acting against their own best interests out of pride, this is a very male fight on the surface, but its outcomes affect wives and grown-up children as well, some of whom inherit parental grudges, taking these cumulative issues into the next generation. Writing in *The Guardian* shortly after broadcast, the writer explains that 'overly simplistic snapshots often wrongly suggest that there is a homogenous uniformity to the people, their experiences and their views. My home county is as complicated, paradoxical and inconsistent as anywhere else.'[6] Graham's purpose here is to show the consequences of short-termist government policy, and while that may change every five years with personnel shuffling through ministerial and related positions even more frequently, the impact of this becomes far more significant at a local level. What happens in a community, Graham's drama shows, happens to everyone and it lasts for decades.

Graham frames this drama within the same process of demographic change affecting political support and representation that recurs in his writing, noted in *Labour of Love*, *This House* and *Monster Raving Loony*. The Conservative Party candidate Sarah Vincent argues on constituency doorsteps that Labour can no longer rely on working-class votes, that the 'Red Wall' has fallen and traditional support has dissipated. Graham links this directly to the strikes and while national failures in government policy have not addressed the removal of this community's core industry, the aftermath of the strikes has created deeply held personal enmities that have turned voters away from their usual political allegiances. *Labour of Love* explores this in more detail, and the failures of modern party-political structures are discussed in Chapter 2, but the issues of vested interests and the hard line taken by lobby groups are also implied here. Sarah actively changes party, moving from an Independent MP to become a Conservative candidate which Graham rolls into this discussion of changing demographics that emerges directly from the experience of this village since the 1980s. Admitting she was always a Conservative thinker but felt unable to openly campaign before voting behaviour altered, Sarah's concern links latent fear in this community that equates political beliefs and actions with possible violence and intimidation. This impression of modern Britain is an insightful one, a place deeply rooted in its complicated and emotional national and regional past which continues to shape an uncertain present while struggling against widespread political and social changes that are disconnecting people from the clearly defined groups that were once part of, and even challenging the ways in which people can or should identify themselves in relation to others.

While much of Graham's work explores assaults launched by the media on traditional and legitimate power structures, *Sherwood* exposes anti-democratic approaches undertaken by the Establishment to undermine perceived threats to society. The possible existence of a 'spy cop' in the village exposes a government-sanctioned practice in which undercover police officers penetrated radical groups during the miners' strikes to provide intelligence that could undermine the protest. The writer situates this in the troubled and deeply suspicious relationship between the police and local residents in the drama, something that investigation lead Ian St Clair must overcome in order to progress with his double murder case. Graham explored the deep conventionality of the police force in *The Angry Brigade*, set in the 1970s, in which their actions were all legal and quietly systematic in their attempt to track down and stop the bombing campaign undertaken by The Brigade, but in *Sherwood* the activities of the police are far more complex. Running across two time periods with the characters of St Clair and Metropolitan Police officer Kevin Salisbury appearing in both the 1980s and contemporary strands of the story, St Clair sets the tone for the modern investigation during a briefing in Episode Two in which he reminds his team that policing can only happen by consent and, even thirty years later, they are still trying to win back local trust following brutal tactics employed by the imported

Metropolitan Police to set down the strike. Throughout the remaining episodes, Graham analyses the fractious relationship with local residents and the particular history with the police as a result of the 1984 action that has consequences for the effective operation of this Establishment service today and against which St Clair's team must continually react, treading carefully in the enaction of their duty. The nuance that Graham includes between reactions to different sections of the police force, here the Nottinghamshire Constabulary and the still hated Metropolitan Police Force, is important in explaining the long-held resentments and refusal to cooperate that make it harder to undertake the active criminal investigation in *Sherwood*. But Graham also includes a series of protected regional identities that resent external interference from a London-based force imposing a central governmental agenda without fully understanding the local context. It means that St Clair's character is grudgingly accepted by the civilian characters who traverse the two time periods in this story because he represents the local police force and has some understanding and respect for this community's history and its impact in ways that Metropolitan Police Force officers like Salisbury cannot.

The role of the police in creating the contemporary social and political conditions in this village is crucial to understanding the outcomes of this drama and the responses they provoke. For modern Britain, Graham shows that the police are not independent and morally unambiguous guardians of democracy, that law enforcement cannot be indivisible from the context in which it operates, often compromising its effectiveness and neutrality when tasked with imposing controversial government policy within the short-termist intentions of any administration. Unlike politicians, *Sherwood* shows that police personnel are often a constant, remaining in the organisation and moving through the ranks for decades, bringing with them the taint and experience of a past they share with their communities, often bridging the gap between central policy and the real human experience of crime and its effects. The weight of that is significant for the police characters in *Sherwood* who are unable to act without acknowledging the more personal world in which they exist rather than the cleaner institutional rules and national laws which only provide so much protection. But, in responding to that ever-changing political directive and regional context, the police are also led to act in ways that are undemocratic in the pursuit of evidence to secure a conviction, sacrificing their neutrality to undertake 'political policing.' And while Graham presents a much purer version of police work in *The Angry*

Brigade, focusing largely on procedure and recruitment, *Sherwood*'s analysis of the spy cop activities reveals covert surveillance undertaken against citizens who had committed no crimes at the time that the undercover officers were sent into communities because the government wished to undermine and destabilise them using police personnel to report on their actions and find reasons to arrest dissenters. A Bafta-nominated drama that was quickly renewed for a second series due in 2024 Graham insisted: 'It's not for me, or a television drama, to judge whether it is time to forgive and forget. The suffering and the anger emanating from both the strike itself, and the social and economic devastation that came after, remains all too real for many people.'[7]

There is a connection here between the activities of the character of Dominic Cummings in *Brexit: The Uncivil War* and the actions undertaken against UK citizens by their own government in *Sherwood*. Both cases are an example of the Establishment working outside of traditional democratic structures and the legitimately delegated authority given to trusted institutions in an attempt to elicit personal data by nefarious means. The unregulated overstepping of the boundaries of their office has significant ramifications for modern society as boundaries continue to blur between the responsibilities of the State and the freedom of the individual. Frequently in Graham's work it is the individual who suffers the consequences of interacting with monolith organisations or concepts bigger themselves, so when anarchist characters try to undermine the Parliamentary political model, democracy restores order or when the Ingrams take on television and lose. But in *Sherwood*, the writer exposes arguably unprovoked pre-emptive attacks by democratic institutions on citizen organisations which have a freedom to speak and to protest. The outcomes are significant, creating a confederacy between the government (even successive governments who had not acknowledged the practice), police and security services that redraws the boundary between State threats and lawful public political expression. Establishment attempts to redefine and confine the definition of protest are a timely concern, but *Sherwood* presents a pattern of government overstepping and its consequences not only for public trust in the organisations designed to protect it but also for understanding proportionate methods of social control in twenty-first-century Britain.

Sherwood has one further contribution to the discussion of Graham's work and that is in the representation of working-class lives in the public domain. Graham rarely focuses exclusively on class, but it underscores much of the writer's work, determining how social structures operate in modern society and the opportunities open to individuals across the scenarios he creates. 'In the Thatcher years, this image of a divided country became deeply etched in the popular consciousness,' writer Aleks Sierz explained in his assessment of *Blood Brothers* noting a similar duality in Willy Russell's depiction of a Liverpool family that 'is both radical in its image of working-class endurance, and conservative in its fatalistic picture of a doomed generation of powerless youngsters.'[8] Sierz and co-editors Martin Middeke and Peter Paul Schnierer expanded on the influence of Thatcherism onstage representations of class in their 2011 anthology of British dramatists noting that writers 'have laid bare the disenchantment with old political certainties, witnessing the failure of party politics and especially the inadequacies of both communism and capitalism.'[9] Class, educational opportunities and politics are also frequent themes in Graham's work, finding a similar duality in the strength but voiceless inevitability of character's lives, referenced in most of his democracy and anarchy-focused plays musing on the changing class structures of traditional political parties and their voter base as well as the very similar background and schooling of British leaders since the Second World War. Jason Price argues that across twentieth-century writing, the visibility of working-class issues led to a more radical political focus in playwriting, and like his predecessor's Graham's theatre becomes a 'mouthpiece for subordinated peoples to speak against power.'[10] Class underpins much of the assumed division between the Labour and Conservative Whips in *This House* from Bob Mellish eating sausage and chips as he packs up his office and making references to an 'Austin Allegro,' it is an indication of his no-nonsense, down-to-earth vocabulary that sets him apart from opposite number Hugh Weatherill who uses cricketing metaphors and jokes about northerners being unable to sit properly in their chairs. Graham uses vocabulary to magnify the differences between groups of rivals across class divides in his plays and the pervasive superiority that more affluent characters often assume over their working-class counterparts. In an introduction to the Student Edition of *This House*, Nicholas Holden notes that social indicators of class including 'wealth, education and occupation' are built into the play's dialogue to further convey the social boundaries of the two parties. Reference to public school education appear frequently in Graham's work which, with the financial privilege they represent, Holden notes 'implies that these institutions offer superior education and more affluent futures for their pupils.' And while *This*

House is not entirely concerned with class, Holden explains how Graham's characterisation of his political subjects 'demonstrate how class underscores the play's narrative and remains consistently bubbling at the play's surface.'[11] It is a theme picked up in *Monster Raving Loony* when Snooty, a public school education character, who distinguishes himself from Sutch immediately by using class to emphasise their differences while dismissing the significance of his duologue partner:

Snooty: Oh gosh, frightfully sorry, I don't speak – wherever it is you're from.[12]

It is a conversation that continues to place a separation between two people from the same place but worlds apart in terms of education and aspiration in which Snooty uses the illustrious list of Prime Ministers attending Harrow School to reminding Sutch that there are limitations placed on working-class lives, stating 'There are those who are born to listen, and those born to play,'[13] a statement that nods to Jim's extended speech in *The Angry Brigade* about violence in the routine of working-class lives that seeks to keep people in their place. In Graham's work, then, class is defined as a set of actions, restrictions or expectations placed upon characters by others based on their economic status and perceived place in a fixed social hierarchy. This external definition and imposition of what class means creates societal segregation with governments often failing to see or understand the needs of communities very different from their own, who are instead overlooked and dismissed by those that Snooty represents.

Graham's work is a corrective to some of that, telling compassionate working-class stories that give his characters a level of emotional depth and complexity often lacking in equivalent dramas. And there are strong connections across these plays that link the experience of David Sutch with Bob Mellish, Jim from *The Angry Brigade*, Larry Lamb from *Ink* and the Sherwood villagers along with the five men at the centre of *Boys From the Blackstuff* (2023) discussed in the next chapter, all of whom have modest working-class backgrounds, seeking recognition and acknowledgement of their existence from a system led and controlled by elites who have very little understanding of the people they govern, assuming power from an early age that is reinforced by education, parental success and ultimately their social status. Class in all of Graham's work determines what roles individuals are permitted to hold in society, what opportunities they have for personal development and even their perceived social value in political decision-making. This alignment between class and power is an important one, further reinforcing a separation between the Establishment that Graham explores and those who are expected to abide by its laws and values while given limited voice in which to determine their own best interests or to protect themselves when the State decides to turn against them. The long aftermath of short-term government decision-making continues to define and confine the day-to-day experience of ordinary people as a result.

The regional and personal picture that emerges in *Sherwood*, therefore, explores the feeling of powerlessness that residents continue to feel more than three decades after the government intervention in the area caused the deep wounds in the village that have failed to heal and continue to define the ways in which sections of this community interact. In looking at the make-up of both types of mining families and the two police forces operating in the area, Graham presents a complex picture of modest but decent lives contending with larger forces and social waves imposed on them from outside. This representation of dignity and respectability in working-class lives works quietly through Graham's output, challenging some of the persistent national narratives that demonise the working class and attempt to exclude their voices from larger discourses about the effects of social change and public policy. There are conversations taking place within *Sherwood* about social mobility in which former mining families enjoy a more recognisably middle-class lifestyle in the modern sections, as well as important clarifications about those who could and could not afford to join the 1984 strikes and the closing-off of opportunity in the local area that sets some families behind and leaves them with nothing in its place except the long-standing bitterness and rivalry emerging from the strike itself—as one character remarks, 'what else is there to do around here but remember?'[14] The same impression of forgotten communities and the impotence of those living with the consequences of successive ineffective government appear repeatedly in Graham's work from *Sons of York* onwards, creating an impression of modern Britain in which class is still a determining factor in who has access to opportunity and progression. This creates a stark contrast between the government and the governed, the limits of which emerge through the writer's characterisation of these long-standing patterns of class division, financial deprivation and exclusion from national conversations about their own future. As a result, the remoteness of Westminster and its perceived lack of empathy directly causes the political apathy, disconnection and feelings of abandonment that Graham's television dramas so vitally expose in this raw examination of enmity and stagnation. These are the same emotions that the Cummings character taps into in *Brexit: The Uncivil War* and it is in *Sherwood* that Graham explains the root of those feelings and makes an impassioned case for the value of the ordinary lives that Britain is not only leaving behind but failing to acknowledge in its approaches to public policy and national conversation.

Notes

1. Graham, James. 2018. *Brexit: The Uncivil War*, Channel 4.
2. Ibid.
3. Graham, James. Peter Piper has a Plan. In Graham, James et al. 2018. *Sketching*. London: Methuen Drama, p.41.
4. Channel 4 2018. Interview with writer James Graham for Brexit: The Uncivil War. Channel4.com, December 28, https://www.channel4.com/press/news/interview-writer-james-graham-brexit-uncivil-war.
5. Graham, James. 2018. *Brexit: The Uncivil War*, Channel 4.
6. Graham, James. 2022. I Wrote Sherwood as a Warning. When Communities Are Divided, the Pain Endures. *The Guardian*, June 29, https://www.theguardian.com/commentisfree/2022/jun/29/sherwood-communities-divided-miners-strike-brexit-rail-dispute.
7. Ibid.
8. Sierz, Aleks. 2021. *Good Nights Out: A History of Popular British Theatre Since the Second World War*. London: Methuen Drama.
9. Edited By Middeke, Martin, Schnierer, Peter P., and Sierz, Aleks. 2011.*The Methuen Drama Guide to Contemporary British Playwrights*. London: Bloomsbury, p.xv.
10. Price, Jason. 2016. *Modern Popular Theatre*. London: Palgrave, p.23.
11. Holden, Nicholas. In Graham James. 2021. *This House* (Student Editions). London: Methuen Drama.
12. Graham, James. *Monster Raving Loony*. Part One. In Graham, James. 2016. *James Graham Plays: 2*. London: Methuen Drama, p.322.

13. Ibid, p.323.
14. Graham, James. 2022. Sherwood. BBC. Episode Four.

CHAPTER 7

Conclusion: The State of the Nation

The collective power of James Graham's work is in its broad-ranging and ongoing state-of-the-nation commentary that explores who holds power in contemporary society, how these organisations and groups sustain control and the extent to which power is shared across a selection of democratic institutions and unelected commercial firms or entities that wield considerable and unaccountable influence. Graham is both historian and analyst in his assessment of power structures, examining not only where these influences exist but using theatre to understand how these came to be. This anatomy of Establishment organisations is diverse, addressing those given power by society to act on behalf of the public, including Parliament, the justice system and the Police, as well as those assuming a level of societal importance through the control and management of information, including how and when that information is shared and in what format. This latter category comprises media organisations, particularly television and newspaper firms who reach far beyond the influence of the traditional holders of democratic influence to engage with voters, and non-voters, influencing the freedom and independence of State functions. Graham's skill and importance as a playwright is in the dispassionate presentation of these discussions, challenging audiences to engage with conceptual notions of power and their often-compromised reality while charting the post-war changes in British society that have shaped the nation today. Often setting his drama in early periods of

© The Author(s), under exclusive license to Springer Nature 259
Switzerland AG 2024
M. Philpott, *James Graham*,
https://doi.org/10.1007/978-3-031-59663-6_7

twentieth-century history, the portrait of Britain that Graham presents is highly complex, complicated by issues of regionalism, class, economic deprivation and inequality that affect the national interest, yet the playwright remains convinced and ever-hopeful that the existing structures and organisations, if managed well, still provide the blueprint for effective social functions. In doing so, the political label often ascribed to his work must be expanded to encompass a much broader concept of state-of-the-nation playwriting.

Playwright and academic Dan Rebellato argues that in the period of Graham's career 'the political context in which the state-of-the-nation play was developed has changed, and as a consequence political theatre has changed.' Arguably, Graham has been at the forefront of this change, blending state-of-the-nation assessment with entertaining and populist approaches to theatre-making. And while Rebellato argues no formal definition of state-of-the-nation playwriting exists, he proposes a set of characteristics that fit the scale and importance of Graham's theatre:

> State-of-the-nation plays tend to be (a) large-cast plays with (b) a panoramic range of public (and sometimes private) settings, employing (c) epic time spans (years rather than hours or days), and (d) usually performed in large theatres, preferably theatres with a national profile.[1]

Joshua Abrams in his analysis of state-of-the-nation plays notes that 'today Britain is filled with questions about the ongoing viability of its political systems and way of life,' a statement that aptly summarises the nature of Graham's drama throughout his career which attempts to 'grapple with these issues and… try to find a productive way forward.'[2] *Dear England* is one of Graham's most acclaimed and popular plays, securing a rapid transfer to the West End soon after opening at the National Theatre in June 2023 and became the first play at the Prince Edward Theatre for 75 years when it opened in October of the same year. Charting the fortunes of Celebrity-Protagonist Gareth Southgate navigating the challenges of being England football manager during three crucial competitions in 2017, 2021 and 2022, *Dear England* has been successful in attracting new audiences to theatre and establishing Graham as a writer with broad popular appeal, earning nominations in nine Whatsonstage Awards categories selected by public vote and winning two Olivier Awards. Popular and political theatre have rarely had the same market in mind; Theatre writer and critic Aleks Sierz in his assessment of popular theatre has considered them quite separate and incompatible forms. Political theatre, Sierz argues in his 2021 text *Good Nights Out: A History of Popular British Theatre Since the Second World War* is 'rarely popular: political theatre is good for you, and therefore often to be avoided' while popular theatre is 'the real thing: people love it, enjoy it, clamour to see it.'[3] Jason Price takes a less divisive view about the forms seeing popular theatre of the kind Graham makes as a route to public engagement with complex societal challenges: 'Given the inherent invitation for participation, the popular theatre's strengths rest in its ability to draw people together and offer up opportunities for fun and/or for reflection upon issues of concern.'[4] Perhaps more skilfully than any other contemporary playwright, Graham has traversed these artificial boundaries by producing work that addresses major national challenges by drawing on popular culture references, from recreations of television gameshow *Who Wants to Be a Millionaire* to the inclusion of recognisable Incidental Celebrity characters, headlines from *The Sun* newspaper to famous political scandals but within an overarching political purpose, and *Dear England* brings the experience of a national sports team to the fore in order to discuss and debate the state of the nation.

Dear England is the culmination of Graham's reflections on twenty-first century Britain and the nature of a complex British identity that is challenged, undermined and simultaneously inspired by its past. As Gareth Southgate selects and works with a generation of young football players drawn from different clubs and with very different backgrounds, the writer actively unpicks the complex construction of class, socio-economic deprivation and feelings of disenfranchisement that distract from national unity or cohesion and repeatedly undermine team performance—the football team acting as proxy for the country. *Dear England* attempts to get to the heart of who we are as a nation, what it means in practice to be English and the issues of representation when few of the players feel any sense of pride in where they are from:

Dele Alli: Milton Keynes.

Jordan Pickford: Washington, Tyne and Wear.

Jordan Henderson: Sunderland. Being able to see the ground over the roof tops. Stadium of light.

> Marcus Rashford: Absolutely folding [sic] people in the streets after school, in Wythenshawe.
>
> Gareth: (*writing some down*) Wythenshawe, exactly, these places we're told sound like shit places -
>
> Eric Didier: Some of them are shit places – Milton Keynes.
>
> Gareth: - but they're our shit places, they're the fans' places.[5]

As with *Sherwood* explored in the previous chapter, Graham uses this discussion to identify the drivers of inequality in Britain particularly in a sport that has a strong working-class community association and is largely the social grouping from which the players are drawn with which they continue to interact throughout the play. And the divided impression of different areas of Britain, of urban decay and the lack of opportunity for collective or personal improvement flows through Graham's work from the circumstances of the central family in *Sons of York*, through the political cycles of decline and abandonment experienced by the Nottinghamshire town represented for decades by David Lyons in *Labour of Love* to the villagers of *Sherwood* enduring the loss of their major industry 30 years before with nothing to replace it. This is the context in which the young player characters including Harry Kane, Dele Alli, Marcus Rashford and Jordan Pickford of *Dear England* grew up, and Graham draws a direct line in the play between the team and the nation's inability to function on a national stage, inhibited and weighed down by the baggage of inequality and social stagnation they carry with them.

What it means to play for a national team thus becomes an incredibly pertinent debate in the highly political context that the writer builds around his characters, and the resultant limitations he imposes upon them. Two of these cut across the motivational conversations that Graham stages in *Dear England*, focusing initially on the idea of 'your' England, unpicking the composition and unbalanced concept of nationhood that the players contend with, leaning into stereotypical dreams about village greens and rolling fields:

> Jordan Pickford: Ok so what, we're just saying words, do we – England, it's, fucking, the Queen, and, cups of tea and –

Harry Maguire: Nowt wrong with a cup of tea, tea's boss.

Jordan Pickford: I would *never* say owt bad about tea, Harry, I'm just saying! –

Physio Phil: Green and pleasant land etcetera.

Gareth: Exactly those – that's what I'm saying, but is that *your* England. I… I don't come from a, a little cottage near a, a village green, I'm proud of that.[6]

Instead, Gareth encourages his team to think about and take pride in the reality of the England they know and are from, using their public position as players to accept and then represent all the things that England really is in the twenty-first century rather than the ungrounded myths and projections inherited from previous generations:

Harry Maguire: I thought 'the past', and the like, the 'weight' of it was the thing we were trying to, like, be 'free' of.

Pippa: But if you know it, it gives you a better chance of owning it. Even – changing it. Like Raheem's saying, we inherit all these symbols and… like this place, named after St George. And the three lions on the shirt, that's –

A few lines later Gareth completes the thought with a call to action:

Gareth: But for you… go out, and represent as you. Connect, with the fans – as *you*. Your roots, stories, truth. Including… social media, if you must -[7]

This is a core theme in Graham's work, exploring the separation between concepts of English and Britishness propagated by governments and media outlets, the bombastic rhetoric used by Eden and his cabinet in *Eden's Empire* (2006) to justify their activities in the Suez Canal, as well as the Leave Campaign orchestrated by Dominic Cummings in *Brexit: The Uncivil War* (2018) explored in the last chapter that, although set 60 years apart, evokes a similar spirit of glory and backwards-looking beliefs in Britain's superiority as a world power, notions that the writer suggests are as deluded in 2016 as they were in 1956. Across his work, and again here in *Dear England*, Graham reiterates the vastly different reality, the physical decline and growing division between the government and the governed in this period that fails to address the pervasive political failures that his work has highlighted. The character of Gareth Southgate adopts the author's voice, encouraging the young players to face the truth of who they are and what their Englishness means as a result. 'The English football team feels perfectly formed to become a metaphor for Englishness, and for the health of the nation, psychologically or otherwise,' Graham explained in a 2023 *Esquire* interview ahead of the play's premiere at the National Theatre, 'it's about how you use institutions as a microcosm for something bigger about our national identity.'[8]

This call for a national self-reckoning contends with the second core idea in *Dear England*, the problems caused by the weight of the past which here is both England's long history and the very specific problems arising from the story of English football in the post-war era. It is Gareth who articulates the alignment of these two inter-related tracks within the play:

> Gareth: England's problem. We're always starting here (*Underlines 'Act Three'*). Everyone wants us to be there already. Because we have all these old stories, about being the Best, being First, that we've absorbed and are trying to recycle, and retell. Because we had one bloody good day in 1966, when no one in this room was even born.
>
> So, we are going to write our own history. Our own story. Which is going to take time.[9]

Graham builds the English football problem into the play far earlier, and like *Eden's Empire*, creates an international stage on which failure has defined both the trajectory of the national team and the careers of individual players, not least Gareth himself who opens *Dear England* with his own penalty miss in 1996, a problem and psychology of failure that haunts the character and the team throughout, unable to entirely shake off this weight to become the team they need to be. Graham aligns this pressure with the country's failure to accept its own changing identity and address the problems of the past:

Pippa: Don't get me wrong, some fear is necessary, of course. But it can force us to make poor decisions. As people, institutions... countries, even. If it comes from a place of panic, frustration, resentment.

For me the real tragedy of fear – if we don't use our power to harness it – is not what it *does* to us. It's what it *takes*....

So much of the modern world now is actually geared around helping to escape decision-making. That's why there's this feeling right now – isn't there. Of 'paralysis', everywhere?[10]

The football team, the nature of government and the nation are facing the same ingrained problems, and the state-of-the-nation assessment Graham provides through the play is the culmination of the writer's work to date.

In the context that *Dear England* presents, there is a direct association between the overwhelming shadow of the 1966 World Cup win which follows the team through the show and the nation's inability to reconcile its own more powerful and Empire-driven past with the complex reality of modern Britain. In both instances, the waning influence of the country is exacerbated by a continued failure to live up to a more illustrious sporting and political past. Across two-decades of writing, there is an identified tension in Graham's work between tradition and change, critical moments at which the nation's development hinges on and is shaped by forces pulling in opposite directions. The Celebrity-Protagonist innovation cycle outlined in Chapter 4 explains the ultimate failure of changemaker characters like Larry Lamb, Charles Ingram and Gore Vidal to control the forces they unleash, often stymied by the traditional socio-political structures in which they operate. In *Dear England*, Graham problematises the national inability to pull forward while looking backwards as a clash between personnel within the England team set-up, both players and staff who refuse to believe in or trust Southgate's more radical psychological approach to training. The young players soon reveal resistance to the new training regime which, like the schoolchildren of *Tory Boyz* explored in the Early Works section repeating political opinions from their parents, reveal inherited ideas about training methodology:

Delle Alli: ... Ok, uh. Well, I don't think *I* want to talk about 'doubts', though. I don't want that in my head. It's about being positive, innit....

Eric Dier: I do think this is bollocks, sorry. Can't we just fucking go train?...

Raheem Sterling: Nah, can I just say, I don't like, need to invite you all into my head, my negative thoughts, Ok. I can handle them my way.[11]

And as a result the culture of the team is slow to change, Graham using the nature of the players' interaction—filled with ribbing and banter which is part of the masculine positioning within the play—as an extension of the troubled and combative discourses that began to normalise in *Best of Enemies* outlined in the Television chapter. What emerges through *Dear England* then is a pointed state-of-the-nation assessment about the reluctance to change, a reliance on tradition and the toxicity of language in which status, difference and individuality are expressed, pulling the team apart rather than uniting them, and us, in a common cause.

In identifying these self-destructive tenets of British identity, Graham's play uses Southgate's model of improvement to posit ways in which England as a nation can also develop by accepting the past and not succumbing to a false psychological pressure to be the nation we (perhaps incorrectly) believe we once were. Much of this emerges from Southgate's attempts to first correct and realign the team's vocabulary, encouraging them to find commonality rather than difference in their experiences of different clubs and places:

Gareth: People of England, listen up!

Players, it has been decided, no longer will you be allowed to just sit in your 'clubs'.

Players: Oh what / Fuck / Noooo.

Gareth: Look at you – City, United, Arsenal, Spurs. You – are – *England*, now. A team. Musical chairs, up on your feet please, move![12]

Later, Graham actively explores the diversity of Englishness represented by the players by drawing attention to the racist and exclusionary responses to their footballing performance as a process of transitioning towards a broader concept of nationality than characters in other Graham plays have experienced:

Raheem Sterling: For me, this stuff happens and we talk about it, and everyone feels good about it, but nothing changes. And today, it's, like, oh well, we are playing abroad, abroad that happens, but I'm like – no. No this happens at home too.

Bukayo Saka: Yeah

Raheem Sterling: But we don't talk about *that*. And I know no one wants to hear *that*.

Jordan Pickford / Harry Kane: I wanta hear about that.

Gareth: And, we can give you whatever back-up, or support you need. As a team.

You all have a right to speak up. We've been giving you these platforms and now… if you can use them, to say what you really wanta say. I'll stand alongside you, and speak up too.[13]

There are direct allusions here to the exclusiveness of privilege outlined in *Monster Raving Loony* in which politicians are shown to share a similar class and educational experience (see Chapter 3) to prevent 'others' from entering the Establishment. This closing of ranks pushed *Ink* Celebrity-Protagonist Larry Lamb to innovative extremes to claim his place in a closed world (see Chapter 4), but Graham suggests, it is only by embracing the reality, merits and demography of modern Britain can the nation both accept itself and move forward. This culminates in Gareth's titular 'Dear England' letter published widely in the media in 2021 which is given a central part in the play, a rare but important soliloquy of a length not seen in Graham's work since *The Angry Brigade*:

Gareth: It's been an extremely difficult time. It's given us all a new understanding of the fragility of life. In the grand scheme of things, perhaps football doesn't seem so important. And what I want to speak about is much bigger than football…

I tell my players that what they are a part of, what we are all a part of, is an experience that lasts in the collective consciousness of our country….

It's about how we conduct ourselves, And how we bring people together. That lasts beyond the summer. That lasts forever...[14]

The writer finds considerable resonance in his character's call for tolerance and mindfulness, and through the dramatic staging of this play makes *Dear England* his own 'Dear England' letter to the country, echoing Southgate's sentiments in a similar call for tolerance and engagement with the reality and problems of contemporary England. While other Graham plays address the solutions for improving the resilience of State functions and increasing trust in the political and judicial framework discussed later in this chapter, *Dear England* prioritises a shift in our engagement with the national representatives of Englishness, a personal and individual responsibility to absorb the lessons of the play and be better. The popular appeal of *Dear England* and the broad audience attracted to it, present an opportunity to more widely share the hopeful and optimistic messaging that ultimately underpins Graham's work.

7.1 Working-Class Masculinity as the State of the Nation

One of the core experiences that Graham has charted in his work is the changing and evolving nature of working-class masculinity across the post-war era, explored through his character experiences and activities within multiple dramas. From *Sons of York* set in 1978 to *Boys from the Blackstuff* set in 1982 and *Dear England* taking place from 2017 to 2022, the economic restrictions of Britain are reflected in the opportunities available to male characters in Graham's plays and the very different ways in which society responds to them. Across the canon of work, definitions and limitations applied to working-class masculinity are synonymous with state-of-the-nation experiences as a whole and go to the heart of Graham's work on this topic, explaining the power dynamics that work across society—whether legitimately delegated or assumed by unelected corporations—and examining the consequences for the men in his plays. They explain the trickle-down effect of decision-making and theoretical discussions about public policy over more than 70 years and its consequences for the declining structures within which working-class manliness operates.

In *Sons of York*, discussed in detail in Chapter 1, the men of the family depicted find themselves at the centre of a significant change moment where older forms of masculinity reliant on inheriting professions, a stability of economic circumstances and a belief in hierarchical structures within families leant heavily on traditions and practices handed down between generations. Set on the cusp of the Thatcher era, much of what the older characters experienced and relied on is about to be shaken up by a Conservative government that sought to reform industrial employment across Britain, and it was a frustration that explodes into domestic violence within the play. The consequences of those policy decisions and the significant effect it had on the lives of ordinary men is subsequently explored in *Boys from the Blackstuff*, a unique example in Graham's work to date of a fictional television story by another writer being adapted for the stage. Based on the five-part series shown in 1982, there are considerable commonalities across the themes, focus and ideas expressed in Alan Bleasdale's and Graham's dramas forty years apart, making *Boys from the Blackstuff* an important collaboration in the wider development of the latter's state-of-the-nation drama. As Nicholas Holden shows, 'working-class communities were subject to widespread hardship, as the economic policies of the 1980s and 1990s decimated industry and plunged huge numbers of the population into unemployment with little sign of support from the established Conservative government.'[15]

Premiering at Liverpool Royal Court in September 2023 and set entirely in the city, *Boys from the Blackstuff* finds strong resonance between the play's early-1980s setting and the present day in which economic restrictions and the impact of national political policy have direct implications for ordinary working people. Having established an imbalance of power across State functions and influential global companies, this is the first example in Graham's major works where the impact of those structures and policymaking approaches are shown from the perspective of working-class experience, extending work undertaken in both his Early Works and more recently in *Sherwood*. *Boys from the Blackstuff* follows five men—Chrissie, Yosser, George, Dixie and Loggo—as they navigate unemployment and pursuit by State officials working for the Dole Office who are keen to prove the men are employed illegally and whose weekly maintenance payments can be halted as a result. The original television series delved into the wider story of each character in turn, studying the personal circumstances driving their behaviour and the extremes to which long-term unemployment had led them. Like *Labour of Love* and *Sherwood*, it is the closure of traditional means of employment—here the docks and construction opportunities—instigated by Margaret

Thatcher's first period in office from 1978 to 1983 that sits under the events of this story, ending the certainty of life-long employment in core industries and putting inherited ties with previous generations under strain when fathers and sons can no longer work in the same occupation—concerns that have punctuated Graham's work throughout his career. The collaboration with Bleasdale is an important one and *Boys from the Blackstuff* is the place where the two writers meet, Graham recasting the structure of the television series and adding new material while retaining Bleasdale's compassionate advocacy of working-class decency. 'It was about giving a sense of the whole city – and also I wanted to see if I could write an Alan Bleasdale scene. It was almost like listening to Alan's music, pressing pause and seeing if I could continue the tune,' Graham explained in an interview for *The Guardian* in September 2023, something Bleasdale affirms: 'When I read the scripts. I realised James had seen things about the city that I hadn't. And it's because I live here.'[16]

Rearranging the anthological nature of the television series into a sequential drama with multiple perspectives, the characters in Graham's version of the story are living out the consequences of political and social failure with important implications for both their inherited notions of masculinity and associated English and British identities. Completing the thought began in *Sons of York*, different kinds of masculinity interact across the play as characters from multiple generations cross paths in the search for work. The sense of frustrated impotence resulting from the inability to shape their own lives or even to have choice about it cuts across the drama as they all experience the closing down of opportunity and a growing reliance on State functions that are increasingly suspicious of their desire for financial support. Like Terry in *Sons of York* who clings to traditional beliefs about a better life in the past, the men in *Boys from the Blackstuff* celebrate a working connection that bought them together and appears fundamental to the types of masculinity they represent, one couched in a sense of dignity and pride arising from their ability to earn wages legitimately to support their families. As Graham's work has demonstrated throughout his career, poor male behaviour and even violence stem from challenges to this ability to exert control over their lives and throughout *Boys from the Blackstuff* the friends are pushed to different, often moving, extremes of desperation as they struggle to control their impulses with significant implications for their family lives and their own equanimity. 'What I took most from Alan was his challenging of the cliche of how working-class people express themselves,'

Graham explained, 'they are lyrical and articulate and humorous and emotional – and that's what Alan showed in these characters. And I wanted that in this.'[17]

The action takes place in a series of male spaces that are emblematic of state-of-the-nation concerns including construction sites, public houses and crucially the Dole Office where many of the constrictions on the freedom of the men are applied. The economic struggle to afford basic living costs and the deep suspicions of State actors and the ways in which working-class characters are demonised has particular resonance in contemporary Britain and Graham retains a compassionate impression of characters much as Bleasdale had done 40 years earlier:

> We technically have very low unemployment – although the stats are complicated. But clearly there are huge issues of quality of life, job security and wealth inequality. The circumstances differ but the despair is the same. During the run of our show, the Labour party conference will gather here in Liverpool and ask: 'What do we want to do and why?' This is the time to ask those questions.[18]

Central to this is the depiction of challenged masculinity that references *Sons of York* in the, sometimes exploding, violence and eventual confrontation across the events of the play. In this presentation of struggling masculinity as a proxy for the state of the nation, two ideas emerge that are resonant across Graham's collective works. The first is the backwards-looking notion of a better world lost, recalled by the men in conversation, a sense shared with many characters in Graham's work. It is depicted starkly in the conversation between George and Chrissie at the side of the Mersey, the former union leader, held in great acclaim by his companion, who makes a pointed statement about national failure. The second is a challenge to male mental health through the sensitively told story of Yosser Hughes, given a far larger and more nuanced role in Graham's drama.

The character is both Bleasdale's and Graham's representation of the State's constriction of working-class men, a character who struggles to support his young family and unable to find work due to the removal of his trade-based skillset when both tarmacking and construction work become economically non-viable. Yosser is most overtly ground down by the activities of the play, and Graham expands a Bleasdale scene in which Yosser visits the Catholic church conceived in the television series to include a counterpart in the Protestant church as part of Yosser's search for help, believing that even God has abandoned him and his family. Yosser's deteriorating mental health is portrayed with sensitivity and compassion by Graham, and although this escalates into Terry-like violence, echoing concerns about undirected male anger expressed in *Sons of York*, it also extends discussions begun in *Dear England* about the implications of social and economic failure on ordinary people. As Bleasdale notes in an interview for The Observer 'perhaps the biggest sadness for me is that in the 40 years since I wrote Blackstuff, we might have hoped that things would get better.'[19] The social decay that Graham's work has charted across his career, the failure of institutions with legitimately delegated power to improve the lived experience of those in Britain, is manifest in the pressures exerted on the mental health of his characters in *Boys from the Blackstuff* and *Dear England* in which the struggles they experience are a direct result of those pulses in society embedding the issues that prevent society from developing:

> Gareth: We're – 'stuck'. Doesn't it feel like we're, like, stuck? Unable to, to – move on, move forward?
>
> And, and it's more than just a series of – setback. More than tactics, talent, technique. I think - ... I think we *all* have a problem, with what it means to be England, at the moment.'[20]

This charting of working-class experience through changing conceptions of masculinity is an important marker of state-of-the-nation analysis in Graham's work, and across his collected plays reflections on Britishness, national identity and the cycles of decline deterring social development have revealed embedded and complex power structures that have affected society. A growing separation between the government and the governed has created cycles of decline experienced by the characters in each of Graham's plays are at the heart of the writer's state-of-the-nation assessment with *Dear England* and *Boys from the Blackstuff* analysing the consequences for working people and the changed nature of British and English identities in the twenty-first century.

> Pippa: Collective trauma is real, it can get passed down through people, it – it sits, in a place, in its walls. Its streets. It can pass through... well, the 'soul'...[21]

Both plays highlight a sense of nationhood built on a backwards-looking reliance on tradition and custom that shape behaviours and responses to change and are at the heart of the challenges facing a country that, as *Dear England* suggests, needs to accept all of the urban faces that constitute modern Britain and the more diverse forms of Britishness that exist. As the character of Gareth Southgate insists 'England needs – a new story.'[22]

7.2 Britain Today

So, what does Britain mean today and is there any real notion of British identity in the twenty-first century? Graham's collective works present a fractured and difficult picture of a country held back by its past. The romantic and glorious picture of empire, control and the disproportionate influence of Britain in the world evoke feelings of pride but these are somewhat mythological ideas of a past that exists largely beyond living memory and are often hijacked for political purposes. Graham outlines the consequences of Britain's inability to live up to this hollow version of its past, but it has been a driving force in society since the Second World War, this work argues, shaping national responses to everything from the Suez Crisis depicted in *Eden's Empire* to the national football team's cohesion in *Dear England*, a persistent social driver that sits at the heart of who Britain thinks it is and appears to be handed down from generation to generation, bolstered by media influences such as newspaper headlines and judgements about State policy and purpose that actively shape public debate and concepts of identity in the twenty-first century. That this unlikely ideal results only in continual disappointment and further decline is clear in Graham's work, suggesting how deeply rooted this misplaced belief has become. Graham shows how this problematic idealism drives government policy, public responses and community apathy in a country that strives to recreate its illustrious past but feels disconnected and disenchanted with authority systems when the Elysian Fields never bloom. Between the changing administrations, social developments and economic shifts that characterise the post-war era, the notion that Britain was better 'before,' a persistent but largely unspecified time, that there was a period when everything was alright and now it is not. In Graham's 2018 play *The Culture* set in Hull during the handover of its City of Culture status, local volunteer Gerald explains:

> Gerald: I just meant it's been a long time since I felt a part of anything. Any purpose. And... You know, thirty years ago, you'd walk down Hessle Road, on your three days of dry land, pub to pub, The Anchor. Rayner's, everyone'd know you, stop to say hello, before it all changed, things stopped. Folk... 'retreated', back inside, shut the curtains, stopped...[23]

Some of that, the character of Janice intimates, is the result of globalisation and an encouragement to move away from traditional communities. 'That's the problem with expanding people's horizons,' she argues, 'they see the horizon and they want to bloody go there.'[24] But it is also the outcome of the very traditional concept of society that Graham writes about with its ancient buildings that contain centuries of expectation about how things ought to be. This deference to tradition sits across Graham's work from the ancient functioning of Parliamentary democracy to rituals and ceremony that still elicit individual and national pride, explained by Lennie a Yeoman Warden at the Tower of London in *Sketching*:

> Lennie: ...that's not just wearing a silly red uniform for tourists, it, it, it it's a service! An ancient service! You don't get to be the Raven Master if you haven't proven yourself, I've *proven* myself, I've *repented*![25]

Likewise in *This House*, Labour Whip Cocks speaks of similar traditions that have been absorbed into the fabric of British identity:

> Cocks: The Ayrton Light, above the clock. Shines when Parliament is seated; put out when it rises. Lots of funny rules and traditions here, you'll start to learn.[26]

In the segue between Act One and Act Two when the clock malfunctions, Cocks returns to the clocktower to strengthen its importance:

> Clockmaker: It's a clock, Mr Cocks. They break. What's it matter?

> Cocks: What's it...?! Ha ha, yes, no you're right, not important, eh, it's not a, a, symbol of anything, doesn't mean anything, only carried on ticking through all the bloody, all the great wars, the biggest crises, any time our backs were against the wall, oh yeah.[27]

The tradition inherent in British State functions is an important theme in Graham's work, examining the connection and consistency with past values that they embody but also their more complex role in a modern society struggling to operate. Whether these inherited practices define Britain, provide the boundaries for its functions or hinder its development is a constant tension across the writer's work as characters utilise and chafe against these practices:

> Silvester: I can see why he's so worked up, all that ceremonial stuff. I wish we could just do away with it. Modernise the place, make it more professional, less… less –
>
> Atkins: I sympathise, Fred, I do, but remember, we are gloriously unique, this country, in not having a written constitution. What we do have are *traditions*, gentlemen's agreements. They help us do what we do best. Muddle through.[28]

The discussion from *This House* precedes further debate about accepted customs of democracy that form part of the organisational identity of Parliament, with dissent labelled as ungentlemanly and, by extension, not in keeping with solid British values of decency and fair play:

> Silvester: Some might wonder why on earth we should be taking so many of our boys out.
>
> Harper: Yeah, they might. But they wouldn't be people of honour, would they? Upholding an age-old tradition.[29]

Conservative Whip, Weatherill, feels the restrictive pressure of those expectations when he exclaims 'oh "centuries old", "thousand years old", "you can't do this", "must do that",'[30] and it is a thought echoed by anarchist The Prophet in *The Angry Brigade* when questioned by The Branch, choosing to reflect on the power that tradition exerts on society and its role in maintaining public order:

> The Prophet: We cannot fight against that which will not fight back. Other countries, we charge, they charge back. But you lot. You just wouldn't bloody do it. You just wouldn't ruddy let go. You stand there, rigid, in

your lines. It's as if you know. It's as if it ran through your veins. The lines will hold. They've held for centuries. Nothing to see here.[31]

Tradition as an active form of social control is similarly evoked by Snooty in *Monster Raving Loony* in response to Sutch's schoolboy belief that the Second World War provided an opportunity to start again. 'Well. My father says the most important thing is – tradition,' he states.[32] Yet, Graham's work shows that it remains important, essential even to national character and conduct, so whether an inspiration or a burden, tradition is so tightly woven into modern British society that living without it is inconceivable, or, as Sutch's mother Annie notes: 'You need all this old junk as much as me, and you know it.'[33]

As a result of this dependence on and refusal to depart from tradition, Britain is a country enduring cycles of decline punctuated by short-lived moments of hope such as the arrival of a Data Centre in *Labour of Love* designed to bring prosperity to a former mining community. Yet traditions only mask the fact that very little changes for ordinary people and the status quo always resumes with those in power seeking only to reinforce their position at the expense of other communities, a state-of-the-nation assessment explained by fishmonger Phil in *Sketching*:

> Phil: It's them up there what's fucked it for you, boy. When they fuck up, up there, we get fucked down here, that's how it works. Trickle-down-fucking they call it. And your generation, you're at the bottom of the pyramid, you get all the shit.
>
> When I was your age, you could go into a trade, profession, work your way up, pride, job security. Now look at yer. Zero hours, moved here, moved there, tossed around like a salmon in a net. You have my sympathy.

Graham's character inherited his profession from his father but the rapid changes in modern British society have created a shift from manual industries to elite financial services that has also altered the physical shape of London, creating a sense of tangible loss for traditional communities pushed aside by this new focus:

> Phil: Hundreds of years ago, ships would bring in food, spices, gold and silver to this dock.

Now up there, in them towers, they trade them, but it ain't real, it's imagined, they never touch it, they never smell it, they never see it, and that's why the whole thing got fucked, 'cause it ain't real. Down here, this market, these fish, they're real.[34]

And it likewise shifted not only where people live but the ways in which people live alongside one another. Referencing Hilary's speech in *The Angry Brigade* about the replicated flats she observes from the bus stop, Graham includes a similar exchange in *Sketching* in a sequence describing the journey Phil takes to work:

Actor Four: He looks up at the passing skyscrapers, now lining the bankside –

Phil: Ugly fucking things.

Actor One: New apartments, rising up, up, ones he could never afford himself.

Actor Four: Barely any of the lights on. No bugger home.

Actor Five: Well yeah, 'cause they *aren't* homes, are they. They're 'safety deposit boxes' for the super-rich, in lands far away.[35]

These examples explain how power has narrowed its focus through the control of assets, moving opportunity away from traditional communities and instead emphasising a volatile economic prosperity based on an 'invisible' trade. And this feeling of powerlessness extends far beyond London characterised by a feeling of decline and stagnation across the country. 'It's not the getting things wrong that's the problem,' Ian St Clair in Sherwood complains, 'it's the sweeping under the carpet and refusing to look at it and learn from it.'[36] Likewise, the monitoring and evaluation officer in *The Culture*, summarises inhabitants' opinions of Hull before its City of Culture status, but Lizzie's assessment could equally apply to many similar places that have experienced years of underfunding and dismissal in the national picture:

Lizzie: Because internal pride from residents towards their city was, was low. Hull – geographically, politically, culturally – has often felt 'excluded'. You know, the whole end-of-the-line thing.'[37]

What emerges strongly across Graham's work, then, is an impression of a nation divided on several fronts and primarily between the government and the governed in which political elites have presided over a sustained and largely unchecked period of decay that has created further separation between those with power and those without it. And while Phil in *Sketching* observes the rise of financial services in London as one of the causes of that distance, very little has changed in the rest of the country or has become progressively worse in both an economic and social sense with communities fractured by the outcomes of government policies as David Lyons explains to a Chinese investor in an exchange from *Labour of Love* set in 2011:

> David: We... areas like this, the economic down- ... we're particularly vulnerable, with so many jobs in the public sector, to cuts from this new government, it's the same cycle we went through, areas like this, under the *last* Tory governments, time and time again, and –
>
> Shen: Since the quarry closed, and before that the coal mines – the main source of employment has been these new government centres, am I right?

And Shen goes further a few lines summarising the futility of government policy in David's constituency that has achieved very little lasting change for residents:

> Shen: So, before, there was government money pouring into these quarries, and mines, across the land, digging for things you no longer needed. Your answer was to fill in those holes and build on top these 'centres'. Which you didn't really need. And... now they're closing too? Is that not work for work's sake?[38]

Graham's collective works have powerful messages about the true state of the nation particularly for working-class communities across the country where the sticking plaster approach of successive government policy has created cycles of failure so deeply rooted that real change seems a remote possibility.

Graham's importance as a playwright has been in consistently and clearly articulating contemporary disillusionment with the effectiveness of the State to solve problems it has been directly responsible for causing, exacerbated by the assumed and unchecked authority of the media in actively manipulating and polarising public discourses to drive its unaccountable commercial agenda. Together these dual forces acting on society are directly responsible for Britain's obsession with tradition, custom and belief in the country's lost greatness. In *This House*, two narratives run in parallel—the increasing chaos of the incumbent government trying to keep its weakened administration afloat by any means necessary, and the symbolic importance of the clocktower acting as a proxy for British identity. This is an important track in Graham's work suggesting the enduring value of this emblematic and steadfast asset which is only enhanced by the short-termist and desperate manoeuvring of the Labour Whips to preserve a temporary power that they will inevitably lose while the clocktower remains. And this idea recurs frequently in these plays as groups feel increasingly left behind or excluded, they cling harder to notions of how Britain used to be and the traditions or belief that everything was better. When Charles Ingram leans into his military life for reassurance and stability of purpose during the traumatic events of *Quiz* or when Hugh Cudlipp and his fellow Fleet Street editors cling to the old ways of print journalism in a time of populist flux in *Ink*, even when the devastated villagers in Sherwood seek the collective reassurance of their old union allegiances giving them a clear sense of belonging to something or when Hull volunteer Gerald wistfully remembers the friendly neighbourhood he still yearns for, these are people seeking comfort in an idea of Britain's shared past where rules and expectations felt much clearer and every generation could expect to live like its predecessors. Graham argues that those notions persist because post-war Britain brought and continues to bring uncertainty against which a collective faith in the past is the only refuge—the same desire for constancy and control that became a political driver in *Brexit: The Uncivil War*. To be British in the twenty-first century is to look to this romantic and simpler version of the past because the reality of what Britain is today and how to fix it is too difficult to comprehend.

The result is to make modern Britain a very fragile place, a word that recurs with some frequency across the writer's plays as the established institutions, systems and practices that Graham examines feel the weight of a vastly changed society. Even the most ancient (another term that occurs again and again) establishments feel more vulnerable now than they ever did and while democracy overcomes anarchic incursions from citizens, the assumed power of media and data management platforms present a far greater threat to the effective government of the country and its concept of justice. But Graham also argues that democracy is under threat from its own processes and, crucially, its personnel who seek to fulfil individual ambition or enrichment at the expense of the national interest. Graham's plays are peopled by councillors and politicians seeking advancement to different roles that bring additional power and influence, while the nature of fixed-term Parliaments prevents any long-term national planning or investment. Instead, it supports only a desire for re-election. The ease with which human beings can derail the processes of democracy is the subject of Graham's drama through deliberate actions, chaotic reaction, accident or purposeful criminal intent and so it makes the structures and institutions stagnate, weak to the threat posed by those bigger forces who want to harness democratic influence for commercial or personal gain and therefore unable to respond to the demands of modern society, tackle the decades of decline or repel attack on its integrity.

This collective analysis of the failures of modern Britain may seem insurmountable with its disenfranchised communities, cycles of decline, separation between the Establishment and ordinary working people, and the destabilising effect of distinct democratic functions by global media corporations, but Graham is ultimately an optimist, believing that the State could function as it should if the effect of human error and ambition were reduced. 'It has to *mean* something… right?' Presiding Officer Stephen asks in *The Vote*, 'It has to matter,'[39] a sentiment echoed by Labour Whip Harrison in *This House*:

> Harrison: Do you know, I think it'd all work fine, this thing. British democracy. If it weren't so damn reliant on *people*.[40]

Sam makes a similar statement of faith towards the end of *Tory Boyz*:

> Sam: But I *have* to believe that every day, in little ways… I have to believe that things can get better. That tomorrow will be better than today.[41]

And Woodley QC says it best of all at the end of *Quiz*:

> Woodley QC: I work in the law. And I have to believe in – 'rationality'. In finding quantifiable truths based in evidence.

I have to believe in the institutions we trust to be fair and functional. Whether that be the judiciary, the police, the media... That they should all be able to resist the temptations of a more entertaining lie, over a less extraordinary truth.[42]

And this is Graham's significance as a state-of-the-nation playwright, not only in holding up a mirror to our times to expose the dysfunction and decline that hampers modern Britain, but in showing that mechanisms already exist to make things better; we just need to find a way to make them worthy of our trust once more.

Notes

1. Rebellato, Dan. From the State-of-the-Nation to Globalization: Shifting Political Agendas in Contemporary British Playwriting. In Edited by Holdsworth, Nadine and Luckhurst, Mary. 2008. *A Concise Companion to Contemporary British and Irish Drama*. London: Blackwell Publishing, pp.245–246.
2. Abrams, Joshua. 2010. State-of-the-Nation: New British Theatre. *Performing Arts Journal*, 32:2.
3. Sierz, Aleks. 2021. *Good Nights Out: A History of Popular British Theatre Since the Second World War*. London: Methuen Drama, p.2.
4. Price, Jason. 2016. *Modern Popular Theatre*. London: Palgrave, pp.183–184.
5. Graham, James. 2023. *Dear England*. Act Two, Scene One, pp.66–67.
6. Ibid, p.66.
7. Ibid, pp.68–69.
8. Collinge, Miranda. 2023. Playwright James Graham on 'Dear England' and the "Shakespearean" Gareth Southgate. *Esquire*, June 2, https://www.esquire.com/uk/culture/a44066219/james-graham-dear-england-gareth-southgate-play/.
9. Graham, James. 2023. *Dear England*. Act One, Scene Three, p.32.
10. Ibid, Act One, Scene Two, pp.17–18.
11. Ibid, Act One, Scene Three, pp.33–34.
12. Ibid, Act One, Scene Four, p.43.
13. Ibid, Act Two, Scene Three, p.79.
14. Ibid, Act Two, Scene Three, p.80.

15. Holden, Nicholas. In Graham, James. 2021. *This House (Student Editions)*. London: Methuen Drama.
16. Lawson, Mark. 2023. 'The Despair Is the Same': Alan Bleasdale and James Graham on Bringing Back Boys from the Blackstuff. *The Guardian*, September 15, https://www.theguardian.com/stage/2023/sep/15/the-despair-is-the-same-alan-bleasdale-and-james-graham-on-bringing-back-boys-from-the-blackstuff.
17. Ibid.
18. Ibid.
19. Thorpe, Vanessa. 2022. Go on, Gizza Play: Boys from the Blackstuff Lives Again—On Stage. *The Observer*, July 2, https://www.theguardian.com/stage/2022/jul/02/go-on-gizza-play-boys-from-the-blackstuff-lives-again-on-stage.
20. Graham, James. 2023. *Dear England*. Act One, Scene One, p.9.
21. Ibid, Act One, Scene Three, p.39.
22. Ibid, Act One, Scene Three, p.31.
23. Graham, James. 2018. *The Culture*. London: Methuen Drama. Act Two, pp.71–72.
24. Ibid, Act Two, p.72.
25. Graham, James. Peter Piper has a Plan. In Graham, James, et al. 2018. *Sketching*. London: Methuen Drama, p.21.
26. Graham, James. *This House*, Prologue. In Graham, James. 2016. *James Graham Plays: 2*, London: Methuen Drama. p.15.
27. Ibid, Act Two, Scene One, p.68.
28. Ibid, Act One, Scene Three, p.42.
29. Ibid, Act One, Scene Four, p.51.
30. Ibid, Act One, Scene Five, p.66.
31. Graham, James. *The Angry Brigade*, The Branch. In Graham, James. 2016. p.148.
32. Graham, James. *Monster Raving Loony*. Part One. In Graham, James. 2016. p.325.
33. Ibid, Part Two, p.363.
34. Graham, James. Peter Piper has a Plan. In Graham, James, et al. 2018. p.23.
35. Ibid, pp.17–18.
36. Graham, James. *Sherwood*. 2022. BBC. Episode 4.
37. Graham, James. 2018. *The Culture*. Act Two, p.83.
38. Graham, James. 2022. *Labour of Love*. Act One, Scene Two, pp.26–27.

39. Graham, James. *The Vote*. Part Four. In Graham, James. 2016, p.312.
40. Graham, James. *This House*. Act Two, Scene Five. In Graham, James. 2016, p.115.
41. Graham, James. *Tory Boyz*, In Graham, James. 2012, p.60.
42. Graham, James. 2018. *Quiz*, London: Methuen Drama. Act Two, p.99.

Bibliography

Plays

Graham, James. 2005. *Albert's Boy*. London: Methuen Drama.
Graham, James. 2022. *Best of Enemies*. London: Methuen Drama.
Graham, James. 2023. *Dear England*. London: Methuen Drama.
Graham James. 2006. *Eden's Empire*. London: Methuen Drama.
Graham, James. 2017. *Ink*. London: Methuen Drama.
Graham, James. 2022. *Labour of Love*. London: Methuen Drama.
Graham, James. 2012. *James Graham: Plays: 1*. London: Methuen Drama.
Graham James. 2016. *James Graham: Plays 2*. London: Methuen Drama.
Graham, James. 2018. *Quiz*. London: Methuen Drama.
Graham, James. 2018. *The Culture*. London: Methuen Drama.
Graham, James. 2013. *This House*. London: Methuen Drama.
Graham James. Edited by Holden, Nicholas. 2021. *This House (Student Editions)*. London: Methuen Drama.
Graham, James. Westerman, Naomi., Srivastav, Sumerah, Ojha, Himanshu, Langley, Ella, Mi Lin Ewart, Chloe, Gordon, Alan, Hughes, Adam, Douglas, Aaron. 2018. *Sketching*. London: Methuen Drama.

Books

Adiseshiah, Sian and Lepage, Louise. (Editors). 2016. *Twenty-First Century Drama: What Happens Now*. London: Palgrave.
Bennett, Susan and Massai, Sonia. (Editors). 2018. *Ivo van Hove: From Shakespeare to David Bowie*. London: Methuen Drama.

© The Editor(s) (if applicable) and The Author(s), under exclusive license to Springer Nature Switzerland AG 2024
M. Philpott, *James Graham*,
https://doi.org/10.1007/978-3-031-59663-6

Billington, Michael. 2022. *Affair of the Heart*. London: Bloomsbury.
Billington, Michael 2009. *State of the Nation: British Theatre Since 1945*. London: Faber and Faber.
Christie, Ian and van den Oever, Annie. (Editors). 2018. *Stories: Screen Narrative in the Digital Era*. Amsterdam University Press.
Deeney, John F. and Gale, Maggie B. (Editors). 2015. *Fifty Modern and Contemporary Dramatists*, London: Routledge.
Esslin, Martin. 1978. *Pinter: A Study of His Plays*. London: Eyre Methuen.
Grochala, Sarah. 2017. *The Contemporary Political Play: Rethinking Dramaturgical Structure*, London: Bloomsbury.
Holdsworth, Nadine and Luckhurst, Mary. (Editors). 2008. *A Concise Companion to Contemporary British and Irish Drama*. London: Blackwell Publishing.
Klaic, Dragan. 2012. *Resetting the Stage: Public Theatre Between the Market and Democracy*. Intellect.
Lonergan, Patrick. 2012. *The Theatre and Films of Martin McDonagh*. London: Bloomsbury.
Luckhurst, Mary. 2006. *Dramaturgy: A Revolution in Theatre*. Cambridge: Cambridge University Press.
Middeke, Martin, Scnierer, Peter P. and Sierz, Aleks. (Editors). 2011. *The Methuen Guide to Contemporary British Playwrights*. London: Bloomsbury.
Price, Jason. 2016. *Modern Popular Theatre*. London: Palgrave.
Rebellato, Dan. (Editor). 2013. *Modern British Playwrighting 2000–2009*. London: Bloomsbury.
Sierz, Aleks. 2021. *Good Nights Out: A History of Popular British Theatre Since the Second World War*. London: Methuen Drama.
Sierz, Aleks. 2011. *Rewriting the Nation: British Theatre Today*. London: Bloomsbury.
Turner, Alwyn. 2021. *All in it Together: England in the 21st Century*. London: Profile Books Ltd.
Woffinden, Bob and Plaskett, James. 2015. *Bad Show*. Bojangles Press.

Articles, Interviews and Reviews

Abrams, Joshua. 2010. State-of-the-Nation: New British Theatre. *A Journal of Performance and Art*, 32:2.
Adiseshiah, Sian. 2013. The Revolution will not be Dramatized: The Problem of Mediation in Caryl Churchill's Revolution Plays. *Hungarian Journal of English and American Studies (HJEAS)*. Fall 19:2.
Adiseshiah, Sian. 2005. Utopian Space in Caryl Churchill's History Plays: Light Shining in Buckinghamshire and Vinegar Tom. *Utopian Studies*, 16:1.

Almeida Theatre YouTube Channel. 2019. Anne Washburn and James Graham in Conversation: Writing Political Theatre, https://www.youtube.com/watch?v=OcTFetDoxqc&ab_channel=AlmeidaTheatre.

Aspden, Peter. 2022. When American ideologies collide: James Graham on his play Best of Enemies. *Financial Times*, November 10, https://www.ft.com/content/90a535fb-d96d-4281-818b-63f72fecbf0f.

Billington, Michael.2017. Quiz review—James Graham explores the thin line between courtroom and showbiz. *The Guardian*, November 12, https://www.theguardian.com/stage/2017/nov/12/quiz-review-exploration-of-the-thin-line-between-courtroom-and-showbusiness.

Billington, Michael. 2008. Sons of York. *The Guardian*, September 8, https://www.theguardian.com/stage/2008/sep/08/theatre2.

Cavendish, Dominic. 2010. The Man at Finborough Theatre, Review. *The Telegraph*, June 2, https://www.telegraph.co.uk/culture/theatre/theatre-reviews/7797433/The-Man-at-Finborough-Theatre-review.html.

Channel 4. 2018. Interview With Writer James Graham for Brexit: The Uncivil War. *Channel4.com*, December 28, https://www.channel4.com/press/news/interview-writer-james-graham-brexit-uncivil-war.

Clapp, Susannah. 2017. Labour of Love Review—The Left Does the Splits Gracefully. *The Observer*, October 8, https://www.theguardian.com/stage/2017/oct/08/labour-of-love-review-james-graham-martin-freeman-tamsin-greig.

Collinge, Melinda. 2023. Playwright James Graham on 'Dear England' and the 'Shakespearean' Gareth Southgate. *Esquire*, June 2, https://www.esquire.com/uk/culture/a44066219/james-graham-dear-england-gareth-southgate-play/.

Crompton, Sarah. 2021. Best of Enemies Review—James Graham is Back, Doing What He Does Best. *Whatsonstage*, December 10, https://www.whatsonstage.com/news/best-of-enemies-review-james-graham-is-back-ng-what-he-does-best_55516/.

Crompton, Sarah. 2017. Review Quiz (Minerva Theatre, Chichester). *Whatsonstage*, November 11, https://www.whatsonstage.com/news/review-quiz-minerva-theatre-chichester_45120/.

Gardner, Lynne. 2013. Tory Boyz—Review. *The Guardian*, October 3, https://www.theguardian.com/stage/2013/oct/03/tory-boyz-review-gay-tories-westminster.

Graham, James. 2022. I Wrote Sherwood as a Warning. When Communities are Divided, the Pain Endures. *The Guardian*, June 29, https://www.theguardian.com/commentisfree/2022/jun/29/sherwood-communities-divided-miners-strike-brexit-rail-dispute.

Graham, James. 2017. What Happens to Trust and Truth When Justice and Entertainment Combine? *Quiz*. Theatre Programme, Chichester Festival Theatre.

Herrin, Jeremy. 2022. *Best of Enemies*. Theatre Programme, Noel Coward Theatre.

Grochala, Sarah. "Conclusion." *The Contemporary Political Play: Rethinking Dramaturgical Structure*. London: Bloomsbury Methuen Drama,

Holdsworth, Nadine. 2021. Disrupting Monopoly: Homelessness, Gamification and Learned Resourcefulness. *The Journal of Applied Theatre and Performance*, 26:1.

Lawson, Mark. 2023. The Despair is the Same': Alan Bleasdale and James Graham on Bringing Back Boys from the Blackstuff. *The Guardian*, September 15, https://www.theguardian.com/stage/2023/sep/15/the-despair-is-the-same-alan-bleasdale-and-james-graham-on-bringing-back-boys-from-the-blackstuff.

Lukowski, Andrzej. 2016. Monster Raving Loony. *Time Out*, May 18, https://www.timeout.com/london/theatre/monster-raving-loony

Mahoney, Elisabeth. 2009. A History of Falling Things. *The Guardian*, May 16, https://www.theguardian.com/stage/2009/may/16/review-history-falling-things.

Manzoor, Sarfraz. 2018. James Graham Interview: My Town Was One of the Top 10 that Voted Leave—I Have to Represent Both Sides. *The Standard*, September 20, https://www.standard.co.uk/lifestyle/james-graham-interview-my-town-was-one-of-the-top-10-that-voted-leave-i-have-to-represent-both-sides-a3938766.html.

Pressley, Nelson. 2018. The British Political Comedy 'Labour of Love' Translates Well in its U.S. Debut. *The Washington Post*, October 1, https://www.washingtonpost.com/entertainment/theater_dance/the-british-political-comedy-labour-of-love-translates-well-in-its-us-debut/2018/10/01/a86fee52-c574-11e8-b1ed-1d2d65b86d0c_story.html.

Rawnsley Andrew. 2015. Writer James Graham Talks to Andrew Rawnsley About His TV Drama Coalition: 'I Love Humanising Politics'. *The Observer*, March 22, https://www.theguardian.com/stage/2015/mar/22/james-graham-interview-coalition-x-y-finding-neverland.

Sierz, Aleks. 2010. The Whisky Taster. Bush Theatre. *The Arts Desk*, January 27, https://theartsdesk.com/theatre/whisky-taster-bush-theatre?page=0%2C1.

Taylor, Paul. 2006. Eden's Empire, Finborough Theatre, London, 93.2 Fm, Royal Court Theatre, Upstairs. *The Independent*, September 12, https://www.independent.co.uk/arts-entertainment/theatre-dance/reviews/eden-s-empire-finborough-theatre-london-93-2-fm-royal-court-theatre-upstairs-london-415671.html.

Taylor, Paul. 2016. This House, Garrick Theatre, London, Review: Dazzlingly Intelligent, Scrupulously Well Researched and Funny. *Independent*, December 1, https://www.independent.co.uk/arts-entertainment/theatre-dance/reviews/this-house-garrick-theatre-review-james-graham-conservative-lib-dem-coalition-a7449831.html.

Thorpe, Vanessa. 2022. Go On, Gizza Play: Boys from the Blackstuff Lives Again—On Stage. *The Observer*, July 2, https://www.theguardian.com/stage/2022/jul/02/go-on-gizza-play-boys-from-the-blackstuff-lives-again-on-stage.

Tönnies, Merle. 2017. The Renewal of British Political Theater in the Twenty-First Century: Indirect Narrative Approaches to Ideology and Power. *Storyworlds: A Journal of Narrative Studies*, 9:1–2.

Williams, Holly. 2015. The Angry Brigade, Bush Theatre, Review: A Real Play of Two Halves. *Independent*, May 7, https://www.independent.co.uk/arts-entertainment/theatre-dance/the-angry-brigade-bush-theatre-review-a-real-play-of-two-halves-10233653.html.

Index

A
ABC News, 16, 19, 220–222
Alli, Dele, 261, 262, 265
Ambassadors Theatre, 34
Angry Brigade, The, 6, 7, 11, 15, 25–27, 29, 99–101, 116, 117, 122, 125, 127, 131, 132, 134–138, 141, 248, 249, 251, 253, 255, 267, 275, 277
Arron Banks, 246

B
Baldwin, James, 169, 170
Best of Enemies, 2, 5, 16–19, 21, 22, 24, 26, 122, 148, 150, 157, 166, 168–170, 174, 175, 178, 181, 188, 197, 200, 201, 203, 210, 211, 219–221, 224, 227, 229, 230, 235–237, 248, 266
Blair, Tony, 31, 59
Bleasdale, Alan, 269–272
Bowen, Jim, 163, 165, 214
Boys From the Blackstuff, 22, 45, 255, 268–270, 272

Brexit: The Uncivil War, 109, 244, 245, 249, 253, 257, 263, 279
Brinkley, David, 168, 228, 235
British identity, 11, 16, 22, 38, 261, 266, 273, 274, 279
Britishness, 38, 263, 272, 273
Brown, Gordon, 243
Buckley, William F., 18, 19, 24, 167, 169, 174, 181, 182, 185, 188, 189, 192, 200, 201, 219, 222–227, 229, 231–234, 236, 237
Bush Theatre, 3

C
Cameron, David, 243
Chichester Festival Theatre, 204
Churchill, Caryl, 100, 127, 129
Churchill, Winston, 3, 27, 29, 30, 32
Class, 7–9, 16, 36, 39, 40, 42, 45, 55, 67–69, 101, 106, 109, 117, 120, 121, 172, 173, 197, 200, 250, 253–256, 260, 261, 268–272, 278

Clegg, Nick, 243
Coalition, 7, 55, 81, 91, 150, 243
Conservative Party, 6, 8, 9, 33, 36, 66–68, 114, 121, 150, 246, 250
Cronkite, Walter, 168, 220
Crown, The, 243
Crowther, Leslie, 163, 165, 166
Culture, The, 148, 273, 277
Cummings, Dominic, 109, 244–249, 253, 263

D
Dear England, 21, 22, 43, 122, 150, 176, 183, 186, 190, 260–262, 264–266, 268, 272, 273
Didier, Eric, 262
Donmar Warehouse, 70

E
Eden's Empire, 3, 11, 15, 22, 27, 29–31, 37, 45, 105, 149, 263, 264, 273
Eden, Anthony, 3, 12, 13, 27, 29–31, 38, 149, 263

F
Farage, Nigel, 246
Finborough Theatre, 3, 24, 38
Franklin, Aretha, 168, 169

G
Gove, Michael, 246
Grange, Pippa, 177, 184

H
Hare, David, 29, 51, 52, 92, 198
Heath, Ted, 33, 35, 149
Henderson, Jordan, 121, 125, 131, 178, 261

Herrin, Jeremy, 65, 236
Heseltine, Michael, 155
History of Falling Things, A, 23, 24
Huntley, Chet, 168, 235

I
Ingram, Charles, 5, 21, 165, 175, 176, 180, 204, 205, 209–213, 215, 218, 227, 229, 231, 233, 237, 265, 279
Ingram, Diana, 10, 163, 170, 180, 190, 208, 216
Ink, 2, 3, 17–19, 21, 26, 150, 156–158, 160, 162, 163, 169, 170, 172–174, 180, 181, 186, 187, 197, 199–201, 203, 218, 220, 235, 248, 255, 279

J
Johnson, Boris, 246

K
Kane, Harry, 178, 262, 267
Kennedy, Robert, 168
King, Martin Luther, 115, 168

L
Labour of Love, 1–3, 6–8, 13, 30, 36, 52, 53, 55, 56, 62, 63, 65–69, 79–81, 84, 244, 250, 251, 262, 269, 276, 278
Labour Party, 6, 8, 9, 53, 55, 56, 60–63, 66, 68, 82, 89, 271
Lamb, Larry, 16–19, 157–161, 172–177, 180, 181, 186–189, 192, 199, 201, 203, 235, 255, 265, 267
Le Tissier, Matt, 192
Liverpool Royal Court, 269

M

Macmillan, Harold, 31, 37, 105, 106
Maguire, Harry, 263
Man, The, 3, 24, 28, 43, 45
Mirror, The, 181
Monster Raving Loony, 4–7, 9, 14, 15, 99–101, 103, 104, 106–108, 111, 112, 114, 116, 117, 120, 124, 135, 138, 139, 141, 149, 245, 246, 248, 250, 255, 276
Moore, Brian, 183
Moore, Dudley, 105
Murdoch, Rupert, 16, 162, 170, 172, 173, 180, 181, 187, 200–203, 218, 235

N

National Theatre, 3, 4, 92, 260, 264
Noel Coward Theatre, 65

O

O'Connor, Des, 163, 165

P

Parkinson, Michael, 110, 111
Parliament, 1, 4, 16, 52, 54, 80, 91, 93, 111, 119, 121, 151, 154, 155, 259, 275, 280
Peter Cook, 105, 106
Pickford, Jordan, 261–263, 267
Powell, Enoch, 168
Prince Edward Theatre, 260

Q

Quiz, 2, 4, 5, 9–11, 17, 21, 24, 25, 114, 122, 150, 162, 163, 165, 166, 171, 175, 179, 189, 197, 203–205, 212–215, 217–219, 221, 222, 224, 227–229, 237, 243, 244, 279

R

Rashford, Marcus, 190, 262

S

Saka, Bukayo, 190
Sancho, Jordan, 190
Sherwood, 2, 38, 45, 249, 251–253, 256, 257, 262, 269
Sketching, 247, 274, 276–278
Smith, Howard K., 19, 119, 124, 128, 132, 133, 168, 221, 222, 225–227, 229, 232
Soho Theatre, 3
Sons of York, 3, 28, 38–40, 42, 43, 45, 256, 262, 268, 270–272
Southgate, Gareth, 176, 183, 190, 260, 261, 264–266, 268, 273
Sterling, Raheem, 266, 267
Stonehouse, John, 152–155, 157, 158, 161
Sun, The, 16–18, 157–160, 172, 173, 177, 180, 187, 188, 200, 261
Sutch, David, 4, 9, 14, 100–116, 126, 132, 138–141, 246, 255

T

Tammy Faye, 148, 197, 203, 210
Tarrant, Chris, 179, 180, 208, 210, 216
Television, 2–4, 9–11, 16–19, 21, 22, 24, 26, 53, 138, 148, 151, 157, 163–166, 174–176, 180, 182, 183, 189, 190, 193, 197–206, 208, 209, 211–214, 216–229, 231–237, 243, 249, 253, 257, 259, 261, 269–271

Thatcher, Margaret, 4, 38, 39, 41, 113, 150, 155, 254, 269, 270
Theatr Clwyd, 3, 24
This House, 1, 3, 4, 6–9, 11, 13, 14, 23, 30, 33, 34, 36, 38, 52, 53, 55, 61, 66, 68, 74, 81, 82, 84, 85, 89, 91–93, 149–151, 154–158, 161, 162, 169, 220, 244, 250, 254, 255, 274, 275, 279, 280
Thorpe, Jeremy, 154, 155, 157, 158
Timothy, Christopher, 157, 158, 201
Tory Boyz, 1, 8, 9, 27, 32–36, 55, 66–69, 149, 265, 280

V
Vidal, Gore, 18, 19, 24, 167, 169, 174, 181, 182, 185, 189, 192, 200, 201, 219, 222–225, 227, 229–237, 265
Vote, The, 5, 6, 9, 13, 30, 52, 70–72, 74, 75, 77–81, 84, 244, 280

W
Warhol, Andy, 148, 167–169
Wasserberg, Kate, 24
Whisky Taster, The, 3, 23, 25–28, 32, 34, 35, 42
Who Wants to Be a Millionaire, 9, 21, 163–165, 170, 175, 179, 185, 204, 205, 207, 209, 213, 215, 216, 261
Wilson, Harold, 58, 89, 150

Y
Young Vic, 225

www.ingramcontent.com/pod-product-compliance
Ingram Content Group UK Ltd.
Pitfield, Milton Keynes, MK11 3LW, UK
UKHW030624250125
453989UK00003B/6